'The founders of every society created social norms and cultural visions either to educate or as a way of keeping the group cohesive, and exercise control and authority. Biased and gender-based regulations have suppressed sections of society and hindered our ability to grow spiritually and emotionally. This has resulted in a lack of communication, appreciation and recognition within us of being divinely-created humans.

Fotoula's *Golden Book of Wisdom* can be viewed as a spiritual evolutionary guide for self discovery. Her knowledge, stories, spiritual exercises and inspiring poetry help us to reflect and connect with our ancestors, cultural heroes, gods and goddesses of different ancient traditions. Taking the serpent as a metaphor, she takes us deep into the cycle of birth, death and rebirth. In this journey of the soul every birth and event can be a door of learning and initiation which gradually takes us beyond family and society into the infinite realm of divinity and complete freedom.

Fotoula is not only a teacher but a walker of the path she shares. She took part in my Shamanic workshop in Nepal and then we went on a pilgrimage to Tibet. She said to me, "I am here to experience. I am ready to go to the places the spirits have chosen for me". This affirmation of 'trusting in spirit' shows how deeply immersed Fotoula is in her own spiritual journey, and how far she can take an aspirant.

I highly recommend this book as well as Fotoula's courses and retreats on shamanism and the teachings from ancient Egypt.

Wishing you all my best in this journey of evolution and self-revelation. May the primordial shamans, ancestors and cultural and spiritual heroes accompany us all into clarity and divinity. Namaste.'

Bhola Banstola, 27th consecutive generation
indigenous Shaman, Jhankri,
Nepal Shaman Association www.nepal-shaman.com

'It is time to find your wings and become a flying serpent. Shed the old skins and conditioning that serve no more to bring your authentic self to the Feast of Life.

Fotoula Adrimi is a true mystery school teacher. She uses powerful material (ancient and modern) to lead others to the magical place where spiritual alchemy occurs. A true shamanic teacher only opens the door for the greatest teachers of all – the compassionate helping spirits. This book is a rare opportunity to benefit from her life's work in your own home and following your own timeline, one chapter at a time. Let me add that Fotoula is from Greece: she knows the gods of ancient Egypt and Greece as well as her own family members. I cannot wait to hold my own hard copy of this book in my hands.'

Imelda Almqvist, international teacher of shamanism and sacred art, author of Natural Born Shamans: A Spiritual Toolkit for Life

'Having known Fotoula for many years I write this endorsement with a swelling of gratitude in my heart. Fotoula has been the wisest, most compassionate and loving presence in my life. As a shamanic practitioner, she has patiently ushered my soul back home and guided me through my underworld, shedding light where there was darkness, supporting me to retrieve myself. As a teacher of the ISIS practices she has been an amazing mentor. She shares the teachings with such generosity and devotion to her path that she embodies for me a true priestess sister calling me back home to the inner Temple.

Above all these qualities and her many gifts as a practitioner, the most precious for me is the purity of her heart. If I can claim to know one person who would pass the judgment of Ma'at it would be Fotoula. Her book is more than a valuable resource for shamanism and other teachings and practices, it is a pure transmission of love, light and joy to the world and those fortunate enough to be touched by it.'

Nicoletta Abatte, Therapeutic Counsellor and Psychotherapist

'In this clearly written guidebook through the stages of the spiritual journey, Fotoula Adrimi leads us to the recognition of our wholeness as Divine-physical beings. Her shamanic eye snakes us through all worlds on, below, and above earth – mirroring the conscious, unconscious and superconscious realms of understanding. She lands us back wholly transmuted into our most original selves with a greater appreciation for the magic of life itself.'

Rev. Kristin Powell, spiritual trip and nature retreat guide at Unity Rising and lead Minister at Unity of Walnut Creek in California, USA.

'For 30 years I suffered from undiagnosed chronic illnesses & pain. During this difficult and challenging period, I had squeezed all the joy out of my life. When I met Fotoula, her level of happiness made this lack evident and I contemplated how to recapture this emotion. After finding out she had been on her own challenging journey, I started listening to and observing her very closely. I recommend this book for those looking for healing, happiness and change in their life. Fotoula not only has walked the path but speaks with an authentic voice.'

Jane G. Doyle, author of award-winning You Heal You: Inspirational & Miraculous Healing Stories of Modern Day Warrior

'Fotoula shares her insight and experience within this book, helping people to break the chains of their conditioning in order to become more balanced. This results in harmony, joy and a meaningful life, and ultimately a more authentic self.'

Madeleine Black, author of Unbroken

'What a journey into the expansiveness of our consciousness Fotoula is taking us on. She has dedicated her life to listening deeply, and in a very holistic way has tapped wisdom from earth, soul, mind and spirit. We hear the ancestors, and we hear the wisdom that shakes up our very personal form, to enable us to listen to the "bigger" that guides us through the many birth/deaths of our growth.'

Meredith Little
www.schooloflostborders.org
www.lostborderspress.com

Fotoula Adrimi is our inspired and seasoned guide on a transformative journey toward self-discovery, spiritual empowerment, and reclamation of our inner radiance. Her skilled navigation ushers us beyond the constraints of our cultural and personal-historical conditioning, toward recognition and expression of our deepest authentic knowing. Invoking her deeply-lived experience in the realms of healing, meditation, shamanism, and ancient Egyptian spirituality, and her own indigenous Greek shamanic lineage, she expertly guides us on an initiatory pilgrimage. Using engaging stories and accessible, practical, and experiential methods, Adrimi compassionately awakens us from our cultural trance, empowering our own inherent sources of healing and wisdom. A must-read for novices and seasoned practitioners alike, who will find inspiration on this passionate journey to authenticity and spiritual connection.

Leslie Conton, Ph.D, anthropologist,
shamanic teacher and practitioner.

The Golden Book
of Wisdom

ancient spirituality and shamanism
for modern times

FOTOULA ADRIMI

Publisher : The ISIS School of Holistic Health

About the author

Fotoula Adrimi, *BA(Hons) MSc*, is the director of The ISIS School of Holistic Health, an international school of healing arts, spiritual development and inner transformation. Originally a town-planner, graduate of the Sorbonne Paris-IV, Fotoula, at the age of thirty, had a spiritual awakening. The experience of resurrection and initiation changed the course of her life and opened her path as a healer, shamanic practitioner and spiritual teacher. Fotoula radiates the light of compassion, dedicating her life to awakening from the veil of the conditioning, and to the healing and raising of the collective consciousness.

Fotoula is a spiritual teacher of transformational wisdom teachings including the Path of ISIS – The Seven Gates of Awareness: teachings channelled from the ancient Mother Goddess leading to awakening and enlightenment through the power of unconditional love.

Fotoula's other passion is Shamanism; working with her helping spirits for the highest good of All. She is also the teacher of the Rays of Divine Consciousness that activate our DNA to its inherent state of Oneness. Fotoula is re-introducing the lineage of the Priestess of the Moon, offered to her by the spirits of Cailleach Bheur and ISIS, bringing together the ancient Egyptian, Greek and Celtic spirituality.

Fotoula currently lives in Scotland. She travels around the globe to visit sacred sites following the calling from her helping spirits. Fotoula also returns to Greece often to visit family, appreciating Greek dancing and her mum's delicious cooking.

Published in the United Kingdom by:
The ISIS School of Holistic Health
www.theisisschoolofholistichealth.com

A CIP record of this book is available from the British Library.

First printed March 2018

Cover design by Eryn Strachan, Moonwood Arts, www.moonwoodarts.co.uk

Layout and design by Heather Macpherson,
Raspberry Creative Type, www.raspberrycreativetype.com

Published with the help of Indie Authors World, http://indieauthorsworld.com

ISBN 978-1-9996410-0-9 (pbk)
ISBN 978-1-9996410-1-6 (ebook)

To my Mum Jenny and my Dad Giorgos
who have been my early mentors,
teaching me about earthly life.

To my spiritual mother ISIS
who has been guiding me in many incarnations,
teaching me about myself.

Author's Note

The case studies in this book are true but some names have been changed to protect the identities of those involved.

For simplicity the pronoun 'she' has been used throughout the book.

Contents

Foreword

The Golden Book of Wisdom: ancient spirituality and shamanism for modern times

Walking a spiritual path in the western world can be both exciting and challenging. Realising that there is more to life than the dictates of our consumerist society, we may be guided to shamanism and other spiritual practices by an inner yearning that seeks expression. But how do we follow the voice of the heart and find our soul's calling when we have no reference for this in our everyday life, and when we are faced with the doubts and fears of the conditioned mind?

Fotoula's book is a roadmap of the path up the spiritual mountain. Within her, she carries knowledge of the ancient, indigenous, and western ways. Born in Greece, into a family with a shamanic lineage, she has learnt some of the traditional rituals that have been fast disappearing.

However, following her family's expectations, she turned her back on her spiritual gifts and studied town planning, immersing herself in the collective dream. Then one night the illusion was shattered by an initiatory dream. Could she trust spirit? Could she trust her intuition? The mind said she would be insane to do so. She had a comfortable life.

But spirit had found her and she started learning, in some cases relearning, what she knew inside. Fotoula has an incredible commitment to her spiritual path. She breathes and lives spirituality and shamanism in her everyday life. She has been studying these ways with western teachers, including myself, as well as indigenous shamans and Buddhist lamas. Fotoula is also grounded, the town planner is still inside her. She is practical, down-to-earth and at the same time expansive and spirit-guided, with a wealth of teachings to offer us. She understands the human mind and the challenges of our western life. She has been immersed in them herself. In her spiritual work, she straddles both realities, the physical and the spiritual, with the innocence of a child and the wisdom of an elder.

Her book is written for us, the spiritual seekers. How can we heal? How can we fly up to the sky? How can we return to Earth and keep the lightness of spirit? How can we find our inner radiance?

In order to answer these questions, Fotoula borrows metaphors from her own heritage as well as other ancient traditions. In searching for metamorphosis, she comes across the serpent, aptly choosing the ancient Greek and Egyptian symbol of wisdom and healing.

In the first part of her book, Fotoula invites us to shed the old skin by becoming more aware of ourselves, the way we think, act, and live our lives. The shadow is healed through compassion, love and forgiveness, integrated and not rejected. For Fotoula, illness, death, and life are a journey towards awareness and soul evolution. When we see the higher perspective, she says, we become aligned with our life purpose, remembering why our soul chose this life.

Through spiritual awakening the snake becomes a flying serpent. It travels, towards what the ancient Egyptians called "the upper regions of the sky," to find wise spirit teachers who explain the human predicament and open doors to soul evolution. The teachers speak through journeys, dreams, and meditations.

But Fotoula does not leave us hanging in a spiritual paradise. We come back to Earth, integrating the learning by bringing the spiritual wisdom into our body. This third part is about living life with awareness of the eternal nature of the soul. She talks about integrity and personal responsibility. Our world is crumbling due to our choice of short-term egoic gain over long-term, sustainable ways of living. This is a wake-up call to realise the eternal nature of our being and emerge from the collective dream. The snake becomes the ancient symbol of ouroboros, the circle formed when it bites its tail. Fotoula invites us to see ourselves as this circle, a being of no beginning and no end.

In the last part, the book steers us onto the runway to take off into the sun, moon and stars, immerse ourselves in our Holy Spirit and embody inner radiance. Fotoula speaks about the limitless nature of the human being, our inner Divinity. The snake is no more, but becomes the rainbow spirit, the conscious being.

Fotoula's book is a valuable body of work, a source of learning for the spiritual practitioner of our time. Her message is not just written in narrative, but true to the shamanic path of direct revelation, she invites us to explore ourselves through the concepts she presents. Chapters contain exercises and poems taking us deeper into our own experiences. This is invaluable. In my experience, traditional shamans and mystics not only learn a theory and adopt a methodology but also open themselves up to the voice of spirit. Learning develops into an art. Fotoula, safely and consistently, shows us ways to work with energy, spirit, and our inner voice. In doing so we can access an incredible pool of wisdom that exists within us.

Throughout, Fotoula's guidance comes through the wise voice of her helping spirits. This is another point in favour of this book, the originality of this work. The exercises and methods that help us dive into ourselves are unique. They have been practiced and developed by Fotoula and her guides to help her and others in the spiritual journey to wholeness. The guidance of ISIS, the ancient Egyptian Mother and Thoth, the ancient Egyptian god of wisdom and learning, as well as other enlightened spirits make this book a cornerstone for spiritual learning.

I have had the wonderful opportunity to train Fotoula as a shamanic teacher. I loved her presence in my Training. She is a humble woman so filled with wisdom and a sense of adventure. Fotoula has such a love for learning and also sharing shamanic ways in her community. She is passionate about the work and has such a deep sense of compassion for what her students and clients need. Fotoula was once my student and now she is a treasured peer.

This book is original, brilliantly written, thoroughly researched and at the same time, exciting and illuminating. The energy and light of Fotoula and the enlightened spirit helpers, coupled with a pragmatic voice and down-to-earth approach make this book a must-read for spiritual and shamanic practitioners.

Sandra Ingerman
Santa Fe, New Mexico USA
November 2017

Preface

My first inkling of my gifts was in childhood. I was empathic. I knew why people acted in a certain way. I had insights about their life. I also had enormous compassion for all human suffering and a deep faith. During mass, I would bathe in the loving presence of God, raising my head to the painted dome with His image and feel His agape radiating. I would lose myself in the beauty of the byzantine chanting and the mysticism of the ritual.

I was born in Greece in the 1970s to a family with a remarkable lineage of psychic gifts. Many ancestors practiced shamanic rituals such as bone divination, weather prediction, and extraction of negative energies. Our family name, Adrimi, means "of the oak tree" (*drys*, in ancient Greek), and my first name Fotoula means the "light of epiphany." Aptly named, I was born with gifts of clairvoyance, psychic awareness, and an inner knowing that I brought from previous lives. I later had my own shamanic calling, and I am now an international teacher of enlightened wisdom—incorporating some of the shamanic knowledge from my ancestors.

My main spiritual guide during the early years of primary school was Mother Mary, who accompanied me everywhere. Mother Mary told me the time when I asked, ensured I won the raffles at school, and kept me safe. I could also see God in my mind's eye, who appeared as a kind, old man. Years later, when God asked me to look into his eyes, I saw many universes and understood Oneness. God is everything that exists, and we are part of Him. Ancient Egypt was another source of fascination. In my mind, I would often fly to the ancient temples, accompanied by radiant Egyptian deities such as ISIS, the ancient Egyptian Mother Goddess.

As a teenager, I shifted my focus to the demands of school life, university exams, and planning my future. My mind overtook my voice of intuition. Around the same time, the Greek Orthodox priest told me that my psychic gifts were calling the devil to me, and I became wracked by fear.

For the next sixteen years, I rejected my spiritual gifts and silenced my inner voice to lead a normal life. I went to university in Volos, Greece, studied at the Sorbonne in Paris, became a town planner in Glasgow, Scotland, got married, and had a mortgage.

Then, at thirty, I was drawn back into the spirit world. Within a few months of practicing meditation, Reiki, and crystal healing, my gifts returned. I felt joyous and empowered, as if I had come home to myself. In 2006, two years later, I reconnected with the ancient Egyptian Mother Goddess ISIS. She reminded me how she had always been with me, since my childhood when I was journeying in my mind to Egypt. ISIS showed me previous lives that I had spent as a spiritual teacher in Egypt and Atlantis. She invited me once again to be her teacher and channel, to bring back the ancient wisdom that has been lost, and to spread the teachings of Ascension by showing people how to engage with what ISIS calls, the "Living Light".

One night, towards the end of 2006, I woke up with the bed shaking and moving from side to side due to an energy column of golden light entering my body. My only thought was what would happen if I moved my body away from the column. And when I did, the bed's shaking intensified. I put my body back underneath the column, and then, I blacked out.

ISIS told me that during the night, through the column, she had embedded the blueprint of the wisdom teachings I was going to channel and the programme for my future life. The experience unleashed an inner drive, an all-consuming fire, to work on myself and change my life. My new path would reflect my wishes and my soul's calling. I studied the spiritual arts and channelled spiritual wisdom from ISIS including the teaching called the "Seven Gates of Awareness," a path to enlightenment. For the next six years, I practiced and taught this spiritual wisdom, alongside my town planning career.

Although baptised in the Greek Orthodox faith, since my return to spirituality I have been a channel for ISIS and other enlightened spirit entities from a plethora of traditions. These wise beings emphasise the value of direct revelation rather than blindly following dogma. The enlightened ones also said I did not have to be a devotee of a particular faith to communicate with them. Thus, I work spiritually with buddhas, rinpoches, Indian gurus, native American shamans, Christ, and ancient Egyptian deities. They all share the one Divine essence. It is our human mind that segregates them into different religions.

In 2012, I resigned from my job as a senior planner in the public sector. And for the next three years, I travelled the globe, seeking places where the ancient energy I had been channelling was still active. I learned about myself through ceremonies such as the vision quest, firewalking, and the sweat lodge. I delved into my inner light through meditation in ancient temples in Tibet, Peru, Greece, Brazil, Nepal, Egypt, and elsewhere, receiving empowerments, attunements, and initiations from shamans and rinpoches. I have found magnificent light in the Great Pyramid and the ancient Egyptian temples, and encountered the divine in Buddhist shrines, ancient stone circles, forests and lakes. My western shamanic teacher Sandra Ingerman and my colleague and co-traveller in the Path of ISIS, Fi Sutherland, were also instrumental in my spiritual growth.

At the same time, I continued to work with the enlightened entities from ancient Egypt. Although ISIS has been my main guide, other beings such as Thoth, the god of wisdom and learning, and Anubis, the protector of the hidden realms, were helping me develop my healing work with others. With their assistance, in 2013 in Glasgow, I founded The ISIS School of Holistic Health, an international school of the ISIS Seven Gates of Awareness path to enlightenment, The Rays of Divine Consciousness, and other spiritual and healing arts, shamanism, and meditation.

The different stages of my life have been part of a script that my soul had written before I incarnated as me—Fotoula Adrimi. My soul wanted to experience growing up in a loving family in Greece, near the sea, tasting the fruits of material life, and also remember its calling of spirituality and working for the world community.

In 2015, I was compelled by a vision to write a book about the journey of the soul, life, death, and spiritual awakening. In my vision, a spiritual master, sitting in a great temple, instructed me to write a book to help people heal their body, mind, and spirit. I said that I would. The result is *The Golden Book of Wisdom: ancient spirituality and shamanism for modern times*.

My goal with this book is to help readers understand their personal journey, know the meaning of life, and help heal the collective consciousness. I believe that when we find our own inner balance, we can affect positively the collective consciousness and the world may become a place of harmony and joy.

Introduction

The Golden Book of Wisdom takes readers on a journey of self-discovery and inner connection. This book summarises my many years of spiritual development, study, therapeutic practice, and teaching of the esoteric arts of healing, meditation, shamanism, and ancient Egyptian and indigenous Greek spirituality, as well as my shamanic lineage. I have been guided by the spiritual wisdom and enlightened teachings of my main guide, the ancient Egyptian Goddess ISIS, an aspect of the Divine Mother essence, whom I have channelled and worked with for many years; by Thoth, the ancient Egyptian god of wisdom and learning; Anubis who acted as a spiritual protector and revealed the hidden realms; a being of light called Hthoth, assigned by ISIS to help with the book; and an early Athenian saint called Dionysius Areopagitis.

Through twenty-four spiritual lessons readers are shown tools to embrace their life purpose and reveal their innate luminosity. Each lesson is introduced through my clinical insights and personal anecdotes, and followed by the guidance of the enlightened spirits I channel. Other testimonials from relevant sources are cited, to offer a rounded view. In writing the book I researched applicable approaches from modern psychology, psychotherapy, ancient spiritual teachings and modern spiritual seekers. References are provided throughout the book.

The narrative is followed by self-guided exercises to help readers experience and thereby, better understand, the wisdom of each lesson. The exercises are of two kinds: purification, a clearing out of the conditioned habits and patterns that do not serve us, and empowerment through opening our heart and connecting with our Divine essence. Many formats are used, such as visualisation, meditation, questions for self-reflection, ceremony, and journeying. With practice, overall, readers may increase their spiritual power, discover their inner voice, and learn to work safely with spirits of the light.

Twenty-four lessons, across four parts

The lessons focus on different states of the evolutionary process. They track the journey of the soul from its Divine state of spirit to a physical being on Earth; from the fall from grace through the shaping of the conditioned mind and the egoic self; and, the return to grace through spiritual awakening and the development of compassion and unconditional love. The evolutionary journey is described metaphorically by the serpent, the ancient symbol of wisdom and healing.

In the beginning, Part I – Shedding Skin, we become aware of the journey of life and adopt a higher perspective on the aspects of personal power, ego, healing, life, death, and karma. Everything we experience is a learning for our soul. Like a snake, we shed the old skin so we can empower our life purpose.

In Part II – Into the Spirit, we continue expanding our perspective of life, by delving into our spiritual nature. The snake that has shed its skin becomes lighter and heads for the sky. Through its wings of spiritual light, it learns to access other worlds and initiates itself as a spiritual being, the mythical flying serpent.

In Part III – Back to the Body, the snake descends, returning to Earth. It integrates spiritual experience into everyday life, seeking wholeness. It realises that the soul journey is eternal, spanning many lifetimes. It links past, present, and future into a continuous circle, the snake swallowing its tail, becoming the ouroboros.

In the fourth and final part (The rainbow spirit), the eternal being exits the wheel of reincarnation. Spiritual expansion beyond the conditioned mind enables awakening into radiance. The ouroboros becomes the rainbow spirit, also known as "Divine Consciousness".

A journey of awareness, connection and evolution

This book initiates a journey of awareness, connection, and evolution; awareness about the soul that has come to Earth to experience birth and death and the illusionary nature of life, the collective dream; connection between the physical and spiritual realities of existence, through which the soul chooses to travel; and, evolution through the spiritual path, which helps the soul embrace the Divine within.

Although we are born in a state of expanded awareness, we can quickly lose this connection through our interactions with other people and the world around us. However, stepping onto a spiritual path, we gift ourselves an opportunity to realise there is more to life than the dictates of the social conditioning. The path reconnects us to the voice of our intuitive heart and we gradually evolve into a spiritual being radiating joy, compassion, grace and peace.

The book is a tool to become conscious of, understand, and overcome the conditioning of the mind, which is the way out of the collective dream. There are two types of conditioning: personal, derived from our unique life experiences, and social, instilled by adopting the values of our family, community, peers, culture and nation.

Conditioning is when we react to the present based on our beliefs and experiences from the past. Our thoughts and behaviours become self-reinforcing, learned patterns. For example, Matthew, an office worker, asks for an appointment with his boss. His boss is busy that day and does not return Matthew's call. Matthew perceives his boss's silence as the old, familiar rejection he experienced as a child. His mind tells him that his boss does not value him and will never promote him. Matthew has been conditioned to equate a lack of attention from an authority figure with being abandoned. Matthew's mind does not consider alternate scenarios, that his boss is busy, simply forgot to return the call, or did not get the message. As a result, Matthew may become angry, disheartened and lose interest in his job, alienating his boss and creating the reality his conditioning dictates.

Social conditioning occurs on a collective level and each culture has its unquestioned rules. For example, when a woman buys an expensive house, some people may think she should not rise above her station. This belief, held in the United Kingdom, is a holdover from feudal times. Logically, a person should be able to buy any house she wishes and can afford—regardless of whether she is born wealthy or not.

All conditioning, the agreements we made ourselves and the collective agreements influenced by the world, affects how we think about ourselves and others, how we treat one another, the decisions we make and ultimately how we live our lives. It is deeply ingrained and slow to dislodge.

The book explores the conscious journey out of the conditioning, the path of returning home to the authentic self, and the reclaiming of inner luminosity.

I share these insights with you to help you in your hero's journey of realising your own radiance. I am very happy that you have chosen to read my book, and I hope it will speak to you.

Part I.
Shedding Skin

In Part I, the snake licks its wounds. For years, it has been slithering on the hard earth, carrying the pain. Now it is time to shed the old skin and heal.

We are taken into a journey of purification and healing of the inner self. Through self-awareness, forgiveness, and esoteric teachings, we open to new understandings about ourself and the flow of life. Have we taken responsibility and carried the blame for others' actions, lost parts of our soul, dimmed our light to conform to the social conditioning of our culture? This is the story of the human predicament. Deep down, we long to heal and to discover our radiance and destiny in the world. The old patterns have to die so that we can experience the rebirth of the authentic self.

In this first part, we reclaim our power, vocation, and life. We learn about karma and illness, life and death. We discover our life purpose.

1

Reclaiming Personal Power

Spiritual Lesson 1: Relinquishing the chains of fear,
I step into my power

Shedding skin: In healing myself, I discover areas of heavy energy inside the body. "What are these parts?" I wonder. My spiritual guide replies, "It is misused power." These parts have a story to tell. I look closer, and I see the faces of people I forced to do my will. Unconsciously, I have carried their power within me. Lovers who I could not let go of, work colleagues who I insisted did my bidding, my mother who would give me what I wanted if I stopped crying. Elsewhere in my body, I see gaps, lifeless holes. My guide says, "These holes were created when you gave your power away." I look inside the gaps. I hear myself saying yes, when I meant no, doing things to please, complying out of fear. I start my healing journey by releasing the energy I have taken and reclaiming my power.

We are born with a finite amount of vital life force energy, known by the indigenous medicine people, the shamans, as our "personal power." As we age, our life force usually diminishes through a variety of means, until little remains at the time of our death. We can lose this vital energy through the body's natural decline, environmental factors, accidents, and by misusing it due to fear. In our day-to-day relationships, fear manifests as either giving our power away to others or taking power from others. In both scenarios, we lose personal power and become more vulnerable to emotional upset, anxiety, disease, and misfortunes.

POWER GAMES

As we grow up, we enter a massive power game that defines the majority of human relationships and reflects our social structures. Unhealthy, co-dependent relationships form, in which people, motivated by fear and insecurity, covertly or overtly, wrestle for or cede power and control. As a result, both parties experience a loss of energy and vitality. According to B. K. Weinhold and Weinhold (2008), co-dependency is present in an estimated 98% of the adult population and is responsible for most human misery.

An unhealthy, co-dependent relationship is one where we need the other person to comply with our ideas of how she should behave, so that we know we are accepted, loved, and appreciated. We fill an emotional gap created by childhood trauma, by projecting our needs onto the person. We cannot afford to lose control and are devastated if the relationship ends. Spiritually, we form an etheric cord from our solar plexus chakra, the chakra of personal power, to the other person's solar plexus. This cord carries an unhealthy exchange of life force energy. (Chakra is a Sanskrit term to describe an etheric doorway, shaped as a wheel, that transfers life force energy from the environment into our body and vice versa).

Conversely, an interdependent relationship based on mutual acceptance and unconditional love forms a heart connection that does not need to control but loves the other for who she is.

We are meant to retain our personal energy in relationships. We can only be happy and content when we are authentic, honest, and take care of our needs; when we are in our power. A hallmark of an insecure person in an unhealthy relationship is doing something to please another, whilst ignoring her own feelings. Likewise, a more dominant but still insecure person may use fear to control someone by pushing her energy into the person. If successful, the victim carries part of her aggressor's energy, creating more fear, resentment, and a tendency to ruminate on the abuse. The power of the aggressor is an energetic intrusion in the victim's body, which unsettles the victim's energy.

The aggressor also takes energy from the victim, undermining her own power. This energy is like a dead weight that cannot fill the gap she created when she pushed her own energy into the other person. Only a return of her energy can fill this space. Most people play both roles of victim and aggressor in different areas of their life.

For thousands of years indigenous medicine people have practiced power and life force retrievals and the removal of intrusions. An energetic intrusion is an influx of external energy, which can be extracted from a person's body by a shamanic practitioner or healer. Sometimes foreign power is easy to remove. Occasionally it is more complicated. Following removal of power intrusions, shamanic healers may perform power retrievals to recover lost life force energy and heal energy gaps.

Shamans believe that both gaps and intrusions, if not healed, manifest as imbalances in a person's body and life, and will eventually lead to disease and unhappiness. The exercise at the end of the chapter provides a way to release intrusions and restore energy.

FEAR: THE MAIN CULPRIT

We lose personal power when we act out of fear. Fear of others' rejection, abandonment, and opinion stops us from discovering and being who we really are. Unfortunately, many of us live in societies that cultivate fear addiction. From early childhood, people may have been raised in fear by the carrot-and-stick principle, whereby parents reward compliance and punish disobedience. This method of parenting creates unhappy, insecure adults and has been found inferior to parenting based on restorative dialogue, that promotes autonomy and self-reliance (Faber & Mazlish, 2012).

When we live in a state of stress, constantly feeling on edge, our focus shifts to future possibilities instead of enjoying life in the present reality. Being mindful and aware is rarely an option and subconsciously, we may urge ourselves to keep busy, and turn to addictions to numb our insecurities (Cresswell & Lindsay, 2014). In this state, we can become egotistical. We may feel the need to continually defend ourselves from a perceived outside enemy.

Fear is like a bad habit. It becomes ingrained in our cells and keeps reappearing and growing like a cancer. Once conditioned towards fearful thinking, we have less capacity to perceive a situation wisely and to think and act clearly. Controlled by emotion and damaging thoughts, we may make unhealthy choices.

Dumping our fears on others drains everyone's life force energy. For example, if I am frightened of having a car accident, I may warn my children to drive carefully, sharing my worries by citing examples of what could go wrong when they drive. This may appear logical and reasonable, but I have not recognised that the fear is my problem and instead I transfer it, potentially making my children nervous about driving. The transfer of fear has increased the likelihood of an accident for any one of us. Fearful drivers make more errors (Taylor, Deane, & Podd, 2007). A wiser approach would be to recognise that I find driving stressful because of my unconscious beliefs and seek ways to overcome the fear.

Fear of others' opinion of us is linked with low self-esteem and can create the belief, "I'm not good enough." This manifests in the expectation that horrible things happen to me. When they do, the belief is reinforced and our confidence falls further, creating a vicious cycle of conditioned self-doubt. Consequently, people can be stuck in helpless situations, unable to make decisions for positive change. For example, some people remain in damaging co-dependent relationships, fearing that they will not be able to survive on their own or will never find another partner.

Spiritual practice has helped me to face and release my fears. By practising meditation regularly, my awareness increases. I observe my feelings and negative emotions. My confidence has been renewed by realising I am not my fears. In meditation, in the quiet space, immersed in high vibrational energies, the negative emotions dissipate, and my mind eventually quietens; I become one with my higher power. My soul is able to communicate with me, showing me the workings of my mind. Solutions can arise to any problems, which become less overwhelming. I am able to detach and be the observer of my life. This awareness stays with me even after meditation. I retain my inner power by accepting, understanding and releasing the fear and its motivation, rather than denying it or pushing it into others.

POWER LOSS: FANNING THE FLAMES OF FEAR

What causes fear and, therefore, power loss, is the tendency towards control that exists in the collective consciousness, and is expressed in our co-dependent personal and professional relationships. We want to be in control even when there are so many uncertainties in life. We find it hard to let go and trust life, lest we become vulnerable. We attempt to rid ourselves of anxieties by transferring them onto others, rather than dealing with our emotions.

When a person lives in peace with herself and life, she is in her power. She has a positive relationship with life and enjoys a certain degree of happiness, no matter what happens to her or what material goods she may possess. As a result, she is more likely to respond to life and others from a position of power. When she meets an insecure person who wishes to control her, she is better able to deal with any attempts to unsettle her due to her inner strength.

When I was writing this chapter, I had a dream where I was shown how we can give our power to others out of compassion, to ease their pain and bring them joy. Sometimes, unhappy people refuse to take responsibility for their life choices, and blame others for their misery. If you are not "helping" them, by doing what they want, they can be manipulative, and you can feel guilty and at fault, when it is their behaviour that is the problem. These people have an agenda, and can use their words and moods in a passive-aggressive manner to create an atmosphere of fear and exercise control. In this way, they deflect their issues towards you, and if your feelings or behaviour changes to accommodate them then you are absorbing their energy (King, 2012). This is a one of the common traps in giving one's power away to keep others happy.

Power Gain: Saying no to Power Exchange

In order to grow our personal power, it is essential to release any life force energy we have taken or accepted from others. Like a cancerous growth, other peoples' energy can live inside us for many years. Ultimately, prolonged exposure to foreign energy disturbs our emotional and mental balance, unsettles our physical body, and impacts our general wellbeing.

Through spiritual development, we can become aware of our choice whether or not to take on the energy of another person. If we agree, are we doing so to avoid an uncomfortable situation? Do we feel threatened? Are we intimidated by overt aggression? Can we feel the energy pushing into our boundaries? Choosing to cede to hostility welcomes negative energy into our body. The person's energy now resides in us, and will coerce us to be more compliant in the future. Slowly, our life force fades as we continue the pattern, repetitively absorbing another's energy.

Now, imagine being in this situation again. This time, see the situation logically rather than emotionally. If you accept another's terms against your better judgement, you lose power. If you feel the other is right and you realise it is a good thing to do, then there is no exchange of power.

Sometimes, we may feel that we do not have the option to say no, especially if violence is a factor. In abusive relationships, our best option is to leave, and if leaving is impossible, we can use stealth. We can pretend to comply but at the same time, make a pact with ourselves that we are acting out of self-preservation and we will not offer any power to the aggressor. For example, during the medieval era of religious persecution, people pretended to observe the Church's doctrine in order to escape death. Galileo stated publicly that the Earth did not revolve around the sun; yet, he knew otherwise.

Regardless of the circumstances, we break through power losses in the same way. First, we recognise the pattern: that is, do we tend to give away power or take power? Second, we agree within ourselves to stop playing the power game. Third, we act according to our commitment.

SUMMARY

When we feel insecure, we tend to either give our power to others or try to control others by unconsciously pushing our life force into their body. In both cases, life force energy is lost due to fear. The power exchange, either through being the victim or the aggressor, weakens us and makes us more vulnerable to disease, physical or emotional. With awareness, we see that the energy loss is unhealthy and unnecessary, and can work to restore our universal power.

EXERCISE: CEREMONY – ALIGNING WITH THE SOURCE OF YOUR POWER

What you need: bowl of water

This exercise leads you through a ceremony to align with the unlimited Divine source of universal power and love that lies within you, and heal any power loss and any resulting energetic intrusions.

Before starting a ceremony, shamans and indigenous healers establish what is called "a sacred space"; they ally with the Divine power to create a container that holds, protects and enhances their ceremonial work. There are many ways to create sacred space in the plethora of the world's spiritual traditions and you may already have a favourite, which you can use. In this first part of the book, a simple way to create sacred space is to invite the Divine, in whatever way you understand this, into your room. I will be talking more about sacred space in chapter 9.

The second most important part of any ceremony is to set a clear intention. This is the area of your life that you are asking the ceremony to heal. In this ritual, your intention could be to heal the imbalance of power within you; restore power you gave away and release power you took from others. Whatever intention you choose, it must be right for you and touch your heart.

Having created sacred space and set your intention, you are ready to start the ceremony. Place the bowl of water in front of you. This is where you will release the foreign power.

In this quiet space, focus on your heart. Imagine a brilliant light existing in your heart. This is the eternal light that creates all life, the seat of the Creator in the body. You have the power of the stars and universes, the sun and moon, the thunder and lightening, the wind and the rain, and the Earth. You do not need anyone's energy but your own, when you acknowledge yourself as the Divine light.

Forgive yourself completely for accepting other peoples' power. If any specific situations come to mind, apologise to yourself and forgive others. (You do not need to contact people to either apologise or forgive. You can do this mentally during the exercise).

Forgive yourself completely for forcing anyone to carry your energy. Release yourself from the power game. If any specific situations come to mind, apologise to the other person in your mind and ask for their forgiveness. This also applies to people who have died. If you sense the person does not wish to forgive you, or they are angry, toxic, unhappy, respect their choice and let them go. You have done your part by apologising. Most importantly, forgive yourself.

Now you have balanced the scales and it is time to consciously heal yourself and any imbalance of power within you. Imagine the brilliant light from your heart expanding throughout your body and filling every cell. Any foreign power is unseated and starts to leave your body. Release any energy that belongs to someone else by blowing it into the water. It can no longer stay inside you when you are filled with the radiant light of the Creator within. Keep blowing this energy out until you feel your work is complete. Then, sit quietly for a few minutes, sensing how you feel without others' energy.

Make a commitment to restore your personal power, by saying to the universe and yourself words to the effect: "I wish to have my life force fully restored. I will no longer give my power away. I will keep my energy inside my body. I forgive myself for the past. I intend to live a happy life, in accordance with my life purpose. No matter how much power I gave away, there is always an abundance of power in the universe and its centre, radiating out of my heart." Feel again the power of universal love inside your heart, expanding and restoring your energy. The light inside you fills every gap, every part of your body and aura. Stay in this space for a little while.

You have now completed the ceremony. Thank yourself for restoring your power in your body and in your life. Thank the Divine outside and inside of you and in this way, close your sacred space.

Finally, take the water from the ceremony out into nature, preferably to a large body of water or river to be released. As you pour the water, thank all the people involved for their contribution to your life experience. Ask that their energy be released into the universe, and pray that they may also find their personal power when they are ready. Give thanks again to the Divine and yourself for the ceremony.

JOURNEY TO PERSONAL POWER

I am carrying a heavy burden.
In my heart are the wishes of my family, my partner's dreams, my boss's demands.
They are the musts of society.
The shoulds of the world.
The need to be accepted by others.
Live in accordance with my upbringing.

Before I know it, I am trapped;
buried in the coffin of depression.
There is no happiness in my life
when I deny my inner self.

My voice whispers
of the power I have given away,
of the years that I have yet to live.
If I go with the past, I have nothing to hope for.

I cannot see a way out of this mess,
unless I stand in my power.
Look at myself and what I have become:
a servant of others.

There is no pleasing them.
They always demand more.
A piece of my soul.
My own flesh on a plate.
Until all that is left is a skeleton.

And then I rise from the grave of silence;
when I lose everything, I make a stand.
The love I thought I had, was never there.
The desire for new life, that was perished before it was born.
The cycle of unfulfilled hope.

When I lost everything,
I packed my bags.
I left the keys behind,
never to return.

I had no idea where I was going,
where life would take me.
That was still for me to discover.
No one, not even I, knows the way.

I live my own life,
my dreams and my hopes.
Joy returns. Life fulfilled.
I die and birth myself in happiness.

2

From the Ego Shadow to Unconditional Forgiveness

Spiritual Lesson 2: I accept myself. I embrace my vulnerability and find the road to freedom through forgiveness

Shedding skin: In my healing journey, I discover that parts of me are missing. I follow my spirit guides into a dark place, a dungeon, an old oubliette. In these recesses, I buried all that I judged as ugly: the angry part, the stupid part, the frivolous part, the traumatised part, the vulnerable part, an endless list of parts that did not conform to an ideal version of myself. These parts appear like little girls with haunted eyes, torn clothes, and emaciated bodies. 'What do you need from me?' I ask them as they extend their little hands towards me. "We are starved of your love," they say. "If you never accept all of yourself, how can you heal?"

THE EGO SHADOW

My shamanic journeys have shown me that we are born little bundles of unconditional love. We instinctively shine the light of our spirit. As we grow and develop a personality, based on our experiences and interactions, as well as our own inherent nature, we birth the ego shadow—the conscious and unconscious aspects of the conditioned mind.

The terms ego and shadow are used in psychology and psychotherapy by different schools. Below, I offer my own interpretation of the terms and their combined use in this book.

Ego is a Greek word meaning "me" or "I." It implies a separation between the self and the rest of the world. The ego looks after its own interests before those of others. Conversely, in the state of spirit, before birth, the soul experiences Oneness, the "we-all" rather than the "me-me". Part of the healing journey, both for the individual and the world community, is to balance the ego-me with the we-all (Scharmer & Kaufer, 2013).

The ego is rooted in survival mode—seeking pleasure and avoiding pain (Freud, Wilson, & Griffin, 2012). Its priority is to protect us from all danger, including trauma, hurt, and disappointment. The shadow is the part of the ego that carries the suffering from the past that has never been acknowledged or healed, where enemies outnumber friends. It remembers the times we trusted and our trust was abused. It strives to protect us from further traumatic experiences and seeks pleasure to numb the inner turmoil.

The ego shadow makes judgements about itself, finds it difficult to accept itself, and sees the vulnerable aspects of the personality as failings. The ego shadow cannot admit to weakness, which it tries to mask often in inappropriate ways. For example, the ego shadow may be highly critical of another person, focusing on her flaws instead of her positive traits, just to feel better about itself and appear outwardly strong. The ego believes it is beyond reproach, whereas the shadow hides away the dark pool of injuries, insecurities and emotional wounds.

The shadow hinders us from achieving our dreams. It wants to keep us small because growth involves change, and change feels dangerous and risky. Change might expose the trauma that it is desperate to keep hidden. At the same time, the ego wants to be noticed and gratified by authority figures— compensating for past unmet needs from a parent or teacher. It wants to be loved by all, but the shadow is afraid to give love to anyone, including itself, lest it is rejected.

WELCOMING THE EGO SHADOW

So, there is a tension between the ego and shadow that we need to develop a skilful way of navigating. We must accept the ego by revealing and embracing the shadow. However, western conditioning ranges between rejecting the ego shadow as unholy, or gratifying the ego shadow as a driving force in the competitive world of corporate business.

For example, in western religious doctrine, the ego is often regarded as the adversary of virtue, the main obstacle in our path to sainthood and enlightenment. Seeing the ego as the enemy encourages a person to ignore it or further berate herself when it clamours for attention.

The more we push away the ego, the noisier the shadow will become (Holiday, 2016). For instance, in spiritual gatherings, we may try to silence the ego and behave as kind and loving as an angel, while the shadow is emitting feelings of jealousy and resentment. I have seen these "earth angels" throw etheric daggers at others, whilst smiling outwards and ignoring their inner emotional turmoil. The more we try to suppress the unresolved ego, the more our shadow will find ways to surface. The tension between the ego and shadow can find many outlets. The ego clamours for attention wearing a beyond-reproach mask whilst the shadow of the traumatised child with the unmet needs fears the exposure of its imperfections.

Conversely, neoclassical market theories advocate that we have to do what our ego wants. Such theories have been translated by some, in ways that justify selfish and unkind behaviour. It is argued that as the world is in a state of duality, of darkness and light, being egotistical is another expression of the Divine. For the ego to exist, it must be part of God; therefore, its desires and shadow should be exercised. Acting out our shadow, being unskilful towards others, can be part of our learning. For example, neoclassical theories of the homo economicus justify selfish behaviour in the marketplace, where the winner only looks after himself, using whatever means to gather resources from other players (McMahon, 2015).

My belief is that a soul may act out of ego when the shadow carries traumatic experiences from the past that are unresolved and unhealed. The soul eventually, through different experiences, may recognise the pain its behaviour created for itself as well as others. Further, there is a personal cost, as living out of ego does not create happiness. By acting out the shadow, a soul alienates itself from its true nature of unconditional love (Zweig & Abrams, 1990).

There are consequences for ignoring the shadow's pain, either by rejecting the ego as non-virtuous or becoming self-centred to satisfy its voice. If we push the shadow down and ignore it, it becomes larger. If we use it as an excuse to hurt others in turn, we only hurt ourselves more. The ego shadow does not know how to make us happy. Even though it masks the emotional pain and dissatisfaction, the hurt resurfaces at times of stress. Unable to accept itself, the ego shadow projects the pain onto others, blaming them for its predicament. We make peace with our ego by first examining what created the shadow's motivations. What past pain is the ego shadow trying to protect us from? What pleasure is it using to fill the emotional void? The next step is having a dialogue with the ego shadow.

CONVERSING WITH THE EGO SHADOW

The ego is the part of us that wants to retrieve what it thinks it has lost: its personal power. Not knowing where to find it, the ego looks to the external world and at the power of others—all the while ignoring the emptiness within. The shadow wants to heal, reveal itself in the light, but it does not know how and reacts to situations in the way it has learned from others and traumatic past experiences.

Healing the shadow can only happen through self-acceptance and the shadow's integration with the self. We achieve this through personal work, therapeutic healing, spiritual practice, and affirmations.

In the healing process, we can say to our ego, look inside you and see yourself in your Divine light. From that place, accept yourself beyond the conditioning and say to yourself, "I am perfect as I am." My clients often resist, asking, "How can I say, 'I am perfect as I am,' when I hate myself?" I reply, "See the ego shadow as the child you were, when you first experienced trauma." As children, instead of being comforted, we may have been told that we were lacking and that we were to blame. So, to heal, we speak kindly and lovingly to our traumatised child within.

Integration is achieved by practicing self-awareness, and reinforcing self-acceptance. When we experience jealousy and resentment and any other negative self-talk (from our ego shadow), instead of pushing away our feelings as bad, we can look at this part of our experience with love, and without judgment. With compassion, we can ask our ego shadow what it is trying to achieve and what it needs from us. In time, the shadow, through love, may eventually overcome its conditioned response of hiding away or competing against others.

During my studies of clinical hypnosis at the University of West London, I was taught an exercise that I have since adapted and used many times in my therapeutic practice. This exercise is based on the theories of dissociation and neurosis (Phillips & Frederick, 1995). It demonstrates the conflict between the shadow and the ego. Natasha came to see me, feeling she had reached an impasse. She was a talented musician. Playing on stage was her dream, but each time she attempted to make it happen, she would procrastinate, overeat, get drunk and find excuses. She felt blocked but did not know why. During the healing session I invited Natasha to connect to her shadow, the hurt part of her psyche that was displaying the unwanted behaviour. The shadow said she was six years of age, a frightened little girl who still remembered how she had been looking forward to starting primary school but subsequently found it very hard. She was now trying to protect Natasha from further significant life changes. I invited my client to embrace, love and fully accept her shadow, even if this was difficult; her ego was resisting, calling the shadow pathetic, childish, weak. There was a great tension between the frightened shadow that preferred to stay small and hidden and the ego that was driven towards success. I said to Natasha to thank her shadow for what it was trying to do, protect her from further pain and trauma. Then I explained to the shadow that its behaviour may have been a protective mechanism in the past, when she was six, it was now limiting Natasha's happiness, and I enquired if there was a way Natasha could satisfy its needs in a more gentle and mindful way. The shadow made some suggestions, many of which were rejected by the ego, who could not see the point in giving in to the shadow, which it judged as childish, vulnerable and demanding. We then educated the ego that it needed to be less of a strict "schoolmaster" and more of a loving parent to the vulnerable, hurt, shadow child. The ego was repeating the words of an unkind parent and teacher, and we were asking it to change its approach towards kindness and love. The more loving and accepting the ego becomes, the less the shadow needs to act out its hurt against itself or others. At the end, Natasha invited her shadow into her heart, integrating it inside her body.

When the shadow is integrated, we tend to our needs skilfully and appropriately. With confidence, we can form constructive relationships, accept love, and live in joy. If a situation arises that triggers an old ego pattern, we can always return to our personal inner work to reassure and heal our shadow.

Healing the Ego Shadow

Sometimes, when we begin to awaken from our cultural conditioning, we enter a space of inner turmoil. The inner voice of the soul and our ego may be at loggerheads. Past traumas, anger, and resentment may resurface to show us what we carry inside. The ego wants to forget and move on. The inner voice knows it cannot be ignored. The pain is deep and can feel overwhelming. When we arrive at this point, we may experience emotions and flashbacks from the past and wonder why we ever embarked on a therapeutic journey.

Unresolved emotions and memories exist as heavy energy inside us. We can release this energy by acknowledging it and energetically allowing any feelings and images associated with it to move out of our body, forgiving ourselves and anyone else involved in the process. We may have kept this energy in our system out of lingering self-blame, guilt, or fear. When a parent or teacher says to a child, "I would not have done this if you had been quiet. This is your fault," the child believes the adult and blames herself. When an abuser says, "Don't tell anyone about this, or I'll hurt you," the victim stays quiet out of fear. The words of the parent or abuser can become a tape that replays in the person's mind when similar circumstances occur, throughout adult life.

To heal ourselves, we engage with and acknowledge the trauma's origins and offer back the energy to its source—including someone else's words and actions. Six principles of self-understanding that help us in our healing journey follow.

1. My hurt is my responsibility. I stop projecting my pain onto others and instead, I look within. Rather than blaming the world for treating me badly, I acknowledge I am on a healing journey.

2. The hurt inflicted on me is not my fault. When someone is cruel, it is not because I provoked her. People's responses towards me are their choice and their responsibility, not mine.

3. The energy stored in my body attracts similar situations to me. If I hold onto the pain, blame and guilt, this will continue to manifest painful situations in my life. Therefore, I embark on a healing journey to release the hurt and integrate the shadow.

4. Light energy removes heavy energy. The trauma, stored in my body and aura, can be released through therapeutic work and spiritual practices that engage with high vibrational energies.

5.   The highest form of light energy is love.

6.   To truly heal, I forgive and let go.

I have seen my clients transform and increase their level of happiness when they engage with, acknowledge, and take responsibility for the shadow's voice (principle 1). After realising that the abuse she experienced was not her fault (principle 2), Annette felt she had received complete absolution. She then imagined her father sitting opposite her and she told him she would no longer carry the energy of the abuse in her body (principle 3). She expressed her anger towards her father and shed tears of sadness, frozen inside her for many years. She then imagined the abuse leaving her stomach and going to her father, who accepted it. Annette understood that her father had acted out his own anger and trauma by abusing his daughter. This was the first step towards forgiving him. In subsequent sessions, Annette worked to change the word "useless," her father's description of her, to the word "bright" (principle 4). This became her new affirmation, her new mantra. Annette accepted herself as she was and started to love herself by being kind and mindful about how she treated herself (principle 5). In our final session, Annette said she now loved herself enough to be able to completely let go of the past and forgive her father (principle 6). Forgiveness brought her inner freedom and changed her life.

THE POWER OF UNCONDITIONAL FORGIVENESS

In order to release our trauma, we need to both love and forgive ourselves and the other people involved. This is not just modern psychology. Indigenous cultures teach that the combination of love and forgiveness is the key for healing the ego and the shadow, the fragmented, traumatised self. The Hawaiian practice of Ho'oponopono expresses this in four sentences: I love you, I am sorry, please forgive me, and thank you (Smith, 2017).

This is easier said than done. Our shadow may want to hold onto the abuse. Behind the trauma lie other emotions such as anger, sadness, resentment, righteousness, which the ego shadow communicates to us. These emotions are associated with the loss of power we experienced and our inappropriate ways of taking power back. The story of what happened may keep replaying in our mind, causing more turmoil and pain to surface.

In 2007, I attended a talk by a Tibetan rinpoche. The lama likened our anger and pain to poison eating us from the inside, causing dis-ease. Meyer (2008) agrees that we can in fact suffer serious physical illnesses as a result of unforgiveness. I also agreed logically, but emotionally, at the time, it did not help me. I had been furious with a family member and could not forgive her. The lama asked us to bring to mind a person we needed to forgive and then look into his (the lama's) eyes. If we decided to look, we were making a pledge to let go of the hurt and unconditionally forgive the person, no matter what she did or may do in the future. I looked into the lama's eyes. I made the commitment. In the moment, I believed I forgave my relative, but it was short-lived. A few hours later, my anger resurfaced.

Letting go is not always easy. Our anger can quickly reappear and be directed, like a dagger, into the other person, as well as into our own body. Once, I awoke enraged and said aloud to the other person, "I hope you can feel this." I felt so righteous. I told myself she deserved it. Through the energy exchange, I was psychically hurting her and, as the lama said, poisoning myself.

Through counselling and other therapeutic work, I learned why this person was able to push my anger button. I believed, unconsciously, that family members were unfair and selfish, would forfeit my rights, and step over my boundaries. Consequently, each time a family member behaved in any of these ways, big or small, I became furious. My beliefs manifested (principle 3) so that life could show me something about myself. I understood that it was my responsibility to release this belief. My mind had found many ways to justify my anger, but underneath the anger was the pain, and the pain was mine to resolve (principle 1). The pain took me back to childhood and my feelings of abandonment and unfairness when my sister was born. I felt rejected when my parents focused on the new baby. Pinpointing the event that led to my beliefs helped me release them (principle 4), and in the process, I completely forgave myself and let love flow, instead of anger, to my sister (principles 5 and 6).

I recognised my part in creating a story that caused me so much hurt and anger. I had been manifesting events, so that I could perceive and perpetuate my inner reality. In releasing the pain, I made a new agreement with myself. No matter what family members did, I would still forgive and love them. Their behaviour no longer mattered (principle 2), when I loved and forgave myself unconditionally. The pattern fell away. In the years that followed, through karma purification (see chapter 6) and continued personal work, family relationships healed to a degree that I would never have dreamt possible. The lama was right after all.

The ego shadow carries beliefs about ourselves, others, and life. We may not be aware of the beliefs, but life shows us what they are by manifesting relevant situations. For example, if we think we are not good enough, life will orchestrate situations where we feel unworthy. Often, the others involved in these situations have no idea of their part in our life lessons. Life is speaking personally to us. It is our job to listen to life, discover our beliefs, and rewrite any problematic scripts to manifest a different reality in our life.

Now when I feel hurt by someone, I look into my life to see where the hurt has come from and what life is trying to show me about myself. I then decide to stop carrying the cross. I take a few moments of quiet time and concentrate on my breathing. I imagine the person in front of me, and say to her that I release myself and her from what happened. I forgive myself and her. I imagine all the doors of my heart opening wide and an immense light of love flowing from my heart to the person. I continue to send love, and if any other emotions appear, I let them flow out of my body with the power of love. Then I thank myself for being able to release my part in this suffering. I also thank the other person for being my teacher and helping me experience the power of my heart.

Over time, we notice we have become less reactive to and more forgiving of the old triggers and our former tormentors.

Forgiveness from the Deathbed. When a person is dying, she often finds the strength to apologise, forgive, and let go before the onward journey. It is the last opportunity she has in this life. During those last hours, past hurts can become insignificant. The ego starts to disintegrate, and the beauty of the inner spirit shines through.

Spiritually, we can recreate the circumstances of our deathbed. During this time, an energy of grace and forgiveness flows through us and enables us to let go. Our soul speaks of the bigger picture and releases the trauma from the inner self (see exercise 1).

The power of unconditional love: Channelling from ISIS. My spiritual guide ISIS encourages us to develop a practice that reveals our essence of unconditional love. ISIS says:

> The spiritual path can be a lonely road. The majority of the
> world shies away from spiritual and personal development.

When a light shines on you and reveals all that you carry hidden inside you, the inner shadow, most people either switch the light off, run away, or project their shadow onto others.

The shadow's game of hide and seek, name and blame, retrieving and revealing, is part of the human experience. In order to awaken into your divinity, you have many opportunities to integrate, embrace and accept the shadow. To do this, treat your shadow as a cherished part of you, with compassion and unconditional love.

At the same time as healing yourself, you are part of the collective consciousness that creates the world reality. And the world can be a very difficult place for some people.

As you retreat into your own personal work, remember that you are a cell in the body of the whole. As you work on yourself and your own process, extend the same love and compassion towards the world around you. Be fair and kind to yourself and, at the same time, be fair and kind to others. Remember that the greatest power that can change your reality and that of the planet, is unconditional love.

So, no matter what happens in your life and out in the world, take a few minutes each day to connect to the power of unconditional love that you are inside. Consciously ask that this power flows into every part of your body. Let it flow into your cells, into your life, into your family and friends, the people you know and don't know, into the institutions and the governments, into the Earth and all beings, and back into yourself.

If any judgements arise for yourself or others, release them. You do not need to know or judge why you or others behave in a particular way. You are doing this exercise in order to heal and transform. Extend the power of unconditional love to all the places within and outside of you without judgement. This is the greatest power you have available to you right now.

This practice is an act of service to yourself and the world community. Do it without expecting a difference. For example, you may ask, 'If I send love to the world's politicians will things change?' From that premise your love is conditional and ego-driven. You send love expecting a result. This limits the spiritual power of your practice. Instead send unconditional love, because beyond all your thoughts and actions, skilful and unskilful, this is your essential nature. And this practice is a way to tap into your power beyond the conditioning, and reveal your essence.

SUMMARY

Our ego shadow is the wounded part of us that develops patterns of behaviour as a defence against its hostile perception of the world. The ego cannot accept itself as it is, so it cannot accept others. It wishes to mask and avoid pain, and seeks pleasure to numb its emotions. Healing the ego necessitates healing the shadow, the hidden wounds of our past—discovering the motivation behind our behavioural patterns and hurts. Through personal inner work, we realise we can release and resolve the pain we carry. During this process, we are called to develop unconditional forgiveness, for ourselves and the others involved.

EXERCISES ON EGO-SHADOW INTEGRATION

Exercise 1:
Journey – Freeing the Ego Shadow

What you need: candle and matches or lighter

In this exercise, you set free the parts of your soul you locked away, and accept them back. You may not like them, but they are part of your own self. You are your own jailer and can liberate yourself through self-acceptance, forgiveness, and self-love. This exercise aims to help you integrate your ego-shadow.

As before, create sacred space, this time by inviting and welcoming your guardian angel or any other spirit helpers of the light you may have, whether you know them or not. Light a candle and ask for your guardian angel/spirit helper to come close and surround you. Your guardian angel has no judgement of you, no matter what you have or have not done. The spirits see us as a bright light of love, as radiant as when we were born. Now, surrounded by their love and support, you can make the journey of self-discovery and healing.

Start the journey by requesting that you are taken to the jail where you have placed parts of yourself. Imagine this jail in your mind's eye. What does it look like? Notice the parts of you that you have placed behind the bars. How do they appear in your imagination? If they are hungry, offer them food, and if they are thirsty, give them something to drink.

Now it is time to release yourself from this self-made prison and integrate your shadow. Open the door of the cell, and ask your guardian angel to take you and your ego shadow soul parts to a healing place. No matter how many parts there are, take them all with you.

Imagine arriving in a healing place of light and love. This could be a sacred lake, a healing river, a spring, or a temple of light. Let your soul parts be immersed in the healing energy of the place. See them being healed one by one. Notice if they transform into different images. Ask your soul parts what they need from you and how you can best take care of them in your everyday life (such as a daily walk in nature). Wait for the answer to pop into your mind. Reassure them that you will look after them from now on and not return them to jail.

Finally, invite your hurt parts to merge with you, welcoming them back fully into your body, welcoming them back home.

Slowly bring yourself back from the journey, by becoming aware of your body and your surroundings. Thank and release the spirit helpers/guardian angel. Ask them to protect and seal the sacred space and you before they go.

Exercise 2:
Psychodrama – Ultimate Forgiveness through Recreating the Deathbed

What you need: a glass of water or juice

You can do this ceremony alone or with others, making it as realistic as you want. If you invite others to participate, you may wish to assign them roles according to whom you want to forgive, or apologise to, at the time of your death.

In 2015 I took part in a death and dying vision quest in Death Valley, USA. During the ceremony, we were made aware of Mayan teachings on forgiveness, which formed part of an end of life ritual. In the vision quest, I found myself facing death and being asked to forgive everyone I held a grudge against (principle 6). I found the experience incredibly liberating. I have included a similar exercise to assist you in your forgiveness work.

Prior to each exercise, I encourage you to create sacred space by inviting Divine grace to be with you in any way that makes sense to you. You can also set your intention to release old hurts and trauma through forgiveness.

Imagine you are in your final hour. See yourself lying in your bed. The doctor has told you that in an hour's time, you will be dead and your soul will leave your body. Think about your life and invite everyone, alive and dead, with whom you have unfinished business to come close to your bed now. See them in your mind's eye coming towards you, or in real life, if you have participants with you.

Do this without shame, guilt or judgement. Nothing matters now. Say what you need to say to whoever comes to you. This is the time to bring closure and make peace with them before you die.

This is also the time to make peace with yourself. Say anything you wish to say to yourself. You may wish to pray to the Creator, your guardian Angel or your helping spirits. You are about to release your spirit and leave everything behind. Once you finish, stay in silence, cherishing the peace of your final moments.

Then, imagine the doctor rushing to your bedside and giving you a new medicine that restores your life completely. You have another opportunity to live! Drink the medicine (the water or juice), and feel all your cells rejuvenating. You are now back in full health.

Thank all the participants. They are so happy you have come back to life. Celebrate together the gift of another chance to live your life.

Your psychodrama is now complete. Take a moment to close the sacred space by giving thanks to Divine grace who assisted you in your work.

Suggestion: It is traditional to offer something to the exercise participants, as an energy exchange. You may wish to cook a meal for your friends.

I Am My Own Maker

Once upon a time,
a little soul saw a world below;
it was a world inhabited by many,
travelling on a journey through Divine Guidance.

The little soul was an innocent spirit.
It knew nothing about the world.
It may have been there before, long ago,
But it had forgotten it all.

The world looked appealing to the little soul,
displaying many colours,
inhabited by different species,
all travelling on the road of self awareness.

The little soul felt a call:
to go there and try its luck;
to become aware of who she was;
even though she did know deep inside.

An angel came to the little soul,
to take her across the way
to a new life.
Where nothing was certain until the end.

The little soul went with the angel,
through a dark tunnel to another world.
It was beautiful, with many colours.
As she had observed from above.

The little soul remembered nothing about this world,
so she had to take the word of others.
She thought they knew best and believed what they said.
But later she discovered they knew nothing.

The little soul cried for love and joy.
She had these before in the sky.
She tried to find them on Earth.
But she was utterly disappointed.

She saw other souls arriving.
And she told them the same story
that she had been told,
never questioning it.

One day the light shone through the darkness.
The little soul remarked on the beauty outside.
The colours that she came here to visit.
The road of self-awareness.

These colours became brighter.
Dancing around the eyes of the little soul.
As she went back through the tunnel
to be reborn in the other world.

What was your journey about, little soul?
You never saw the colours in your life.
They had gone when you arrived,
to be found again at the end of the journey.

The little soul said
she did not see the colours.
Because they were hidden inside the compartment of her heart,
but she was not brave enough to open it.

She now sees the beauty from above:
the colours in all these souls on Earth, radiating out.
Asking the others down there to notice them.
But alas, they are not meant to hear her.

3

Lessons from the Spiritual Nature
of Illness

*Spiritual Lesson 3: Illness as a teacher, my body reflects my soul's plan
for self-growth*

*Shedding skin: My spirit guides show me that my body has a story to tell. I
track the pain in every cell, every organ, every muscle that has ever felt uncomfortable. My back hurts when I feel unsupported; my feet become ill when I
am disconnected from the Earth; my womb goes into cramps when I reject my
feminine side. Behind the illness and discomfort lies the story of my life and
other lives, patterns and beliefs about who I think I am. My body responds to
my thoughts and reflects my feelings. I understand that healing is not only
addressing the physical ailments but also a deeper disconnection with myself.*

The soul is the architect of its future body on Earth. Before its incarnation,
the soul designs a specific home, selecting its special features. It decides
which body and what conditions and gifts the body will have that will support
the soul towards awakening. The soul's client, the universal law of karma, the
law of cause and effect (chapter 6), also instructs the architect about what to
incorporate within the body's design, the conditions and gifts that will help
the soul purify its karma. The soul then uses the available materials in the

genetic storehouse of its prospective parents and ancestors to customise the house.

At the same time as the physical body is shaped, an etheric blueprint of the body is created. This etheric blueprint is an exact copy of the physical body. It remains in perfection in the spiritual realms throughout the soul's earthly incarnation. The blueprint, like the physical body, carries all the soul memories—all the information the soul needs for its current incarnation, including its life purpose and significant memories from other lives. These memories may become available as the soul progresses in its human life.

Physical afflictions can be preordained by the soul before incarnation (primary causes) or generated by environmental factors (secondary causes).

Soul-Ordained Illness – Primary Causes

Within this classification, the spiritual nature of disease has four spheres of influence. The first is customised to the individual, and the second is inherited through the collective consciousness. The third cause of illness is through interpersonal toxins, such as tolerating an abusive relationship. Lastly, a powerful constellation of illness is self-induced through our beliefs and attitudes, such as negativity.

Customised to the individual. The body reflects the soul's desire to self-actualise (Maslow, 1970) and self-realise. Self-actualisation refers to the wish to fulfil the potential and purpose of each lifetime. I call self-realisation the discovery of one's divinity, becoming the living God, the ascended Christos, by overcoming the conditioning of the mind. A soul-ordained illness is one that the soul has chosen to experience as part of its journey towards self-realisation. Most of us may carry over long-held, unresolved attitudes, patterns of behaviour, and belief systems from previous lifetimes. Often, illness and disease are the soul's way of developing awareness and overcoming these patterns in its current incarnation. Unless the soul learns the lesson behind the illness through personal work, it may not find a cure for the disease.

For example, a soul is aware of a judgemental attitude towards others. Before incarnating, the soul chooses to develop a particular illness in order to become more compassionate. Adam worked long hours and was disparaging of anyone who took sick leave. He was especially critical of people with little understood disorders, such as chronic fatigue syndrome (CFS). Adam's soul gave him the opportunity to learn a much-needed lesson. He developed myalgic encephalomyelitis (ME) and was overcome with fatigue, missing many days of work. Before, he used to call the illness "the me me disease," in a derogatory manner, meaning that people who had ME were only looking for attention. Through personal work and karma purification, over fourteen months, Adam cured himself of ME and became a more compassionate person as a result. He now volunteers to help others deal with the illness.

Inherited. The body reflects the lessons the soul has come to experience on Earth. Some of these lessons are ancestral and manifest as illness and disease. Others are carried over from past lives, where we may have experienced a similar illness or weakness.

For example, thyroid or throat problems among females in a family may be caused by generations of women being silenced by others and having silenced themselves. A girl growing up in such a family may take on the belief that she should not express her feelings and opinions in her relationships and develop a thyroid problem later in life. A soul may choose to incarnate in this family to change the pattern for herself and future generations.

Interpersonal toxins. We may take on an illness because we feel trapped by the difficulties of life, including a problematic relationship. A client, Aliki, endured years of mistreatment from a verbally abusive spouse. At the age of sixty-four, she believed that she was too old to change her circumstances and leave the marriage. Aliki also thought marriage was for life, as her mother had always told her that "a woman should be happy with her lot, no matter what happens." Aliki had been unhappy in her marriage for a long time, suffering in silence, wishing herself dead many times. One day, Aliki tripped and fell down some stairs. Aliki developed a tumour in her body where she landed. A few months later, the lump was diagnosed as cancerous and eventually, Aliki died. Death was her escape route from years of abuse.

Self-Induced Negativity through Attitudes and Beliefs. There is a link between negative thinking and illness (Pert, 1999). In contrast to carrying over ancestral belief systems, negative thinking refers to our attitudes in daily life, whether we see our glass as half full or half empty. Do we have a tendency to moan and complain? Do we feel unhappy most of time? Is the grass greener on the other side of the fence? Negative emotions diminish our energy, our light and may cause illness (Emoto, 2010).

One of the first spiritual books I read was Mind Magic: The Key to the Universe by the healer Betty Shine, (1991). Betty was clairvoyant and could see people's auras. She noticed that, generally, positive people's auras sparkled with light, and they enjoyed health and wellbeing. Most of the time, the opposite was true for those who lived in negativity. Their aura was "heavy," and its colours were duller. What Betty explained through her clairvoyance faculties, has been verified by the scientific community. For example, scientific evidence relates cynical, hostile attitudes to higher incidents of coronary heart disease (CHD) and mortality, compared to optimistic traits (Tindle et al., 2009).

My spirit guides later illustrated Betty's wisdom. When we are caught in negative thinking, the wheels of life, the chakras, slow down and become clogged. As a result, our life force energy is compromised. Our meridian etheric channels are like slow-moving rivers where the water becomes increasingly stagnant. At the same time, our negative thinking surrounds us like an etheric toxic cloud that permeates into the world, affecting our wellbeing and that of others around us.

Education in the spiritual arts encompasses training the mind towards positive thinking. Spiritual practices, such as those of the Path of ISIS: The Seven Gates of Awareness, open the energy channels allowing more light to flow inside the body. At the same time, as we establish a Divine connection, we may become better equipped to deal with life challenges and not feel so overwhelmed when things go awry. Developing unconditional love, the opening of the heart, is key to creating a life of positivity and wellbeing. By reclaiming our personal power (chapter 1) and healing our soul essence (chapter 5), we become stronger from the inside and better able to make choices that serve our highest good, bringing more joy into our life.

ENVIRONMENTAL FACTORS – SECONDARY CAUSES

A secondary illness is contracted from our environment—independent of our soul's plan. It is now accepted that human activities may have an adverse effect on the environment and public health (Reis et al., 2015). Although we do not have primary responsibility for developing the illness, we are part of the collective consciousness that created the environmental pollution. At some level, we may be contributing to it, for instance, by driving a car. As these diseases are largely caused by factors external to us, and not pre-ordained by our soul, they are generally easier to heal.

For example, Nick and Stephen may catch malaria on a trip to Africa, an illness that exists in the environment. Nick's soul had ordained that the illness was part of his earthly journey. Stephen's soul had made no such agreement. As a result, Nick finds himself incapacitated by the illness and it takes personal work and life changes for him to completely recover. Conversely, Stephen responds well to the medication and regains his health shortly after treatment.

Ways to Release Soul-Ordained Ailments

The soul has two medicine cabinets for soul-ordained illnesses: one is ethereal, and one is earthly. The ethereal cures centre on energy healing work, purification and releasing energy blocks. The earthly cures relate to body work.

Ethereal Cabinet: Realigning Cellular Memory. Our etheric blueprint holds our life's plan and remains unchanged throughout our earthly life. As I have witnessed in my practice, the client's etheric blueprint (aptly, light blue) can come down during the healing and momentarily merge with the body to activate or recall a cell memory of wellness. This also reminds the client of her life purpose, and occurs at a point in her life when she can receive it.

Ethereal Cabinet: Purification through Self-reflection. In 2007 I experienced a cure following a five-day mantra retreat, facilitated by a Rinpoche of the Tibetan Bön Tradition. Mantras are chants that invoke etheric power and healing energy.

The retreat involved intense spiritual practice. Each day started at 4am and finished at 10pm. However, the closer to the start date, the more my resistance grew. Why should I waste my annual leave singing mantras instead of lying on a beautiful beach? Eventually I decided to attend, but half-heartedly. I had packed some novels.

The day before departing, I received a letter from my doctor. It informed me that my smear test had revealed cancer cells. I was given an early appointment to attend a biopsy. With the letter there was a leaflet about living with cancer and details of charities and organisations that provided support. I was filled with fear. I prayed to my helping spirits, ancestors and angels, anyone who was there, for help. They told me if I wanted to heal, I had to wholeheartedly attend the retreat, do all the spiritual practices and take the novels out of the suitcase.

And so I did. In the retreat, I avoided all distractions. Insights about the way I was living my life emerged out of nowhere. During the meditation practices, I self-reflected. One night I stayed in the shrine room and observed my dreams, thoughts and the issues that arose. The retreat gave me precious time and space for contemplation through which I found a stronger commitment to my spiritual calling. The subsequent biopsy and successive tests, showed no sign of cancer.

Ethereal Cabinet: Removing Energy Blocks. During a healing session, I often see the negative attitudes—regardless of their source, ancestral or otherwise—as blocks of heavy energy stuck in the client's body tissues. I channel light energy into them so they can be released. During or after the session, the client may experience physical pain, which is caused by the stored emotional hurts leaving the body. The physical pain signifies the release of the unacknowledged deep emotional and mental pain that was stored in the body as cell memory.

In 2015, after her orthopaedic surgeon believed her only option was to have knee operations, my mother sought a spiritual healing for her legs and knees. After the hour-long ISIS energy transmission, she reported feeling an explosion of fire inside her legs. She was in excruciating pain. Naturally, I was sorry that my mother was in pain, but I knew that the fire was breaking up blocks of heavy energy. The pain lasted three days and rendered my mother barely able to walk. And then, her legs healed completely.

Energy blocks can carryover from past lives. In the course of a healing, I sometimes see images of a client's past life when energetic blocks were created in their body. The blocks appear clairvoyantly as black or dirty grey energy blobs or as objects related to a past life trauma. A client with recurring headaches felt a weight around her head, as if wearing a heavy helmet. She described having been a soldier in medieval times. As I guided her through the past life experience, she made peace with everyone she had harmed or been harmed by, thus releasing the karma of that life. She no longer needed to keep fighting or regard others as enemies. I was then able to remove the helmet from her head. And her headaches stopped.

Energy blocks can also be caused by harmful intrusions in the body (Ingerman, 2004). According to Harner (1990), these intrusions can cause pain, discomfort, illness, and rises in temperature. Healing can take place when these energies are removed by high vibrational light flowing through the healer to the patient. On the third night of a four-night vision quest in Death Valley, California, I was bitten by a horsefly and had an allergic reaction. My lip and face began to swell. I connected to the light of ISIS, a healing energy system that I channel from the ancient Egyptian Goddess (see chapter 18, The Path of ISIS). As my hands radiated with the energy, I brought them close to my rapidly swelling face. Then, a vision appeared in my mind's eye. I saw a small, black ball inside my lip, and I understood that this was the poison from the horsefly. I also saw streaks of blue light surrounding the ball. I knew instinctively that I was healed. The swelling stopped and in a couple of hours, completely disappeared.

Other intrusions may be more dangerous to one's health. Sometimes, people make an unconscious agreement to take on the energetic intrusions of others, especially loved ones. A friend was sad to see her mother suffering from breast cancer. As her mother was going through chemotherapy, my friend also developed breast cancer in the exact place. Her mother recovered, but my friend died from the intrusion.

An exchange of intrusions between family members can take place when our love for the other person is so great, we would rather take on the illness than see her suffer. Unconsciously, we may believe that it is not fair for our loved one to be ill while we are healthy. This is different from healthy empathy, in which we are compassionate towards the other person but do not experience the guilt or wish to partake in their pain. We develop energetic attachments or cords to those we feel close to. These cords grow stronger the more we feel guilt about or are emotionally dependent on the other person. Intrusions creating illness are transferred through such cords.

An intrusion can only stay in our body if we have space to accommodate it energetically. "Reclaiming Personal Power" (chapter 1) discusses how we weaken ourselves when we give away our power. Energy gaps are also created when we dissociate from ourselves due to trauma or shock. Indigenous cultures believe that our soul is like a liquid essence, held inside the vessel that is the body. When we experience trauma, the vessel is shaken and part of the liquid-soul can leak out. The resulting gaps and spaces may potentially be filled by an intrusion, if we ourselves do not take steps to retrieve our lost energy. For instance, we can be reunited with lost soul essence through a soul retrieval process (see chapter 5).

Earthly Cabinet: Healing through the Body. The second medicine cabinet in our custom-built house is the body wisdom. The body is an adept instrument, giving us information about our unresolved karmic issues. However, the body's cues may be ignored or prone to misinterpretation and thus, require our deep awareness and practise.

When the soul incarnates, it merges with the body. Through spiritual development, we learn that our consciousness can leave the body. This can create the impression that the body is superfluous to our personal growth. Paradoxically, separation between the soul and the body is not always helpful. The spiritual path entails honouring our body and developing and using the bond that naturally exists between it and our soul.

Healing through the body is a crucial step towards wellness and soul realisation. Unless we become aware of our beliefs and change our attitudes, illness may manifest in different forms in the body. People may be cured of one condition, only to develop another related issue. For example, the body may develop psychosomatic illnesses to avoid situations that we judge as unpleasant or harmful (Shapiro, 1996).

In 2004, I noticed small infections on my feet. First, a toenail became infected, which I treated with prescription medicine. A few months later, another toenail became infected. Again, I used the medicine, and again, the infection disappeared only to reappear on yet another toenail. Eventually, my toenails recovered, but then a verruca appeared. No matter what I tried, traditional and alternative medicine, the verruca remained. My doctor finally said there was nothing more he could do, and I had to live with it.

Almost a decade later, in 2013, while I was camping in the Inyo Mountains, California, the spirits of the plants told me that my foot was infected with the verruca because I was disconnected from the Earth. Shamans believe that plants have a spirit that can communicate with people who are open to listen to them. Harner (1990) explains how medicinal plants can act as spirit helpers. The plants told me I needed to connect to the Earth with my bare feet and become aware of its healing power. During my five weeks in the mountains, I went barefoot as much as possible. At some point, I noticed the verruca was gone. I later found out that people have studied the beneficial effects of the Earth on the human body, promoting a technique called "earthing" (Williams, 2017). I regularly take time now to connect with the Earth, and have not had another foot infection or verruca.

The Last Door (Are We Listening Yet?)

Our human existence in one body is finite, whilst our soul's journey is eternal and infinite. Sometimes illness is a way for our soul to exit this incarnation and continue its journey elsewhere.

Exit Points. Prior to incarnation, our soul can set up different exit points, pre-programmed scenarios in which the soul may choose to die. Most of us are not cognisant of our exit points and are unaware that our soul has made these agreements, although highly advanced spiritual people may know their time of death in advance. Sometimes, exit points become active when a soul has achieved a major part of what it came to Earth to do.

In 2006, I saw one of my exit points. One of my life lessons was to leave a relationship that did not serve me. A month after separating from my partner, I became aware that I had reached an exit point. The spirits told me that leaving the marriage was a major realisation, and asked me if I now wished to die. I decided to stay alive. A few minutes later, I was walking along a narrow street when something stopped me momentarily. The corner of a balcony on the fourth floor of a block of flats detached and landed in front of me. Had I not stopped, I might have died.

Other exit points are put in place in case the soul is not progressing on its spiritual path. The soul sees that there is no point continuing to live in the same way and opts to take the exit point.

It's Terminal. Spirituality affords us a more nuanced perspective of terminal illness, especially when medical interventions and alternative healings fail. In some cases, healing may not help because the soul has completed its life's work, and its next step is to board the ship to the other side, where further opportunities await.

When few opportunities for personal growth remain in the current life, the soul may be able to progress further in the spirit world or through a different incarnation. This was true for Anna. When she first came to see me, Anna had been through months of chemotherapy and radiotherapy. The treatments were unsuccessful, and her doctor told her she had three months to live. I started giving Anna energy healing, and the symptoms and pain disappeared. We then focused on personal development work, looking at her life journey and her beliefs about herself. Anna was a radiant personality, but throughout her early adult life, she had despised herself. This persistent self-hatred had caused her physical and emotional suffering. As we worked through the different aspects of her personality, Anna returned to joy and happiness.

However, despite nine months of her intense inner work, Anna's symptoms reappeared. She entered the hospital and died soon after. I became furious with God. I was angry that Anna's symptoms had initially disappeared and when she had recovered her joy, they returned. In despair, I asked God how he could call himself a compassionate being. God came to me and surrounded me with an energy field of such love and compassion, that all anger left me. God told me that it was Anna's time to go. Her life would continue in the spiritual realms, and all the work she did on herself had prepared her for the next step on her soul's journey.

We are conditioned to think that an early death is a premature death. Each soul has its own journey and time on Earth, which is sometimes fixed and at other times, dependent on how the soul responds to life lessons. Our soul is eternal and occupies many bodies, living many lifetimes. At some point, the soul will leave its current life and continue its journey elsewhere.

Summary

Illness may be part of our soul's journey towards inner-realisation, our karma from past lives, or a means to reassess our way of living. Our body reflects the wishes of our soul for growth. It is chosen by us before incarnation, together with a blueprint expressing all that we are. Our karma, unhelpful beliefs, and negative attitudes about ourselves and our life are stored as heavy energetic blocks in our body and may cause disease. Physical illness may also be a way for our soul to exit the current life, as it has completed all that it came here to learn and has other opportunities for expansion in the spiritual realms. By listening to the body's inherent wisdom, appreciating life's lessons, connecting with the Earth, and taking steps to live life in a positive, respectful and fulfilling way, we are able to create a foundation towards wellness.

Exercises for Healing

Whether illness is generated by primary or secondary causes, working with the inherent wisdom of the body and high vibrational energies can reveal the deeper issues our soul is trying to communicate to us, as well as help us heal. Below, I include two exercises I have practiced in my client and group work. The first exercise is about becoming aware of any deeper issues that are manifesting illness, through self-reflection. The second practice is a journey to the sacred site of the Great Pyramid of Giza in Egypt, where light energies can help in our self-healing journey.

Exercise 1:
Body work – Communicating with the Body

In a quiet, relaxing space, speak to your body as you would address a friend. Acknowledge with gratitude its vital contribution to your earthly experience. Close your eyes and ask your body to appear in your mind's eye, in any form it wishes to take that reflects its needs.

Sometimes, you can see yourself in your mind's eye in a different form, or you may know instinctively what information your body wishes to convey. Acknowledge what your body is telling you and discuss with it how you can take positive action to address its needs. Then give thanks to your body, and come back from the exercise.

When I facilitated this exercise in my shamanic group, some people reported seeing their body as a different gender, reflective of their approach to life. For example, a woman who carried more male energy than female, saw herself as a body builder. Other people have seen themselves as plants or animals. A tree that appeared withered signified that the body felt unloved. Conversely, a healthy tree implied that the person felt nurtured by life. Different animals conveyed various feelings. Be open to see your body in whatever way it wishes to express itself, as this form will be significant to you in some way.

For instance, the first time I did this journey, I saw my body standing at a crossroads. It presented as an old woman with wrinkled skin, who was gasping for water. My body was telling me it felt old and lacked energy because it was dehydrated. At that period in my life, I was drinking a lot of coffee and hardly any water. By showing itself at a crossroads, I realised that I needed to look after my health to be able to go through the life changes I desired.

I have seen people transform their approach to life and health when they action their body's suggestions. Others acknowledge the information but choose not to act on it. Spiritual exercises can be helpful in providing us with insights but their effect increases when we take action. In this way we affirm to our body: "I am listening to you. I acknowledge your insights. Continue to speak to me. I am taking steps to heal".

Exercise 2:
Journey – Using the Light of Sirius to Release Energy Blocks

In an earlier section I mentioned how my mother's knees and legs were healed through the ISIS energy transmission. In ancient Egypt, ISIS was identified as the goddess of healing and was a healer's main spiritual helper. ISIS has a connection to the Sirius star. In those times, healers harnessed etheric light from Sirius, in order to release heavy energy blocks and heal physical illness. ISIS has taught me how to work with the light of Sirius both for healing, and spiritual and personal development. I teach these ways through the Spiritual Path of ISIS, the Healing Path of ISIS, and the Seven Gates of Awareness.

This exercise is a journey into the Queen's Chamber inside the Great Pyramid where the light of Sirius has been anchored by the ancient people. Start by creating sacred space, inviting the unconditional love of ISIS to surround you. Also welcome any helping spirits of the light you may work with. Set your intention to let go of an energy block that is ready to be released.

Close your eyes and imagine yourself in front of the Great Pyramid in Egypt. Ask permission from the guardian spirits of the Great Pyramid to enter the Queen's Chamber. Say to them that you have come to heal yourself at a deep level and release an energy block in your body.

If permission is granted, imagine following the guardian spirits inside the Queen's Chamber. (If permission is denied, ask the guardians why, and what you can do to be granted permission for the healing another time.)

Invite your body to show you any energy blocks which can now be released. You may experience pressure or pain in different body parts as you become aware of these blocks.

Focus on one of these areas, and ask to see the energy block in your mind's eye. The block may appear as heavy, dull energy or shamanically, as an insect or other creature. It does not matter how it appears, as it is only energy. Alternatively, you may have a felt sense of the block, as not everyone is visual. Thank the block for being there, as it has a lesson to teach you. Ask the block what it consists of and how it came to be in your body.

Acknowledge that you no longer need this block. Ask the body if you can release this block for your highest good. Also enquire if there are any changes you need to make in your life to complete the process. (You may have to change the attitudes and beliefs that created the block.)

Inside the Queen's Chamber, you are surrounded by the light of Sirius. It flows through your body in waves, pulsates through your tissues, and breaks down the block. Imagine voices toning ancient chants, which further activate the healing.

At the same time, with outstretched wings, ISIS, the goddess of healing, flies over your body. She brings a ray of high vibrational light into your crown chakra, the energy point at the top of your head. This ray flows into your central channel and meridian system and into the energy block you identified, to break it down so that it can be released. Stay with this process for as long as necessary for the block to be completely removed, or reduced.

When you feel this process is complete, allow the healing energy to flow through you, bringing you into a state of peace and harmony and filling any energy gaps with divine light.

Finally, connect with your heart, knowing the energy blocks were created by your soul for its growth. Let the light of love and peace flow from your heart, filling you with your own radiance. You are like Sirius, a star in the universe shining brightly in the endless space.

Thank the guardian spirits of the Great Pyramid and those of the Queen's Chamber. Thank ISIS and your healing guides as well as your body. Slowly follow the guardian outside the pyramid and bring yourself back from the journey. With every breath, become more aware of your surroundings. Then open your eyes.

Close the sacred space, by asking for the space and you to be protected and sealed before ISIS and any other spirit helpers leave you.

WELLNESS

It has taken many years to find peace;
unhappiness was like a curse that reappeared when least wanted.

A pain that kept coming back,
to remind me of the burdens that I carried inside.

I sometimes thought I alone had this load,
but when I looked, I saw it on many others.

Was I given this by my ancestors,
to carry for them on my life on Earth?

Did I agreed to take it on,
so that I could save others from further suffering?

My heart did not know where the pain came from.
It had been there for so long.

Even if I found it comforting, it kept me small, this pain.
I would go and lie down and cover myself with heavy blankets.

It had been a dear friend in some ways.
Even if it turned sour and sent a knife into my heart many times.

I saw that the knife was held by my own hand.
How many times did I stab myself?

It does not matter now,
I found that my heart had enough room to embrace me.

My body is my own mirror, carrying the wishes of my soul.
unlike me, it is mortal and perishable.

I thank my body for my life:
an adventure, where I meet myself.

4

Surrendering to Death:
Before, During, and Forever After

Spiritual Lesson 4: Surrendering to death, I make peace with life

Shedding skin: After three days of fasting alone in Death Valley, in America, I meet the spirit of death. I asked for this spirit to come. I prayed many times to become aware of my mortality. The spirit of death takes me to another world that is so radiant, my inner vision can only perceive indistinct shapes. Death explains that what I see is the luminosity of the souls returning to the spirit planes after passing. The golden light at the proverbial end of the tunnel that awaits us at death, is the light of our own essence in its primordial form. "How can I experience this light in my earthly life?" I ask Death. Death said, "You are intended to forget this light so you can embark on the journey of finding it again. It is the journey of forgetting and remembering that brings out the gifts of your soul."

We are passengers on ships powered by the wheels of reincarnation. The ships set sail from various dimensions towards the port of Earth, navigating through the portal that separates the spirit realms and the physical world. The ships dock at a port for a short while. In the harbour, other ships with other passengers follow different itineraries. One by one, the passengers disembark and experience life.

When it is time to leave, the passengers board their ship and set sail once again for the spirit realms. Some of us may forget to return to port, and our ship has sailed. We are left stranded in the Earth realm until other ships are summoned to take us home.

Once we arrive back in the spirit realms, we recall our adventures in the port of life—what we did and did not do, who we met, what we saw. Our soul may momentarily merge with the Divine Consciousness of unconditional love, to heal any traumas and disappointments from life on Earth and any memories of physical conditions.

Our next voyage may be to the same port or another harbour in the universe. Our higher spirit, spiritual guides, karma and soul determine where we will go. Sometimes, it is not easy to get a place on the ship and we may have to wait. Eventually, we sign up for the passage. This is how life and death operate.

Chapter 4 discusses the many ways we forget to return to port and miss the boat. Impediments such as fear, emotional attachment, inner turmoil, mistrust, and lack of faith can hinder our smooth transition. The teachings and exercises of this chapter guide the reader towards acceptance of death and a future easy passing.

FRAGMENTED, TRAPPED AND STRANDED SOULS

The best way to die is to die happy and aware. When we accept our time of death, we pass to the other side in a state of bliss. Free spirits know how to let go. For example, in the British Isles, Celtic funerals are upbeat celebrations. Rather than grieve the deceased, we express our appreciation for our loved one's life and toast her health, even though she is dead. This points to a realisation that life continues after death.

For some souls death can be a difficult process. The soul may leave part of itself behind, become stuck in the body, or miss the boat. I refer to these as fragmented souls, trapped souls, and stranded souls. Each circumstance is discussed below.

Fragmented Souls: When We Can't Let Go of Emotional Attachment. Death is the only certainty in life. There are times of departure, the exit points that have been determined prior to incarnation. When we—as a survivor or as the dying—do not accept the inevitability of death, we impede the passing.

When a loved one dies, any energetic cords, between her and those living, break. Once the physical body dies, the connection between those in separate kingdoms cannot be sustained. This connection is a cord between our solar plexus chakra and hers. The pain we survivors feel is caused by the removal of these attachments that now have nothing to hold onto.

I witnessed the pain from the removal of these cords at my ninety-year-old grandmother's passing. In the weeks prior to her death, I had accepted her impending departure. She had developed pneumonia and could only breathe through a machine. My spiritual guides warned me the night before that she was due to die, and I dispassionately agreed it would be for the best. I was at peace. Yet after she died, I experienced intense grief. I could not understand why. The spirits showed me that during my life, I had been attached to my grandmother. Energetic cords were connecting me to her body. At her passing, those cords broke and I felt the loss. Even though I was able to communicate with her psychically in the coming months, our reciprocal energy connection had been forever severed.

The grief we experience at a passing is our own. Sometimes we say, "I am sad for her (the deceased) because she had no joy in her life, or she died when she had so much to live for." Usually, this is our projection of our sadness. It is we who feel adrift. The deceased is probably enjoying a time of peace, healing, and renewal in the spirit world.

In Greece, the cultural tradition is to show anguish at funerals to prove to fellow mourners the depth of our love for the deceased. It is customary for close relatives to beg the deceased to "take me with you," as life without them is deemed impossible. After the service, mourners drink black coffee with no sugar or milk to represent the bitterness of the collective loss.

Survivors' overt displays of non-acceptance can be distressing for the deceased. Because of our pain, our loved one, concerned for our wellbeing, may not wish to board her ship. She may remain around the Earth and try to communicate with us to reassure us that she is well.

As a shamanic practitioner, I often witness how these types of emotional attachments of the dying and the survivor create soul loss for both parties at the time of death. A mourner who did not want to let go may hold back a soul part of the deceased to fill the hole that grief had created. Likewise, the deceased may take part of the soul of her living relative with her, so she will not be alone in the afterlife. Occasionally, both parties may gift part of their soul to each other, worrying the other one will not manage on her own. All of this usually happens unconsciously, as we are conditioned to see death as final and our loss as irrevocable.

Each of the above scenarios of fragmentation is known as "soul exchange," or as "soul loss". My guides showed me how detrimental either situation is both to the living and the dead.

The survivor who took a part of the deceased's soul, even if this was a gift, is weighed down by the burden, feeling unhappy and overwhelmed by life. For the person who died, because part of their soul is still on Earth, she cannot reunite with the totality of her essence. She has to wait for the survivor to either die or release her soul part.

The survivor who lost part of her soul essence to a dead relative is then often stuck in unending grief. She may feel as if something is always missing and develop addictive or harmful behaviours to fill this gap. What is truly missing is her soul essence, which lies with the deceased in the spirit reality. Consequently, it is harder for her to heal and find happiness.

The deceased who received part of the survivor's soul as a gift is not free either and cannot completely heal. As I explained in the first chapter, someone else's soul or power is useless to us. We cannot integrate it and make it ours.

All these soul exchanges create karmic links between people, which they have to address in other lives.

We do not need to die or grieve in order to lose a part of our soul. During life, we may lose soul essence due to trauma, either by experiencing it or perpetrating it (chapter 5). At death, we may be able to reunite with this lost essence, become whole again, and heal. However, if parts of our soul are held by others who do not release them, a complete healing may not be possible. This can hinder our soul's journey and prevent us from being whole in our next incarnation. In my professional practice, I perform soul retrievals for both the dead and the living, to reunite the client with his essence following scenarios of soul exchange, including those due to death trauma. These soul retrievals work beyond space and time, regardless if the people involved are alive or dead.

When a loved one passes, we must let her go on her journey to spirit, undisturbed. We wave goodbye as her ship leaves the port. Maybe, we will meet her again at our own passing. Maybe, we will have a future life together. Or maybe, we will not see each other again as our karma is complete.

Trapped Souls: A Whole-Body Experience. Fragmented souls leave without soul parts (soul loss), but trapped souls have a more traumatic experience. In this scenario, the body dies, but the consciousness remains attached to the corpse (soul trap). There has been no separation of the physical body and the etheric body. This can be distressing for the deceased. Imagine you are in a mortuary box or shut inside a coffin. This can occur when we do not wish to accept our death and have intense fear of dying, like a terror.

When I go to graveyards, I sometimes realise that a person's consciousness is still inside the grave or wandering aimlessly around it. In these situations, my guides will ask me to help the trapped souls pass over. The spirits in the graveyard are summoned by a powerful guardian spirit, an ancestor, or other being of light who appears as one of the trapped souls.

This masquerade is important because these souls may shy away from an angel appearing in the sky, whereas a guardian spirit in disguise is more familiar. The guardian informs the souls that help is on the way and gathers those who wish to move on from their trapped state. I arrive and open the portals between our world and the world of spirit. I sing a power song, following the tradition of the ancient people, singing the souls home. The singing helps the souls pass and maintains the high vibrational energy that assists this ceremony. Afterwards, I close the portal. (The practice of opening the portal for trapped souls to pass is inherently risky, as trapped spirits can slip into our aura and remain. It should only be undertaken by experienced practitioners.)

In another situation, the dying person resists moving on and is slow to separate from their body. However, she may not be trapped as this is her conscious choice. In such cases, we respect the wishes of the soul and do not try to move her on. When my great-aunt Paraskevoula was dying, she welcomed her time and passed peacefully. Paraskevoula had asked me not to take her across to the other side because she wanted to stay around until her funeral. It was important for her to be with the family a little longer.

At the church service, I saw my great-aunt standing outside her coffin in her etheric body, but I knew a part of her soul was still in the corpse. When the priest began chanting, the atmosphere changed. Angels surrounded the coffin, and lifted all of her essence out of the body. As they did, my great-aunt's form grew hazy as she and her essence were taken up to the spirit world. All that remained was the empty shell in the coffin, which was then buried in the graveyard.

Stranded Souls: Sudden and Violent Deaths. Some deaths are unexpected and violent. And unlike fragmented souls who exchange a memento as they board and trapped souls who miss the boat, stranded souls ignore the boat. Not everyone dies comfortably, or at least tended to, at home in bed and surrounded by loved ones. Sometimes, we die without warning and under traumatic and violent circumstances.

If a person dies unexpectedly or violently, she might not realise that she is dead due to the speed of transition from life to death. She tries to speak to the living, but no one appears to listen. She wanders in her energy body, and sees dead relatives who wish to help her pass. Assuming they are ghosts or fictions of her imagination, she runs away frightened. The way to the realm of the light has opened for her, but she ignores it. She misses the spirit path to the other side, and she is left behind on Earth.

Other times, the soul is caught in a time warp. They are around us but they see the place as it was in their time. I have seen this with souls that are stranded in old buildings, which have been subsequently modified. To a psychic, these souls can appear to be travelling through a wall, but in their time, there may have been a door that was subsequently blocked.

Souls that are stranded may inhabit a spiritual world of low vibration, called the "lower astral planes." This world exists around the Earth's etheric field. Souls in these planes continue to exist in a state of suffering, even worse than in the earthly life they left behind. I once visited these lower planes of the tormented souls and was astounded by the suffering that the souls experienced. It is a very sad place, mirroring the sadness of the souls who inhabit it. Due to their own anguished thinking, they find themselves entrapped there. Help may be available to them, but blinded by their sorrow, anger, stubbornness or despair, they may not wish to accept it.

In 2008, I visited an old church in Balquhidder, Scotland, known as the resting place of the eighteenth-century Scottish hero Rob Roy. The site is also famous in Celtic folklore as a place where the veil between the physical and spirit worlds is thin. The seventeenth-century Reverend Robert Kirk was able to observe the faerie realm in that location over many years. As I sat on a church pew, I perceived a spirit monk. He approached me and asked if I would help the stranded souls gathered there to pass over. These were mostly people who had died violently, in skirmishes and clan warfare. They had come together at this special place, waiting to pass. Due to the sadness and anguish of the souls, the whole area felt heavy.

Confused and distressed, I asked the spirit monk, "Why can't you help the stranded souls pass over?"

The monk said, "I need the intervention of a living person. A human being has the capacity to consciously enter the spirit worlds, and can work in both realities—the physical realm and the spirit realm. She is the bridge that helps stranded souls pass over to the other side. In helping the souls, she receives the positive karma from this compassionate action. As the stranded souls leave, the place is filled with light and the whole planet receives a healing."

Out of ignorance, some of us try to make contact with stranded souls for entertainment purposes and thus, will accumulate negative karma. We may use an Ouija board to speak to spirits or take part in a visit to a haunted house. Without realising it, we may be leaving ourselves open to a spirit attack, whereby a spirit person who is stranded and desperate may physically hurt us or attach to our aura, especially if she thinks we are being disrespectful. Sometimes, we experience pain and discomfort after these visits to haunted places. Stranded souls are not there for our amusement. They need our help to move on to a happier existence.

For example, a grieving and distraught client sought healing for a family member, Nicolas, who had died suddenly. I journeyed shamanically and discovered that Nicolas had hung himself. In the spiritual reality, Nicolas was still attached to the rope, waiting to die. His soul was unaware that death had already taken place. I helped Nicolas detach from the rope and spoke to him about his life, asking him to go through the veil to the other side. I said that I would help him part of the way since Nicolas felt unable to go by himself. He was still too traumatised by life events and had lost many soul parts. I asked Nicolas for his permission to perform a soul retrieval (chapter 5), a practice in which I heal and bring back the traumatised soul parts he had lost during his life. He readily accepted. When I brought back his own light essence, his tears of gratitude flowed. The soul retrieval was a huge gift for him, allowing him to recognise the light of his soul and move on.

Suicide may be part of the soul's journey, and yet, death by suicide remains controversial in modern society. In medieval times in England, people who suicided were buried at crossroads with a stake through their heart, and had their fortune seized by the crown. Other times they were buried outside the cemeteries, as it was thought they had offended God. A widespread belief was that suicide victims never found rest but returned as ghosts to plague their communities (Murray, 2000). These old prejudices still influence our thinking.

Suicide can be an exit point for the soul when it has achieved its purpose on Earth. More often, suicide is premature death; the soul chooses to escape its current difficult life. As a result, the soul does not finish its journey on Earth and it may have to return and live this life all over again, sometimes under more difficult circumstances. We cannot escape our karma.

Most souls who suicide, leave in turmoil and end up in the lower astral planes. Even shamans cannot move them to the light without their agreement. Conversely, those who embrace suicide peacefully and consciously, for example, through euthanasia, may have a very different experience and a serene passing.

Dying Well from a Spiritual Perspective

In my death and dying spiritual and shamanic work, I have encountered three key principles that enable a beautiful passing to the afterlife and the smooth continuation of our soul's journey, preventing fragmentation, soul trap and being stranded in the lower astral planes:

• acceptance and preparation for death: making peace with life by consciously preparing for our passing and settling any unfinished business, leaves us free to board the ship without regret;

• healing our energy body from the cell memories of illnesses removes the burdens of earthly life; and

• surrendering in faith to the Divine, opens the door at the final moment.

Acceptance and Preparation: Forgive and Move On. When death comes to us, we want to make peace with it and leave in a good way. This requires preparation. During a death-and-dying vision quest in 2015, facilitated by Meredith Little, co-founder of the School of Lost Borders, I was taught the Mayans' four-stage plan for dying well. The Mayans believe in the continuation of a soul's journey in the afterlife and the existence of a compassionate Divine presence that guides us home.

1. Accept death is knocking on the door, and surrender.

2. Put earthly affairs in order.

3. Withdraw from life's activities. Invite family and community to come and say goodbye. Settle or release grudges, ask and offer forgiveness, share love. Make peace with the world.

4. Withdraw into solitude, and prepare for the spiritual journey home. Make peace with oneself. When the time comes, greet death like an old friend and follow him to the other side.

In our society, we are largely conditioned to fear death and therefore, ignore it. The subject is taboo, even though it is a fact of life. Those of us who fear the inevitable and are close to our transition may fight any awareness of our condition and occupy the mind with mundane details of everyday life.

In the Mayan way, death is a conscious departure to the spiritual realms. Like the eagle, we soar into the cloudless sky, leaving everything behind without remorse.

We do not just need to live skilfully. We also need to die skilfully.

Healing the Energy Body: The Death Cure. Even when we live free, accept the inevitable, and have faith, our death can be painful and compromise our smooth passage. The soul may be in prolonged agony during its final illness.

Sometimes, even though the body dies, some part of us may retain the memory of an illness or physical pain. This memory, including all its effects, is stored in the "energy body," an exact replica of the physical body, made of universal energy. This second body, which the ancient Egyptians called "the double," can be seen psychically and survives after death. Unless the memory of the illness is removed, the dead person may still, psychologically, carry the pain and suffer from a similar condition in their next incarnation. The pain can prevent the deceased from moving into the spiritual realms. Since the energy body is exactly the same as the physical body, the person may not realise she has passed. She may wander around her earthly home in her energy body, plagued by the illness.

Between 2008 and 2011, I attended a fortnightly psychic circle. My guides would bring pained souls to me. Despite having no physical body, the agony of their final illness was intact. This is akin to phantom limb syndrome, when a person feels pain in an arm or a leg that is missing or has been amputated. In the energy body, the limb is still there and has not been healed.

Healing the energy body is not necessary if the soul passes to the spiritual realms of the light, where we instantly heal. When we die, our consciousness moves out of the physical body into its double—the energy body. It is then the energy body that moves into the spiritual realms. In the spiritual worlds of the light, our awareness grows: we are pure consciousness that has manifested this human form. When our consciousness embraces the shining spirit that it is, the energy body is completely repaired, healed and no longer needed. We each experience three states: the physical body, the energy body-double, the pure consciousness.

At the behest of some clients, I perform healings for those who have died, if needed. The process has three stages.

1. Heal the energy body and remove any memories of past illnesses. I have found that the energy body can heal quickly through light. So, I ask the spirit being who is still in pain to step into my aura, and I pull the light of ISIS down through my crown chakra. Through this light, the spirit person's energy body is healed, almost instantly.

2. Soul retrieval to reunite the deceased with all of her essence lost through trauma and also address any soul exchanges between her and loved ones.

3. Invite the soul to move on to the spiritual realms. I never move a soul without its agreement. Sometimes my spirit guides and I may have to persuade the soul to move on, but we do not force anyone through the veil against their will.

I do not recommend performing this healing for the dead without suitable training, as you may take on illnesses from the deceased or carry them in your aura, depleting your own life force energy.

In our culture that prizes the scientific mind, we have no concept for the above practice of healing the dead. In comparison, in ancient traditions healing for the deceased was of vital importance to ensure a soul's passing was uneventful and peaceful. Medicine people were called to support the deceased. Death wives were responsible for delivering the soul back to spirit.

Some of these traditions survive today. When my friend Jeanne, a BönPo practitioner, died, I was asked by the rinpoche to do a forty-nine-day healing ritual to help purify Jeanne's karma and heal her energy body and state of consciousness. As I did the ceremony, I felt gratitude coming from my deceased friend.

The ancient Egyptians too had complex healing ceremonies to ensure that the soul moved to the spiritual realms of the light happy, healthy, and intact. Since my work with ISIS, I remembered some of these concepts that I had practiced in a past life in Egypt and they have been incorporated into the ISIS Path courses.

Having Faith: We Are Not Alone. Living free of attachments paves the way to dying well. The ticket to living free is having faith in a divine love. But what if we do not have faith? What if we do not believe there is "a God or gods"? Or an afterlife? Well, if we think our last breath is the end of our existence, then when the light of spirit comes to usher us to the spirit realm, we may dismiss it.

Faith in a Higher Power helps us in life and offers ease at the hour of our passing. When we die believing in the goodness of the Divine, we are at peace. Even if we die suddenly or violently, a thought towards God will always open the gates to the spirit realm. Trusting in God and the Divine wisdom will help us calm the mind and move forward to the spirit world. The Bhagavad Gita, an ancient Hindu discourse speaks about the death process, and explains the immortality of the soul and the illusionary nature of life on Earth. The ancient text suggests that the way to die well is with the name of God on our lips (Easwaran, 2007).

GOING HOME

So what happens at death? What do we see or experience? And what is the best way we can move on at the end of life?

Trusted Helpers: Follow the Guide. When we are terminally ill and close to passing, spirit helpers and guides visit us. It is common for people who are dying to see their dead relatives and friends.

A few days before my great-aunt Paraskevoula died, her dead sister Filitsa visited me in a dream to advise me of the impeding death in the family. She was coming to help my great-aunt pass. When Paraskevoula entered the hospital, she started seeing her sister, who had been dead for over five years. I said to Paraskevoula to follow her sister the next time she came, knowing that Filitsa was taking her home. Similarly, my granny saw her mother as she was dying. Other people see Jesus, Mother Mary, a spouse or someone who they felt close to in life. One client followed his power animal, a horse, when he passed.

The death process may last several days, even weeks. In those cases, part of our essence moves gradually to the other side, and the veils between the worlds are thinning. At the hour of our passing, when we see our helping spirits and deceased relatives, it might be time to follow them.

Some of us are afraid of death because we believe we will go to perdition. After centuries of Christianity, fear of hell and the day of judgement exists in the collective consciousness. Our fear keeps us bound to the Earth realm. Once I was trying to persuade a "stranded spirit man", who had died in the early 1900s, that there is no hell. He asked me how I could know as I was still alive. I respected his point. So, I asked him if he would trust an angel. As he was a Christian in his life, he accepted the help of an angelic being. In his mind, an angel could never take him into the devil's domain. The angel took him to the other side.

Waking up on the Other Side. My spirit guides have told me that when we incarnate, a large part of our consciousness does not come into the body and remains in the spiritual realms. The immensity of our spirit, the Divine Consciousness of the Creator, always exists complete and whole. This eternal spirit projects a higher self. The higher self then projects the soul, which incarnates on Earth and has a life experience. The higher self is the observer of all that is taking place on Earth. It stays in the spiritual realms as the bridge between the immensity of our spirit and the soul that incarnates.

When my friend Katy was dying, I promised her that after she passed, I would journey to her shamanically and find her on the other side. This was a big comfort to her. The day after she died, my spirit guides took me to a spirit hospital, where I saw Katy sleeping peacefully. This is a place in the spiritual realms where Katy was taken to heal, before moving on and reuniting with her higher self. (Katy died in a hospital, so I believe this is why her consciousness projected a spirit hospital. But this is not the same for everyone. There are endless projection possibilities relevant to each soul who passes.)

My guides asked me to gently wake up Katy. When she awoke, I noticed the amazing brilliance in her eyes. This was Katy as a spiritual being, not an earthly woman. My guides asked me to show Katy that she was alive by taking her to a window and pointing out the sun radiating in the sky.

When I help a person pass, I journey shamanically to her the next day and, with her permission, I wake her up and show her the sun. The helping spirits say it is beneficial for souls to see the sun. This is not the sun of our solar system, but the source of all life, the creative force of the universe, God's consciousness that radiates warmth and love to all beings. Experiencing this spiritual sun, the person feels an inner sense of being touched by the Creator and knows she, too, is the light of the Creator.

Those of us who die aware, consciously embracing death as part of life, do not need help to heal or to be woken up on the other side by a shamanic practitioner. But for those souls who are not aware at death, a spiritual practitioner can help.

When we move to the other side of the veil, we review our life on Earth and merge with the Divine Consciousness and we completely heal and remember who we are. We can also self-heal prior to death through spiritual practice, as described in exercise 2 below.

After we move to the other side willingly, wake up in the spiritual realms and self heal from the experiences of earthly life, we can still visit the Earth plane. We learn to move through the dimensions, as we have no body and are pure spirit. When the consciousness then visits a previous relative, perhaps in a dream or through a medium, it usually takes on the recognisable form it had in the past life. That said, being free to choose its appearance, the spirit may present as a healthier and younger version of the form it once inhabited.

Dying Awake. An authentic spiritual practice, meditation and connection with the Divine, can prepare a person to be more aware at death. This also depends on a person's karma (chapter 6).

Ideally, we would die peacefully, embracing the process, being the protagonist in a new movie that opens up before us. We are aware that we are about to leave the port of life and will soon board the ship that travels to the other side. As we leave our body, we start to see a light, a brilliant white light coming closer. There may be other coloured lights too, but we ignore them. Attracted by this immense light, we step fully onto the ship and travel to the other side. We realise the light we followed is our own soul, free from the body. We are home.

Returning Souls: Death as Lodestar. Shortly after I wrote this chapter, my helping spirit ISIS, the Divine Mother, came to me with her perspective on life and death. These are the words of ISIS:

> The Spirit of Death is a compassionate being, who guides
> souls into a new experience. The spirit is not the grim reaper,
> a skeleton, or anything else people may have described, out of
> their fear of death.

> When death comes, surrender to it, knowing you will be
> guided. Death has not come to cause you harm, but to help
> the soul return home. Death is a friend, not an enemy.

> Long ago, people knew this and celebrated the time of death
> as a time of going back home. Now, many see death as
> something external, something that should be ignored and kept

distant, something that causes harm. This is not so. Death walks with you every day and is part of the human experience. It is the denial and fear of death that causes suffering.

The Spirit of Death is a compassionate being of light who comes to those who need it. Would you rather live in pain? Would you rather miss opportunities open to you in the spiritual realms? Do not fear death.

The fear of death keeps you stationary, avoiding risks that may help you realise your purpose for incarnating. People give up in life for fear of death.

Those who live with the fear of death, fear to live. They fear life. Those who live with the awareness of death, embrace life.

SUMMARY

The soul that incarnates to experience life on Earth is but a small projection of the immensity of our spirit. Each soul's time on Earth is a short journey, which comes to an end at the moment of death. The best way to die is to consciously surrender to death, making peace with life and having faith in a Creator. Emotional attachments to loved ones can prevent souls from moving forward to the unconditional love of spirit and hinder the living as well. Shamanic practitioners can heal these fragmented souls, trapped souls or stranded souls. Healing the dead is as important as healing the living. We are never alone in death when we have faith in Divine grace.

EXERCISES TOWARDS A PEACEFUL END

Exercise 1:
Journey – Visiting the Other Side

To help dispel any fear of death, you can experience the love of your dead friends residing on the other side of the veil whist you are still living. I have used this exercise with terminally ill clients, as well as spiritual practitioners who wish to have a healthy approach towards death.

In the beginning create sacred space by inviting the Love of the Divine to surround you, and your guardian Angel to assist you. Also, as you are visiting the death realms, imagine yourself in a bubble of blue light patterned with streaks of gold.

Set your intention that during this practice, you step into the spiritual realm of the light to meet those who will welcome you home at your death. I suggest you only step into the other realm, and venture no further. It is not your time to move on.

Imagine in front of you is a portal of light, like a gate surrounded by light. The doors are closed, unless it is your time to die. Ask your guardian angel to open these doors into the light, so you can become aware of the process of death. (If the gate imagery feels unnatural, choose another that suits you, such as a bridge over a river, or tunnel.)

In your mind's eye, wait until the doors open. Imagine stepping through the doors, and coming out on the other side. You are in a place of radiant light. Your eyes may not be used to the brilliance of this light. Wait until they adjust.

As your eyes adapt you notice shadows coming towards you. The shadows are the people who will greet you when you die. They may be relatives and friends who have already passed, religious figures, and spirit animals. Wait to see who comes. You may be surprised to see who is in your welcome party.

Listen as the spirit beings greet you. Feel their love radiating towards you. Immerse yourself in the pure love of spirit.

After bathing in the love of your spirit friends for a while, it is time to return to your life. No matter how good it may feel to bask in the radiant light, turn around and walk back through the doors and into your physical body. Imagine the doors closing behind you.

Slowly bring yourself back by becoming aware of your breathing. Thank the Divine and your guardian angel of the light for allowing you to travel to the spirit realms. Ask the angel to close the space, and seal and protect you and the room.

Exercise 2:
Spiritual Practice –Merging with the Creator

This healing can be done as a spiritual practice any time prior to death, to reconnect with the Divine essence. It is also a way to heal our energy body from earthly conditions that you do not want to carry into the afterlife.

Start by creating sacred space, inviting the Love of the Divine to assist you in this practice. Also, as in the previous exercise, imagine yourself in a bubble of blue light patterned with streaks of gold.

Set an intention to merge with the light of the Divine and heal your energy body. Feel yourself detaching from the body and floating upwards towards a central sun, the light of the Creator. This radiant light awaits you.

Merge with the sun, feeling your individuality melting away. You and the Creator are one, there is no you anymore. Everything within you dissolves. You are pure consciousness, the light of the one sun. Stay in this state for a few minutes.

Feel your soul filled with this light and then gently detach from the sun, becoming again an individual. Slowly separate from Divine Consciousness, and flow back into your body. As you return, you may feel a slight physical sensation when the soul re-enters the body, or have an inner knowing that you are back.

Welcome back your soul, now healed and filled with brilliant light. Imagine this incredible light shining in your heart, filling every cell of your body with its radiance. Stay in this space for a few minutes.

Slowly come back by becoming aware of your surroundings. Reaffirm your gratitude to your soul, your guides, and the Divine. Ask that you and your space are closed and sealed.

THE JOURNEY THROUGH THE VEIL

What is on the other side of the veil?
I see a world I do not know, yet this is where I come from.

I am fascinated with this world,
but scared of it and those who inhabit it.

I live life trying to forget that at some point I will die.
I consider myself immortal.

Other people die but not me.
I continue living.

My loved ones knock on my door.
I cannot hear them.

They whisper about this world,
where everybody ends up:

"It is a world of miracles.
Your thought becomes reality, quickly with certainty.

If you are sad when you die, sadness is what you encounter.
Joy is there too, when you hold this state in your mind.

It is a world of many layers, for all states of consciousness.
There is a place for everyone, and yours is there too.

In the midst of it there is a heart and some will know it.
Through the path of love you find the way to it."

5

Soul Retrieval and Soul Reclamation

Spiritual Lesson 5: Reuniting my soul, I become whole

Shedding skin: Lying on the floor, I follow the drumbeat. I am scarcely aware of my surroundings, whilst colours, sounds, and feelings from another world fascinate a different side of me. I need to trust the shamanic practitioner who is journeying next to me, trying to retrieve parts of my fragmented soul. I let go and relax into the process. In a vision, I see myself sitting behind the practitioner, on a galloping horse. My inner eye clears as I travel deep into my past. The shamanic practitioner is on a mission and asks me, "Are you ready to heal?" I say yes, and then he blows vigorously into my heart. I feel a comforting warmth expand within me. The sound of the Native American flute gently brings me back. The practitioner says, "Welcome home," and offers me a cup of herbal tea. Until that moment, I did not know I had been lost to myself for many years.

A LIFETIME OF SOUL LOSS

I was introduced to the practice of soul retrieval in 2007, whilst on a shamanic practitioners' course based on the work of Sandra Ingerman. During the course, I learned that many indigenous cultures believe our soul is vulnerable to physical and emotional traumas, and that parts of the soul can dissociate or leave the body and move into an alternative reality to escape difficult experiences and remain suspended in time.

According to this view, trauma can trigger small or significant soul loss depending on how we experience an event, how sensitive we are, and the extent of violence involved. When soul loss happens, we can become numb to life, existing without feeling like an automaton. In order to fill the gap created by the loss, we can develop addictive behaviours around alcohol, drugs, food, or depressive thoughts. Dr Paine (2012) describes the numbness that follows the trauma by saying that numbness is not the same thing as lack of pain. Instead he asserts that numbness can result from overwhelming pain, sensation and memory of the trauma. He perceives addiction as a symptom of the emotional and spiritual wounding and associated pain. The obsession with the addictive substance is a secondary development to the post-traumatic stress disorder (PTSD), which Dr Paine identifies as a disease of the mind and thinking.

The soul loss may unconsciously keep us attached to the trauma, and we may feel as if something is always missing from our life. We may have difficulty moving on from what happened, and grow sad, bitter, and resentful. We may adopt a victim mentality and start acting out of character. As the years pass, the soul loss can manifest as fear, insecurity, depression, and even chronic physical pain. This is why indigenous cultures believe that unless the lost soul parts are returned (and the sooner, the better), it is difficult for a person to fully heal.

Indigenous cultures are sensitive to the potential for soul loss occurring at any time. They address soul loss as soon as it occurs in order to empower the individual, who may not be her usual self, especially if she experienced an accident or traumatic event, such as the sudden death of a loved one. When travelling in Guatemala in 2007, I visited a Mayan village. Our guide said that once a person becomes aware of soul loss either in herself or in a family member in her care, she visits the local shaman to have a soul retrieval performed. During the healing, the whole community participates by holding space. They sit in a circle around the shaman, chanting and praying for a positive outcome.

The need for soul retrieval healing in the western world became apparent during my aforementioned soul retrieval training. As with most of us, I was carrying traumas, hurts, and disappointments. During the course, I received multiple soul retrievals from fellow students that brought back many soul parts from various upsetting events in my life. I immediately felt shifts taking place within me, but it took several months for these soul parts to fully reintegrate. I gradually became stronger emotionally, more mature, calmer in my mind, and healthier in my body.

In the West, the concept of soul loss is not part of our belief system and therefore, not generally recognised or understood. Without access to the traditional viewpoint and resolution, we may be caught in emotional suffering for a long time. Further, the trigger for the emotional suffering may be suppressed and we may self-medicate with unhealthy substances and behaviours. Medical treatment may be insufficient, whereas a spiritual healing therapy could aid recovery as Dr Paine (2012) discovered.

Left untreated, soul loss can become a vicious cycle. Loss of soul parts can create further difficulties, which creates new trauma and therefore, more soul loss. In cases of extreme violence, either suffered or even witnessed, extensive soul loss can take place, and the mind may erase all associated memories, such as in PTSD. Eventually, however, the soul, wishing to heal, will remind the person of what happened and hidden memories may resurface, sometimes in dreams, flashbacks, and déjà vu experiences.

Soul loss has multiple causes and can occur during any phase of life from conception to death.

In Utero and Childhood. If a pregnant woman is unsure, consciously or unconsciously, about having the child, she can transfer her doubt and insecurity onto the foetus. The developing foetus experiences the mother's emotions and carries the rejection into its future life. My client Kalioppi had been conceived when her parents were separating from an unhealthy, violent marriage. She always felt unwanted, lacked confidence, and suffered from depression. During our hypnotherapy session, Kalioppi remembered feeling her mother's anguish about the pregnancy. As a foetus, she had witnessed her mother's thoughts and emotions. The memory initiated a healing journey for both her and her mother as they undertook personal work and received multiple soul retrievals.

Birth trauma may also create soul loss, especially with the increasingly medicalised and clinical nature of the labour and delivery process that has taken the heart out of this beautiful event. Projected parental expectations can also be harmful. Parental neglect, strict parenting, childhood disappointments, and even the loss of a favourite toy are some of the causes of soul loss that I have seen in my healing practice.

The school years are also potentially traumatic for children. Separating from the family unit, a teacher's inappropriate remarks or behaviour, and playground bullying can create soul loss in the young student. Soul loss at this early age can plant the seeds of unhappiness that may grow into dissatisfaction and depression later in life.

The Teen Years. Teenagers are exploring independence and discovering their individuality. Paradoxically, friendships and a sense of belonging become more important. Sexual awakening can lead to new and difficult experiences. Teens may encounter soul loss during the breakup of a first romantic relationship and through ridicule from and rejection by peers.

Experimenting with alcohol and recreational drugs, especially to the extent of having blackouts and memory blanks, can lead to soul loss. When a person is intoxicated and drugged, her energy bodies open and she may access the alternative psychic realities spontaneously. This can be dangerous for the integrity of the soul. The part of her soul that has travelled into the psychic realms may get stuck there. The resultant gap from the soul loss, could be exploited by negative energies and malevolent spirits, which enter her energy field and cause harm, particularly if she has no awareness of psychic protection. These foreign energies can cause physical and mental illness, increased levels of anxiety and paranoia, and generate patterns of negative thinking. In extreme situations, panic attacks and depersonalisation disorder may follow.

Adulthood. If we experienced soul loss as a child, we may find it harder to grow into mature adults. We may behave like a spoiled child, renounce our responsibilities, and numb ourselves with addictions. We may find ourselves locked in an unhappy relationship, which confirms the beliefs and patterns established in childhood (such as feeling neglected and ridiculed). These are all indicators of soul loss. Unless one engages in personal development work, the patterns repeat, creating further unhappiness and more soul loss. Long-established fears and insecurities can re-emerge and manifest as fear of losing material wealth and social status, in overcompensating behaviour, or as social withdrawal and depression. The soul loss cycle continues.

Elder Years. Traditionally, our final years are a time of reflection. The veil between our world and the spirit realms becomes thinner. Free from the demands of child-rearing and breadwinning, we may have the opportunity to focus on exploring the mystery of life and guiding our descendants on their own path. New soul loss at this end-stage of life can make us resentful and bitter. Unable to make peace with our life, we fear death, which manifests through the breakdown of the physical body and the loss of our peers. Rather than growing into maturity with gratitude and grace, we are fearful of and curse our mental, emotional, and physical decline. We regret missed opportunities and grieve those we have lost.

Throughout Life. Experiencing accidents, misfortunes, violent and abusive acts, and the death of loved ones (chapter 4) can all potentially trigger soul loss in us. However, soul loss can also occur when we intentionally harm another being and silence our voice of conscience. I have found that the souls of people who have harmed others or themselves, for example through abuse, brutality, or murder, also fragment and fly away during the attack. The perpetrator loses some of her light. Unless she repents, she becomes inhumane and may continue her destructive behaviour. The karmic consequences of the act also mean that eventually, the perpetrator will suffer the pain of her victim. This creates a vicious circle, which can only be broken through the realisation of the pain we caused others and taking responsibility for our actions through repentance, forgiveness, reconciliation, and positive action.

Tick (2014) worked with a variety of indigenous methods, including soul retrieval, to help American soldiers suffering from PTSD. His patients described how they felt their soul was destroyed through their experiences of war. Following healing, some of them found it helpful to return to the war zones, such as Vietnam, and offer help to local communities via various peace projects.

METHODS OF SOUL RETRIEVAL ACROSS MANY TRADITIONS

In 2014, in Nepal, I was with a group visiting the ancient city of Bhaktapur, known as the "City of Devotees." As we walked around the famed Durbar Square, an electrical storm broke out, and we took shelter under the roof of a nearby temple. Waiting for the torrential rain and lightening to stop, I sat facing an elaborately carved, stone temple. I recognised the stone temple from a dream I had had six years earlier. The Hindu deity Ganesha had instructed me to perform a ceremony there for the wellbeing of the planet.

I asked the shaman guide to tell me about the temple. He said it was dedicated to the Great Mother Durga, but its most unique features are the two carvings at the foot of the entrance steps. Pointing to one of the carvings, the guide said that it depicted a shaman carrying his client's soul parts during a soul retrieval healing.

Shamanic. Since my shamanic training in 2007, I have performed hundreds of soul retrievals for clients. In my sessions, I journey with my helping spirits to the alternative realities where parts of the client's soul are frozen in time. For example, a soul part of a young girl who had been bullied at school stays at the same age.

Soul parts must first be healed before being returned to the body, lest they retraumatise the client. The healing ensures that the old wounds do not resurface. So, I take the soul parts to a healing place, and I ask them to slowly release their fears and trauma. A transformation at soul level takes place. The parts start changing from their unhappy emotional condition into a luminous state. When a soul part returns, the gifts it carries may also manifest. The soul part may then tell me how the client could develop the gifts.

When I find a lost soul part, I reassure it that it is safe to come back to the person, as usually the life circumstances that caused the soul loss are no longer relevant. For example, the soul may have left during the school years but the client is not at school any more. I remind the soul that its place is in the body, rather than in this suspended state. I explain how the client wishes to heal and find happiness in her life, which would be very difficult for her to achieve if it stays away. I emphasise that the client needs the soul energy to be whole. The soul part may be reluctant to return if it feels nothing has changed since it left. Or, it may stipulate changes that the client needs to make for it to remain. The client may need to demonstrate to her soul part that she is willing to heal by following through with its suggestions. There are times, however, when the client may not be ready for change, for example, the identity of victimhood can be too strong. Then, the soul part may decide not to stay.

During a soul retrieval healing, I am part of a team—along with beings of light and disembodied spirit shamans—working on the client at the same time. They do not always let me know what they are doing, as I am focusing on the journey and they do not wish to distract me. Some spirits may use my body to perform healing, merging with me as their energy flows to the person. Others may show me some of the lost soul parts, while some spirits bring back the soul parts themselves. The spirits may also appear directly to the client offering guidance.

Shamanic Cleansing. Shamanic healing for soul retrieval may also include ritual immersion and herbal cleansing. I once took part in such a healing in Peru. At the Temple of Water in Tipon, near Cusco, three shamans worked together to bring parts of my soul back. First, they swept local herbs over my body to remove any negative energy. Then, they had me sit in a part of the temple where the water flowed beneath me and in front of me. The three shamans placed their feet in the water and chanted. They called my soul back, which was cleansed by the sacred water element, and blew it into my crown. The whole process was over in mere minutes, but I was left exhausted. For the next hour, I lay on the earth to integrate.

Tibetan Buddhism. I have participated in a community soul retrieval known as "La-Lü" in the BönPo tradition of Tibetan Buddhism. According to Buddhism, everything one experiences, positive and negative, is governed by the law of karma. Therefore, the reason a soul part leaves the body and dis-ease settles in, is due to one's karmic debt.

To prepare for soul retrieval, the five causes of karmic debt must be pacified by the practitioners of this art, usually monks, lamas, and rinpoches, although laypeople who have taken refuge and learned the mantras can also be invited to take part. These five psychic poisons are anger, jealousy, pride, attachment, and ignorance. The person symbolically offers food and coins to her karmic causes. The rinpoche fills a copper pot with water, milk, and herbal essences. The pot symbolises the soul lake, where all souls are found. In the lake, an animal made of ghee floats. The animal is either the person's Tibetan astrological sign or a thirteenth animal: the deer, which in Buddhism symbolises harmony, happiness, peace, and longevity. The animal holds a turquoise bead, into which the soul part will be returned. After the soul retrieval, the person wears the bead for the rest of her life.

Invocations and prayers are said and mantras chanted to purify the karma of the person. At the end of the prayers, the rinpoche looks at the animal in the pot. Depending on the direction the animal is facing, the rinpoche determines whether or not the soul part has returned. There are other tests that demonstrate the success of the soul retrieval and of the karma purification, such as a retrieval of a stone from the pot. If the stone is a white pebble, the soul has returned. If the stone is black, more purification is required.

ISIS, the Ancient Egyptian Mother. In shamanism, soul loss is perceived as an essential safety mechanism that protects us from fully experiencing traumatic events. By becoming the automaton, we are able to survive trauma—albeit in a new, imbalanced state. ISIS's broader perspective is that trauma and the resulting soul loss and process of soul retrieval, are part of our journey towards awakening. Our original light can never be dimmed, even though it may feel otherwise during our earthly life.

Aligning with Source. In the second gate of her teachings called the "Seven Gates of Awareness," ISIS offered me a chant that enables the return of lost soul parts. These parts, lost during a person's current life and other lives, come back in a luminous state. The soul retrieval only takes a few minutes to perform, and the client can feel the soul part or parts entering her body. Intrigued, I asked ISIS to explain how the chant worked.

ISIS showed me that we all share the same light. The one Divine flame burns within us all. Even though in the Earth reality we perceive ourselves as individuals, we are all one soul—the Divine soul. In the bigger perspective, my soul cannot be lost or held by another person because victims and perpetrators are connected in the infinite body of God. For instance, I may think my mother has kept my soul part in this life, to control me; however, from the bigger perspective, I am my mother and my mother is me. I am everything that exists—the one light.

In our earthly existence, we are all a projection from the Source of All Life, the Divine Creator. The Source is the light and soul of everything that exists. When the chant is performed during the second gate ritual, it initiates a transfer of the soul part we need straight from Source. This soul light is projected directly into our body. This light is pristine, untainted by earthly life, trauma, and karmic debts. The soul part returns in a state of wholeness. There is nothing to heal because, coming from Source, the soul part is always perfect.

The Seven Gates of Awareness teaching is designed to bring us into a state of complete alignment with Source—our natural state. We are Source incarnated. When I carry out ISIS soul retrievals, I am reuniting my client with the light of Source—beyond individual personality and ego.

Energy Transmissions. In order for the soul retrieval described above to be performed, the practitioner needs to be able to channel high vibrational energy and light. This can be achieved through continuous personal development and spiritual practice as we aim to become a hollow bone for

75

the Divine light to flow through us. As we hold this place of love and integrity, miracles can happen.

Since 2015, The ISIS School of Holistic Health has been holding weekly transmissions of the ISIS energy. The energy transmitted can differ from week to week, and ISIS gives me specific practices for each transmission. During these transmissions, some participants have received spontaneous soul retrievals. For example, Peter had a dream the night before a weekly transmission, preparing him for the process. In the dream, a woman said to him, "I am lost from myself." Peter realised that this was a reflection of his own situation. Just before the transmission, he happened to pick up a book and opened it to a random page. It said that if a soul dies from sudden death, it may stay around the Earth for a while.

During the transmission, Peter felt the presence of many light beings around him, which he later described.

> I felt as if I was being lifted up. Then, slowly I came back
> down into my body. I thought about my dad who had died,
> and I felt as if his part in me was being taken out. (When Dad
> was in hospital, I remember him saying that he wasn't ready
> to die. I think part of him came into me at that time.) During
> the transmission, I was thinking, "Well, Dad is a part of me. I
> don't know if I want him being removed from my body."

> At the same time, I felt as if I was coming back into my
> body after being away from it for a long time. I tried to
> remember the words in my dream, but couldn't. However, the
> words of a song, "I've been outside myself for so long," were
> going around in my head.

Peter's experience is a classic case of spontaneous extraction and soul retrieval. High vibrational energy generated through the transmission, coupled with our intention, like Peter's, make possible—but do not guarantee—spontaneous soul retrieval. We open ourselves to healing for the highest good and surrender. Healings can happen and spontaneous soul retrievals are possible, and each is a gift from spirit.

Before any soul retrieval, spontaneous or planned, we may have a dream or receive a message about soul loss. In the healing, we may link the loss to a real-life, unresolved grief or other trauma. We finally let go and reunite with our body. We come home.

Earth Retrieval. I am often invited by my helping spirit, ISIS, to carry out Earth healings, known as "Earth retrievals." Our planet needs healing because humankind is out of balance. According to ISIS our fragmented souls create global chaos. As we have been hurt, we hurt others, ourselves, and Mother Earth. We create chaos around the Earth in many ways: physically with lifestyles that pollute the environment, emotionally with our anger and negativity, mentally with our toxic thoughts, and spiritually with our disconnection from ourselves and Source.

We can heal the planet by acknowledging the situation and holding an aspirational vision of the Earth, where harmony and love prevail. This can create a shift in our world—the same way that a soul retrieval, regardless of the method, creates a positive change for an individual. Elders and shamans around the globe engage in dreaming the new reality for the Earth and the world community. They connect to Source to manifest a new Earth and hold this vision in their mind. (The second exercise of this chapter is a practice from my helping spirits on how to engage in Earth retrieval).

An Eternity of Wholeness

Life on Earth is an adventure where we learn about ourselves. Sometimes, we learn through joy and other times, through tears. We create positive and negative karma; we experience the outcome of our actions, words, and thoughts. At the end of life, we return to spirit where we remember our Divine origin.

Even though we may lose many soul parts along the way, this could be our soul's choice. Perhaps our soul would have been bored on an uneventful journey.

Eventually, the process of life and death makes us aware of our luminosity. We realise our soul can never be lost because we are the Divine incarnated. When we awaken from the conditioned mind, the physical world becomes an illusion, a dream that we have been sleeping through.

The journey from separation to oneness is the spiritual path. Along the road to wholeness, we find the opportunities to heal from life's adventures. We ponder our actions and choose different ways of living. We become aware that the soul loss we experienced points to another greater loss: our disconnection from Source, the Divine flame inside our chest. We gradually find our calling and walk back home.

Summary

Chapter 5 offers perspectives of soul loss and retrieval across life stages and from different traditions. The diverse practices help explain the states of dissociation and inner alienation many of us feel in the modern world. From the time of our conception, the soul encounters situations beyond its ability to cope. The soul can fragment, and a part or parts will leave the body. As a result, we may carry the unhappiness and pain of a traumatic event for many years, infecting our future with our past hurts.

Soul retrieval can bring stranded soul parts back home into the body. The soul once again experiences wholeness. Different cultures and spiritual traditions use a variety of methods to carry out this healing. ISIS has shown me a way of retrieving our essence by connecting to Source, the Divine light that we each are—beyond our unique personality.

As we heal ourselves, we create shifts at the planetary level. We can engage directly in Earth's healing by imagining a harmonious existence for the planet and implanting it into our current reality. In shamanism we call this "dreaming the new Earth."

In a broader perspective, soul loss is part of our journey towards awakening. We learn through our actions, words, and thoughts and experience our positive and negative karma. The spiritual path offers a way to heal past experiences and uncover the unified and undying flame of the Divine light within.

Exercises: Working with Teachings of Soul and Earth Retrieval

Exercise 1:
A Meditation on Soul Retrieval

Receiving a soul retrieval healing by a competent practitioner can be life transforming and an important step in your healing journey. The meditation below is not a substitute for a soul retrieval healing from a shamanic practitioner; however, it can pave the way to healing and start a process towards wellness.

Set some time aside for this work with a clear intention to reunite with any soul parts that have left your body and are now ready to return. Before you start the healing, you may wish to walk in nature, meditate, chant, sing, or do a familiar spiritual practice. After the healing, I suggest you rest, if needed, and be nurturing towards yourself.

Create sacred space by inviting your guardian angel and the Divine Creator into your space. Say a prayer of your choosing, and include your intention to reunite with any soul parts that have fled due to difficult past experiences and are now ready to return.

Imagine you are radiating the light of the Creator from inside your heart. The light of one-hundred-thousand suns is radiating out at the same time. You are that light. You are the light that creates universes and stars, forests and oceans, and all living things. Everything exists within you. There is no differentiation between you and All. You are All. You are the Creator and the Creation. You are all beings. See yourself as the flow of the rivers, the breeze of the wind, the fire inside the Earth, and the rocks and the crystals. See yourself as the male and the female, as life and death, all uniting into One. You are All, and you are the One Being.

Nothing else exists but your intention. In this space of connection, intend that your soul parts, which have left due to life experiences, now return to your physical body, in their primordial, pristine state. Intend that they flow back into your heart, reuniting and merging with the light of one-hundred-thousand suns. It is time to be whole on the Earth, to be complete. It is time to radiate the light of the stars. It is time to accept yourself and illuminate the world with the light of your soul.

Wait for a few minutes, whilst you receive your soul parts back into the body. Stay present in the process, welcoming the soul parts as each comes home. Welcome back your radiance, the light of the world that you are. Welcome back yourself and the opportunity to live as a luminous being, a being of light, radiating the essence of the Divine.

Now, imagine your soul light radiating out into the cosmos, like a star. At the same time, imagine this light radiating inside your body, nurturing every cell, organ, and tissue, and every part of you.

You can remain in this state for a while, at least fifteen minutes, taking everything in, being in touch with the light of your soul. When you feel ready, slowly come back from the meditation and open your eyes.

As you welcome your soul home, you welcome yourself fully into life. Ask your soul to help you live life with the awareness of who you are.

Finally, give thanks to your guardian angel and the Divine presence and release them. Ask that your sacred space is closed, sealed and protected, and so are you.

Exercise 2:
Dreaming the New Earth into Being

What you need: rattle (optional)

Earlier in this chapter, I spoke about indigenous elders engaging in the practice of dreaming the new Earth. Medicine people I have worked with say that our conditioning of scarcity and fear creates disharmony globally. In this exercise, that I was given by my helping spirits, you engage your imagination in creating a harmonious Earth reality. Similar to the ISIS soul retrieval where pristine soul parts are brought from Source to the client, in this retrieval you implant a pristine Earth into the current reality.

Start your practice by creating sacred space. Invite enlightened spiritual beings who work for the highest good and wellbeing of the planet, to support you. Some people refer to these beings as "Earth Angels," but you do not need to know who they are. Set the intention to perform an Earth retrieval for the highest good of all beings.

Imagine you are looking at the Earth from outer space. Ask the enlightened beings to show you a reality on Earth where all species, including humans, live in harmony. In a parallel universe, an immaculate Earth exists. In that reality life is free from pollution and strife. There is no disconnection from Source.

Focus on specific places on the planet and see how life unfolds in harmony there. Immerse yourself in this meditation, and engage all your senses: hear the sounds, smell and touch the Earth, see how people live, perhaps taste something—as if it is all real. The enlightened beings may show you different aspects of life that could be helpful for you to know for your present life.

Pull back and look at the Earth again from outer space. Imagine that you have grown so big that you can hold the Earth in your hands. In real life, raise your hands and imagine you are holding the pristine Earth. Feel the planet's energy pulsating between your palms.

Blow the Earth you are holding between your palms, into the ground, performing an Earth retrieval and implanting this harmonious state into the current reality. If you have a rattle you can use it now, otherwise imagine you are holding one. In a circular clockwise direction, shake the rattle four times over the ground where you blew in the energy of the harmonious Earth. In this way, you seal the process.

Slowly come back from the visualisation. Thank the spiritual beings who supported you through this process. Ask them to close and seal and protect you and the space before they go. Thank yourself for doing this work, dreaming the new Earth into being.

SOURCE

The light of all, manifested trillions of beings.
Through the process of life I forgot who I was:
the brilliant star in the night that lies within me;
the sun that burns in space creating life.

I was looking for something.
The more I searched, the less I found.
I looked to see what I was needing,
only to realise I had everything.

I thought to look inside me.
Maybe there was some clue
about what I was missing.
I lifted the veil of my unhappiness.

As a sun, I walk on the Earth
noticing many other suns around me.
Most do not know their own brilliance,
like me, searching for something we already have.

6

Karma: What we Manifest in the World

Spiritual Lesson 6: Everything I do, think, and speak, I become. In the game of life, I play out my karma

Shedding skin: I am standing in the woods of Namo Buddha in Nepal, shedding tears of grace. The journey of my soul through eternity is revealed to me, a journey towards awareness that continues through lifetimes with karma as the teacher.

Four years later, in 2012, I am in a retreat centre near Santa Fe, New Mexico, taking part in a shamanic teachers training facilitated by Sandra Ingerman. I am journeying shamanically to become aware of how I create negative karma. I wish to negotiate with the enlightened spirit guides. "Please help me become aware of what I create, so I do not have to live through the negative consequences of the karma," I say.

The guides smile at me and laugh joyfully. They say, "Don't worry. You will create negative karma and live through its consequences. This is how you will learn about yourself. We have already set future events in place, where your ego will manifest. With each experience, by observing your actions and reactions, you will have the opportunity to become a little wiser."

It takes me a while to accept the gravity of their answer. My aim becomes to develop the awareness of the enlightened mind. I am shown that for a lotus flower to blossom, it needs to be fed by the nurturing soil from the swamp of karma.

WHAT I SPEAK, THINK AND DO, I CREATE: THE LAW OF KARMA

Karma is the law of cause and effect that helps us align with our wise self, the higher self. Karma teaches us that our actions, words, and thoughts have consequences—positive and negative. Karma is not punishment. It is not payback. Rather, karma leads the incarnating soul to make wiser choices and evolve. The soul knows and agrees in advance the karmic lessons that it will experience in each life. There might be one main lesson or a multiple debt, depending on the wishes and the level of awareness of the soul.

The first step in working out our karma is to become aware. By acquiring insights of our preordained karma, we can develop mindfulness, grow spiritually, change our patterns and work to dissolve the debt.

Karma affects each level of our being:

- From the human perspective, karma is the challenges and blessings we meet in life that help us awaken from the illusionary nature of this world. Thus, it is instructive.

- From the viewpoint of the soul, karma represents the set of agreements we made about our current life prior to incarnating, based on our previous lives and the plan for the soul's evolution. Thus, it is transformative.

- From the aspect of the higher self, karma affords the opportunity for spiritual growth. Thus, it is divinely inspired.

Inside the portal of time and space (the portal between lives), I meet the lords of karma, spiritual beings assigned to help in my soul's evolution. They show me the brilliance of my soul and what it has decided to experience. "Everything you do, think, and speak becomes karma," the lords tell me. Karma is what we manifest in the world. My karma is the energy I release into the universe, and the energy the universe returns to me. As in a tennis match, I hit the ball out, and through the universal law of karma, the ball is returned to me.

Karma can be offset from lifetime to lifetime. In a simplified example, a wealthy person in one life may be poor in another life.

Within a single lifetime, an experienced soul may work on multiple karmic causes. A less experienced soul may need to repeat the same lesson, until it finally learns from life and the karma is released.

All karmic debt has to be repaid eventually. No one gets away with anything under the law of karma, and no one is exempt from it. This is divine justice.

KARMA PURIFICATION

We partake in different life events, both difficult and joyful, to become aware and resolve our karma. Alternatively, we can engage in purification practices, to work through our karmic debt, and either dissolve it or reduce its impact in everyday life.

Karma purification has four aspects: physical, emotional, mental, and spiritual.

Physical Clearing. Negative karma manifests in the body in various ways, including illness (chapter 3), weakness, and weight gain, and through sensations, such as heat, pain, and emissions. Although we can purify karmic debt by encountering different life lessons, we still need to clear it from our physical body—from our cells.

During intense karma work, we can feel physical pain in different areas of the body, where the karma is held. In my healing practice, when this happens, I direct the client to speak to the pain: ask to see its story and what it is trying to convey. The body connection may reveal images from this life or other lives, exposing the circumstances of how the karma was created.

Lindsay was taking part in The ISIS School's Rays of Divine Consciousness retreat, which incorporates a karma purification ceremony. During the ceremony, Lindsay experienced excruciating pain in her stomach. She had no prior medical issues in this region and was mystified as to its cause. I guided Lindsay to focus her awareness on her stomach and ask, "What karma am I holding here?" Lindsay described the karma as a "heavy, black energy ball hovering inside my body" with an "unpleasant smell."

The ball told Lindsay that it was karma from her first years at school, but she could not remember any incident. I guided Lindsay to again concentrate on the energy and request more details. Lindsay saw images of her father encouraging her to work hard at gymnastics, for which she was naturally talented. Lindsay remembered her anxiety when her father came to the trainings, and feeling jealous of and competitive towards her peers.

As Lindsay became aware of these feelings, I asked her to pay attention to the ball of karma inside her body. While the group chanted mantras and channelled high vibrational energies on her behalf, Lindsay felt the ball in her stomach changing. At the same time, she forgave herself and her father for their competitive fire, apologised to the other children, and prayed for karmic healing. As the karma was being released, Lindsay began to cough uncontrollably and burp loudly, dispelling it from her body. By the end of the ceremony, the pain had disappeared completely.

Other physical acts to support karma clearing are spontaneous crying and even sobbing and bodily shaking.

In some of my groups, I use a shaking exercise as a way of releasing energy that we pick up from our environment. However, the same exercise may spontaneously take us into transcended states of consciousness that release karma from the body, as I found out. In the exercise, I instruct the group to stand and bring their focus inside the body with the intention of shaking off everything that does not serve them. Then we access, by imagining or visualising, the vibrational energy of the Earth flowing into our feet. We imagine the energy starting to shake our body and we start to shake gently on the spot. At some point, the body will shake automatically, without being coerced. Our job is to allow the body to shake, sometimes forcefully, sometimes gently. We trust in the wisdom of the body. We shake on the spot for fifteen minutes.

On one occasion as I began shaking, different muscles started to shake at different times. This was familiar; however, at some point, I started to shake violently and jump up and down. Unexpectedly, I found myself in a vision surrounded by an immense light. Enveloped in the energy of love, I felt emotional. In that place of Divine love, karma does not exist and I could feel its hold dispelling from my body.

Emotional Release. There are three elements that enable karma release at the emotional level: love and compassion, forgiveness, and the light of Divine grace.

Love and Compassion. No matter what we have or have not done, love and compassion are the powers that set us free. We approach the karmic lesson with unconditional love and compassion, for ourselves and the other people involved. Paradoxically, in our western culture, we may have been taught that we should feel shameful and guilty for our "sins." Unlike love, guilt keeps us imprisoned in the emotional patterns we have manifested and prevents us from releasing karma. Burdened by shame, we avoid examining the karmic lessons and may carry the karma over lifetimes.

Forgiveness. Once we become aware of our negative karma, we forgive ourselves, receiving perfect absolution. With humility we also apologise, in our mind, to the others involved and to ourselves. Through unconditional forgiveness, we can release ourselves from the karmic links that bind us to other people.

Grace. The universal law of karma can be offset through the light of Divine grace. Once we resolve the situation through our loving intent and the power of forgiveness, Divine grace releases us from the pattern we may have carried over lifetimes. Touched by the Divine, we may have an emotional release too, as the tears of grace flow.

I helped Lisa access a past life and release the karma between her and her parents. She found herself in an ancient city that was being overrun by foreign soldiers. As she ran into a room, two soldiers followed her. They drew their swords and killed her. In spirit form, Lisa saw herself psychically attack the soldiers. The attack created holes in their energy body and in time, they became ill. She was so angry at being killed, she could not forgive and let go. Eventually, she found the way to the spiritual realms. In front of the lords of karma, she saw the two soldiers standing beside her. The lords said they had to resolve the karma between them. They suggested a future life together, where the soldiers would be Lisa's parents.

In that moment, Lisa knew her parents in this life were these soldiers, and she realised how much she loved them and that they loved her (love and compassion). Lisa could see they were horrified that they had killed her in the past life, and she was shocked she had attacked them. As the love flowed, her parents apologised. "We killed our little girl. And we are so sorry." Lisa forgave them unconditionally and apologised for hurting them. As they forgave each other, they also decided to forgive themselves and no longer carry this karma (forgiveness). The three of them were surrounded by light. Bathed in this Divine light (grace), the karma was released and Lisa returned from the past life regression lighter and freer.

Personal work develops the awareness to identify our behaviour patterns and recognise the consequences of our actions. We work to shine a light on our ego and shadow (chapter 2), to see how they manifest in the world. To neutralise and heal the karma, we recognise, feel, love, and forgive the shadow of the egoic self. Our soul can embrace the needed lesson (of not harming, for instance) through unconditional love and forgiveness. And we may not have to relive this particular situation again, as the light of Divine grace releases the karma.

Mental Reconciliation. Mental purification is centred on examining our thoughts, beliefs, ideas, and attitudes. Like the conditioning, it can be both individual and collective.

Individual Karma. Each lifetime presents us with events to which we can respond skilfully or unskilfully. Each response tells us something about ourselves—if we choose to look. In order to learn the purpose of these events and the consequences of our responses, we examine them from a place of detachment, compassion, and forgiveness, rather than expectation, victimhood, blame. We may observe our ideas and beliefs create similar situations many times, even in many lives, before we recognise our pattern.

As well as purifying negative karma, we also receive the consequences of our kind and compassionate actions to address our positive karma. However, we may resist receiving kindness, even though we are comfortable offering it. Such a situation arose for me in an ISIS School retreat.

During the School's retreats, I like to do everything I can to help participants feel comfortable. I teach, I make tea, and I even help with the cooking. When someone offers me assistance, I tend to refuse and manage on my own. This is an old belief about being self-sufficient. Just before one of the retreats, I stumbled on the stairs and ended up in the hospital with a broken big toe. I had to graciously accept help from the course participants. For the entire retreat, everyone fussed over me and made sure I was comfortable. I had manifested this positive karma, which was helping me release an inner block that resisted receiving the same kindness and help I offered abundantly to others. In life, we reap what we sow, and we have to experience and acknowledge the effect of both positive and negative karma.

Collective Family Karma. This type of karma arises from the consequences of the decisions we make as a family unit. A deceased relative once showed me a pie chart with slices of different sizes. Each slice represented a family member's share of our karma. As we purify our individual karma, we affect and purify our family karma.

Collective National Karma. We adopt the values, ideas and beliefs of our home country. We participate in our nation's collective karma, which becomes another karma pie slice for us to purify.

In 2009, life gave me just such an opportunity. In my birth country of Greece, there is a lot of distrust towards Turkey, and vice versa. This is a collective belief system. One night in Scotland, as I sat in my car at a red light, the driver behind me rear-ended my car. The driver, a young foreign student, was apologetic and immediately took responsibility. He asked if we could settle the matter privately to avoid future insurance penalties.

The next day, we drove to the garage, and he paid the bill to fix the damage to my car. We resolved everything amicably. Driving back, out of curiosity, I asked him his nationality. He said, "I am a Turkish Cypriot." I said, "I am Greek." At first, he thought I was joking, but I assured him I was sincere. Then, he remarked how we had managed to resolve this situation as friends, contrary to the common belief we are bitter enemies. At that moment, all the stereotypes between us fell away. I knew instinctively that through the traffic accident, we both worked our share of our respective nations' karma pie.

Spiritual Purification. In addition to developing skills of emotional maturity and mentally observing our life lessons, we can adopt many spiritual practices that purify karma. For example, meditation combined with high vibrational etheric energies, such as the Path of ISIS practices, can reveal the karmic root causes we carry.

Mantra Chants. Specific mantras within Buddhism, ancient Egyptian spirituality, and vibrational or light language, (an ancient language no longer in existence that I, amongst others, channel), when chanted and combined with meditation, can help purify karma.

Death and Dying Vision Quests. In the spiritual realms of the light, karma does not exist. When we die, we encounter the major events of our lives and the lords of karma explain the lessons. We can go through a similar process in a death and dying vision quest.

Dream Work. Karma purification can take place during our sleep. For example, for several nights over many months, I dreamed that I was asked to make a decision about a work situation. Many times, I made an unskilful choice, skirting responsibility and blaming "the system." At the end of the dream, my spirit guide appeared and showed me that I had failed the test and karma was still there. The same challenge recurred in a similar dream three months later. But this time, I made the skilful choice and purified some of that particular karma. Other aspects of karma endure and continue to emerge. Working with karma is like peeling an onion. One layer falls away, and another is revealed.

Ceremonies. In ceremonies, we work on our karma energetically, rather than meeting it through life events. Even if we still have to live through certain situations, their impact can be mitigated by these rituals.

Spiritual traditions offer many resources for karma purification. The Rays of Divine Consciousness karma purification ceremony and the ISIS practices that I have channelled have been a treasure in my personal karma work and that of ISIS School students.

In a karma purification ceremony, we work with the four aspects of karma, physical, emotional, mental, and spiritual. The participants meet for a seven-day retreat. The first two days, we share spiritual practices and esoteric teachings to understand the nature of our mind and how we manifest karma (mental clearing). We invoke high vibrational energies that reveal our negative karma and the obstacles that manifest in our life as a result of our beliefs, attitudes, and actions (spiritual and mental purification). The third and fourth days, we work as a team to purify each other's karma. We adopt the principle that a person's individual karma is a reflection of the collective karma. As we address our individual karma, we help every other soul in the cosmos. We support each other through chanting, visioning, meditation, and body work. The karma manifests in the body as a physical pain (physical purification). Through love and compassion, forgiveness, and the light of Divine grace that follows, the karmic cause is revealed (emotional release). Spiritually, the high vibrational energy of the practices complete the karma purification.

At the end of the ceremony, an energetic wave is unleashed that will work to bring our life into a state of homeostasis and resolve the consequences of the karma we have carried. Sometimes life circumstances can change instantly, while at other times more karma clearing is required.

For example, in 2013, during the annual Rays of Divine Consciousness retreat, I became aware of an aspect of my family karma that had affected the previous three generations of first-borns, including me. Before the retreat, I had been estranged from my family for two years. Our energetic link was severed and, in a strange way, it suited me to be separated from all the family drama. Then, in the karma purification ceremony our link was re-established. My mother contacted me straight after the retreat, but differences were too great to mend the relationship. The ceremony had revealed our family issues and brought more conflict within the family to the fore. The medicine of the ceremony was working, but not in the way I had envisaged. Purification can be not repairing a torn bond, but seeing things as they are and accepting them in the present moment. In the next purification ceremony the family karma completely cleared. Afterwards, I visited my family in Greece and could not believe the change in attitudes. Instead of the years of judgement and criticism, we shared unconditional love and mutual respect. Life circumstances enabled my family and me to see the immense love we had for one another, beyond ego, pride, and hurt.

These powerful ceremonies take us into a journey to re-establish equilibrium. They work over many months, even years, until balance is achieved. The journey can be eventful and unexpected, as hidden aspects are revealed. In the ancient Greek tradition, karma is symbolised by the goddess Adresteia—'Αδρήστεια "she who cannot be escaped," who establishes sublime and permanent balance out of the forces of love and war.

The Awakened Mind

According to ISIS, the purpose of the soul is to "awaken fully into its divinity and hold the awakened state in this world of duality." The aim of spiritual practice is to help us enter the awakened state, where we perceive ourselves as the flow of universal energy. Karma is a learning tool in our soul's awakening journey. As we observe the consequences of our actions, words, and thoughts, we become aware that we create our own reality. This cannot be done through the mind alone. The mind must be joined with the heart. It is inside the spiritual heart centre that the state of enlightenment exists.

Karma purification does not create awakening or enlightenment, but it clears the way. Imagine walking a path towards awakening. You may not know where the path terminates—around the corner or miles away. Awakening comes with an element of surprise. It cannot be preordained by the mind. It happens when we reach a certain etheric brain wave that takes us into a higher state. All the spiritual practices we do with sincerity and integrity help us along the path, but how short or long the road is for each of us is unknown. Every day, we switch on the light in the room of the heart, and one day, the light stays on.

Karma presents as obstacles and opportunities along the path to awakening. We have come here to experience life and learn from the results of our actions. Negative karma presents as the endless distractions that take us away from our purpose of self-realisation. They, too, are part of the journey. Meanwhile, our positive karma tries to align us with our soul's purpose and spiritual path. These are the wake-up calls, invitations to evaluate the way we think and live our lives, and the doors into a larger perspective.

When we awaken fully from the conditioning, we are no longer bound by the law of karma. We have graduated from the Earth school. We have fulfilled part of our soul's journey, and reached the state of self-realisation where we consciously embody the Divine self.

SUMMARY

The Earth school is governed by the universal law of karma which, simply put, means we will receive the results of our actions, words, and thoughts, both positive and negative. In this way, life helps us realise the significance of our choices and the consequences of our actions. Karmic debt can be purified through such insights. Sincere spiritual practices with physical releases can also transform our karma and clear our path towards the awakened state.

EXERCISE: MEDITATING BEYOND KARMA

Intend to experience a state of being that is free of karma. Your soul essence is the Divine light. Your soul is primordial, pristine, and pure. Although you carry the karma within your body, the soul is not tainted by karma.

Open the meditation by inviting the light of Divine grace to help you and request the presence of the compassionate lords of karma. Intend to experience a state of being beyond karma.

Imagine your spirit rising up out of your physical body. Visualise yourself looking down at your body, meditating. The soul may appear to you as a ball of light, somewhere in the body (perhaps in the heart or central energy channel, known in Sanskrit as "sushumna.")

Imagine diving from above into this luminous ball that represents your soul. You are surrounded by the radiant energy. How does it feel to be encircled by the divine within?

From this core place within you, imagine yourself expanding until the ball of light encompasses your whole body and aura. You are the Divine light incarnated. Stay in this space for a while, experiencing the light of your soul beyond the karma.

Slowly, see the luminous ball that surrounds you, shrinking and flowing back to its original size and place in the body. Say, "I am the Divine light incarnated."

Thank your soul for this experience, and slowly come back.

Give thanks to Divine grace and the compassionate lords of karma that helped you in this practice. Ask that they protect, close and seal you and your room before they leave.

The Lotus and the Swamp

In a muddy swamp; a place of suffering,
the sun rises to reveal a sea of bright pink hues.
How can the delicate blossom exist in this inhospitable place?
I choose to come here, the flower says.

I did not know who I was:
a pink lotus, the open heart of divinity.
I immersed myself in the profane world
to discover my sacred nature.

The Divine hand
made me as the swamp and the lotus.
We feed from one another,
joined together in one destiny.

The sun beckons me to understand who I am.
Effortlessly it shines across the cosmos,
inviting me to reveal my own light.
Alas, the eternal night of my mind is too dark to pierce.

No sunlight can penetrate the depths of the swamp
where I find myself in endless circles,
living and reliving the hurtful memories.
Bound by cause, effect, and consequence.

If I could only lift my head to the sun.
The sunlight could nurture me.
My own radiance would meet the light of the world,
revealing my inner divinity.

7

Discovering our Life Purpose

Spiritual Lesson 7: The more I travel in the footsteps of my soul, the more I experience the eternal sunshine of who I am

Shedding skin: In the space between lives, before incarnation, I meet the three Moirai (Μοῖραι), the three Fates. The first, Clotho, spins the yarn of my life. She chuckles and laughs as the yarn unfurls. The second, Lachesis, asks me what I go to Earth to achieve, what my life purpose is. My soul whispers to her and the words are weaved into the yarn. The yarn folds and unfolds as my soul continues to speak. At some point, the yarn is handed to the third Fate, the mighty Atropos. With her scissors, she is about to cut the yarn and end my forthcoming life. "Wait" I shout, "Tell me, please. Will I achieve my life purpose?" Atropos smiles and looks at the yarn. "There are many opportunities for you to do so," she says, "and many hindrances too, all entwined in the yarn. Life will take you to that door again and again. At the end, it is up to you to walk through it." Before I can ask again, she swiftly cuts the yarn and I find myself back from this inner journey.

I recall the time before being born as Fotoula Adrimi. In the spirit realms, my higher self, spirit guides, and my soul design my life on Earth. It is full of unique opportunities to grow my light, wisdom, and self-understanding.

Mnemosyne, the goddess of memory, offers me the cup of forgetfulness. The social conditioning of the physical world will obscure my soul memory, this blueprint for life, after being born. Losing track of who I am and what my life purpose is, forms part of the journey. I may start to remember again when I step into my power.

Finding our Life Purpose

The journey of the soul is partly predestined, that is, written in the blueprint of our life, the pre-ordained karma, and partly unknown. Certain things are meant to happen to give us the experiences our soul has chosen to continue its growth. The non-predestined parts—what we do not know and we come to Earth to find out—is our reaction to the life events our soul has placed on our path. We would like to believe that we have free will but choice is limited by our responses and not the circumstances. Our soul has designed opportunities, gateways for self-realisation, but our ability to explore them may be restricted by the level of awareness and attachment to the personal and collective consciousness here on Earth.

The soul has a master plan for self-realisation beyond this life. Each incarnation and life purpose forms part of this master plan, which is subject to re-writes, as each life offers the soul new insights. Karma is not the same as life purpose, but a determining factor, the pre-ordained events that the soul will meet towards achieving or relinquishing its life purpose.

Metaphorically, life purpose is a destination in a journey. The soul-traveller decides to go to a particular place. It makes a plan based on its resources. Karma decides how the soul will travel. Will the soul journey on a first class ticket? Will it go on foot or by airplane? Will the soul meet people/events and get distracted from reaching her destination? Will the soul have to carry heavy baggage along the way?

Most of us may not know what our life purpose is. Why has the soul come to this planet at this time? Others may have an inclination, especially if they are already on a spiritual path. When I was told by a shaman that my life purpose was to bring the light of the Divine to Earth, it resonated with me, as I was already living as a spiritual teacher.

Knowing our life purpose and manifesting it in earthly life is not always easy or straightforward. Many of my clients think they have found the magic wand once they discover their inner calling. However, it may take years and trials for our life purpose to be achieved in the material world. Although, the spiritual entities of light will assist us in bringing our calling to fruition, we still need to follow through with appropriate action. It is up to us to make it happen.

Grabbing the Opportunity. In pursuit of our life purpose, we trust in Divine grace and surrender to what life is teaching us. Grace is what brings the right thing at the right time, activating the aforementioned blueprint, or "divine timing" in spirituality circles. These instances are known as "synchronicity," or more commonly, "coincidence." It is as if the universe is saying, "Joe, this is your chance. Take it, even if it makes little sense to you now."

Every opportunity to realise our life purpose is an invitation for us to walk though a door. It is not always easy for us, and may lead to unexpected life changes. In my work, I observe people praying for what the heart wants. And yet, when life gives them an opportunity to claim it, they sometimes shy away because of their fears of unworthiness due to the social conditioning, or beliefs about how the opportunity should come about. For example, in fulfilling my life purpose, working as a spiritual teacher, I had to overcome the social conditioning that said, "stay in a comfortable public sector job until you get your pension."

Some opportunities alight at a low point. Sometimes we grow through joy, and sometimes through adversity. When we refuse to walk through the doors that life opens for us, life will give us more opportunities. However, at some point, life may become difficult in order to limit our options and encourage us to follow our life script.

When I was considering leaving my life partner after six years, I found it very challenging emotionally. I kept putting off the decision that I knew deep inside was best. While I wavered, life became intolerable—to the point that leaving the relationship was the only option.

Each lifetime has a certain span, and our opportunities to fulfil our purpose are limited by the time factor. A point may come when we feel that life is passing us by. We seem to have lost our inner power, our drive, our motivation, and missed our dreams. In each incarnation, we have a certain period to pursue our purpose. Although life supports us by continually presenting doors that will help us attain our purpose, at some point, the last door will close.

When the patterns become apparent and the opportunities for growth appear, are we able to see them? Or, do we ignore them and blame life?

Lighting the Path of Life Fulfilment

When we are born, the light of our soul shines brightly within. However, as we go through life, we learn to dim this soul light. The light is so luminous, it can make us and others uncomfortable. Imagine going into a room and seeing a light beaming on all your fears, guilt, sadness, and insecurities. Some of us would welcome this light, and be glad to see what is hindering our life journey. The majority of us would feel uncomfortably exposed and want to turn off, or at least dim, the light.

It can be difficult to look at and own our issues. We may prefer to keep blaming others for our misfortunes. Many of us have hidden away our problems in a box, attached a heavy lock to the outside, and thrown away the key—in an effort to keep out life. A spiritual path is one where we open our personal Pandora's box and examine every part of us, step-by-step. We learn to embrace our vulnerabilities and renew our strength. We accept our light, and acknowledge and transform our darkness. We refocus our efforts to achieve our dreams and adjust our way of life towards the fulfilment of our purpose for incarnating.

Reclaiming our Life Purpose through Spiritual Death. Mystics and shamans seek to understand the process of death and come to terms with their mortality, as a way to empower their life and achieve their life purpose. In 2015, I took part in a death-and-dying vision quest. Based on an ancient Mayan ceremony known as the "ballcourt," the winning team is sacrificed to the gods. During the event, I symbolically faced my own death. In doing so, I became determined to embrace my life and its purpose. A similar awakening of commitment may also happen following recovery from a life-threatening situation. We become aware of what is important in life and change our ways to accommodate our new understanding.

On an earlier pilgrimage in Nepal, I connected with the essence of my soul. Our group travelled to a holy place called Namo Buddha, accompanied by Nuptul Tenpei Nyima Rinpoche, a Buddhist teacher and monk. Heading there, inside our minibus, Nuptul Rinpoche talked about the history of the site and its importance within the Buddhist tradition. I recount the story, as I remember it, below.

"Namo Buddha"

In his last incarnation before enlightenment, Buddha was a prince. One day, he went for a walk in the forest and found himself on top of a hill. He saw a tiger, under a tree, that had just given birth to cubs. The tiger was exhausted. She had not eaten for days and had no milk to feed her cubs. Buddha tried to give the tiger his food, but the tiger was too weak to eat. He understood that unless the tiger ate and produced milk, she and the cubs would perish. Motivated by great compassion, he cut his arm and offered his blood to the tiger. The tiger drank the blood and slowly began to recover. As milk flowed from her breasts, the prince died.

The king and queen were worried when their son had not returned. They searched the forest shouting his name. All they saw was a healthy tiger and her new born cubs. Finally, they found the prince's body. Deeply upset, they mourned for him, tearing their clothes and putting ashes on their heads. Then they heard a voice calling to them from above. It was their son. He was alive and surrounded by Enlightened Beings. "Why do you mourn for me?" he asked, "Don't you know that I cannot die? I am now self-realised, awakened in the company of the Enlightened Ones. Do not be sorry for me, but celebrate my awakening!"

The rinpoche finished his story, and I thought it was a nice myth, a mere children's story, a fairy tale about tigers and princes. Nobody in our group said much about it.

We arrived at the site, parked, and climbed to the top, where we found a small shrine. We sat on the floor of the shrine, as the rinpoche chanted in Tibetan. I began crying. I did not know why, but I could not stop the flow of tears. When the chanting finished, I walked outside and sat under a tree. I heard a voice: "You cannot die. You cannot be hurt. No matter what happens to you in each of your lives, your soul is eternal, and it can never cease to be. Nothing and no one can hurt your soul, no matter what happens to your mortal body." For the first time in my life, I could perceive the endless journey of the soul. I saw my soul travelling life after life. I trusted in the wisdom of this journey. I touched the eternity that I was. My tears flowed again, but this time, they were tears of grace, of inner knowing, and of immeasurable gratitude for this journey of lifetimes.

Opening the door to the eternity of my existence enabled me to detach from everyday dramas and follow a spiritual path, living my life purpose. That day, I touched the part of me that always exists, my immortal soul. On this planet, we become attached to people and circumstances because we feel we need them. I learned that day that my soul has no needs. My mind creates these conditions. As a result, my love for life became unconditional: no matter whether life is easy or tough, I continue to embrace my time on Earth and live according to my inner calling.

Through this experience, I learned to develop appreciation for life and gratitude for its gifts. Every moment is precious because it is mortal and transient (Causton, 2011). Nothing remains the same; everything changes, including our life circumstances, as Herakleitos argued in the classical era (Botten, 2011). There is no end to the experience of the soul, as it continues to exist and move from lifetime to lifetime. By understanding our own immortality, we are touched by Divine grace. This is a journey of surrender to life and death, a concept Buddhists refer to as "the inevitability of impermanence." Our soul travels like the sun from the east to the west, renewing the journey with each incarnation, as the ancient Egyptians described in their Book of the Dead (Wasserman, 2015).

Releasing Attachments. Parvati, the Hindu goddess of fertility and a manifestation of the Divine Mother, showed me how our attachments to people, material things, and beliefs can hinder our journey towards our life purpose in this and future lives.

In a vision, Parvati took me to a riverbank, where I joined hordes of other people. We were all carrying numerous bundles overflowing with things from our life—people, knowledge, experiences, material possessions, opinions, and so on. The way to fulfil my purpose and move to the next life was over a bridge that was narrow and unstable. Parvati said that if I wanted to cross safely, I could only take five things with me. People were so attached to their stuff, they could not let go of a single item. They were forever stuck on the riverbank, unable to move forward.

Parvati said that people who could not detach, ended up living and reliving the same life and each time, believing it to be a new life. These people could not achieve their life purpose and had to come back repeatedly and try again. She asked me to concentrate on what was important for my life and carefully choose the five items that would help me achieve my life purpose. When I did, I realised what qualities were important for me to concentrate on so that I can fulfil my life, rather than waste my energy in carrying a plethora of unnecessary bundles. The second exercise in this chapter helps you develop your power of discernment and release the "bundles" that obstruct your path.

The Three Flames: Self-Reliance, Self-Empowerment and Self-Awareness

Traveling in the footsteps of our soul is not simple. Doubts and fears may emerge. More than ever, we need to galvanise our personal power and release the energetic cords we hold in our body (see chapter 1). In addition, we have three flames to light our path and lead us to our soul's awakening: self-reliance, self-empowerment, and self-awareness.

Self-Reliance. No matter how many people we meet in our life, and how much of our life we share with them, it is important to live true to ourselves. Stay alert to these tendencies: the more we choose to be true to our inner voice, the more opportunities for personal growth will appear, and the more likely we are to discover and fulfil our purpose and find happiness.

Fighting for the chance to walk our path is part of our journey, as it strengthens our resolve. Having striven through difficulty to achieve our dream, we are less likely to give it up. We start the process of developing self-reliance by trusting ourselves and trusting Life, knowing that no matter what happens, it is just another part of the journey and we will eventually get through it.

Self-Empowerment. A common misperception of social conditioning is that the needs of others come before our own. Many of us lose power by sacrificing our own needs for others'. To follow one's life purpose is the opposite of selfishness. Staying true to ourselves fulfils the divine plan that our soul drew up before incarnation. Despite what others may think, we are not here to fulfil another person's wishes. If we squander our life pleasing others in co-dependent relationships, we will not discover our own gifts.

101

Is self-sacrifice ever appropriate? What about the heroes in history who give up their life for the greater good? Recall the story of Namo Buddha. Motivated by compassion, Buddha cut his arm to save the starving tiger and her cubs, and thereby, fulfilled his life's purpose: transcendent awakening. Should we not try to emulate Buddha? If your soul is telling you to live your life for the good of all, then you will feel good doing it with no residue of resentment or guilt. Buddha did not offer his blood because he was feeling guilty or fearful but through an altruistic intention to rescue the dying cubs. A true hero saves another because his heart is moved to help, not through a misguided motive or belief.

Another common fallacy is that by empowering ourselves to fulfil our life purpose, we will hurt others. This may be true if our relationship with others is unhealthy and out of balance, and we have given them our power. Our growth and happiness makes them uncomfortable, as it upsets the existing balance of power. The skilful answer is not to renounce our life purpose, but pursue it. If the relationship is based on love, they will eventually support our dreams, realising that they are important to us. I have had both male and female clients who renounced their life purpose and happiness because they did not want to change the family circumstances, and "hurt" their children. They live in a lie, pretending all is well. This does not serve anyone including the children, who are unconsciously taught to renounce their power for others' comfort.

To live our calling, we need to take back our power, sometimes from the people we love most, such as our family. If you find yourself in a place of power loss, you will always doubt your judgment, feeling adrift, in a state of indecision. Even when you make a positive move, you constantly ask yourself if you have done "the right thing", unable to find happiness and fulfilment. Understanding how you give your power away and engaging in its retrieval (see chapter 1), will fan the flames of self-empowerment.

Self-Awareness. During our life, we lose sight of our life purpose due to the social conditioning. We adopt the belief systems, behaviours, and feelings of the people and social systems around us, rejecting our wishes and dreams. Our discernment weakens. Thus, we have relegated our inner voice to the collective consciousness: the set of beliefs, ideas, and morality that operate as the unifying force within society, sometimes also referred to as "group thinking" (Combs & Krippner, 2008).

For example, imagine growing up in a society where you were told that happiness did not matter, and money and family status were more important. Even though you want to become an artist, your parents influence you to study law. You squander years of your life in a job you dislike, so as not to disappoint. Sometimes, we absorb the thoughts and feelings of others out of a desire to belong.

The power of the collective is strong and can easily sweep us up in its current. The solution is to bolster our discernment, become aware of our thoughts and limiting beliefs and stay aligned with our life purpose. We fan the flames of self-awareness through meditation and spiritual practice and therefore our alignment to the authentic self increases. The quieter our mind, the easier it is to detach from groupthink and hear the voice of our consciousness. And then we have to act accordingly, even if this means to change the circumstances of our everyday life.

SUMMARY

We come into the world with a blueprint of how to live our life purpose and manifest our potential. Our exposure to the collective consciousness and interactions with others may derail our planned adventure. Nevertheless, life will always bring us opportunities to remind us of our inner calling, sometimes through joy and sometimes though tears. Many times, we may avoid or decline these doors until our options narrow. Time on Earth is finite and at some point, all opportunities to realise our purpose may be lost and all doors close. Fear, especially of death, and attachments can keep us stuck and unable to make any headway in our journey. Paradoxically, the more contact we have with death, the more we can embrace life's opportunities. Furthermore, we can fan the flames of our life purpose by building self-reliance and self-empowerment and developing our self-awareness.

The more we travel in the footsteps of our soul, the more we will experience the eternal sunshine of who we are.

EXERCISES: FANNING THE FLAMES OF LIFE FULFILMENT

Exercise 1:
Journey – Activate Your Life Purpose

In this journey, I will guide you to discover and energise your life purpose. As usual, create sacred space, this time by inviting the three Fates, the three ancient Moirai who weaved your destiny in alignment with the wishes of your soul. Ask them to support you, as you explore your purpose for this life.

Imagine that you are going up a mountain, into the mist. The road is narrow and treacherous. Yet, your steps find the path. As you walk, feel the fresh, cold air on your face. Smell the damp earth and touch the smooth rocks. See the way opening before you, leading into the cave of the three Fates.

Before you go inside the cave, make an offering to these deities, who control everyone's destiny.

The three Fates have been waiting for you and explain how this is an important moment in your life. You are here to re-evaluate your life purpose.

The first Fate explains what your soul chose as a purpose. Do you still wish to pursue this?

The second Fate shows you what you have already experienced as a result of your life purpose, the opportunities realised and those missed. She asks you if there is anything else you wish to be knitted in the yarn that would help you along. However, she may or may not accept your suggestions. If they come from ego, they may be declined. She only works for your highest good.

The last Fate just smiles at you, as it is not her time yet. You still have some time to live on Earth, before she cuts the yarn.

Now that the Fates have done their work, it is time to go. Thank them for their help in understanding your life and its purpose. Slowly exit the cave.

Walk back down the mountain, until you find a beautiful spring. Now drink from its waters, washing away any energies that no longer serve you.

Slowly bring yourself back by noticing your breath coming in and out of your nostrils. Give thanks to the three Fates aloud and say that your work is complete. Ask that your space and yourself are completely sealed and protected.

Following the journey, let go of any outcome. Life cannot be controlled, even by the practices and ceremonies we do. Sometimes we try so hard to achieve our dreams that when nothing happens, we feel we are swimming upstream against an ever increasing current. This is the time to surrender to life and say "may your will be done." Having done all the ceremonies and prayers, we then detach and surrender. We have set our intention and sent it to the heart of the universe, we now need to step back and notice with detachment what happens. In the meantime, life may be testing us, giving us small windows to walk through to realign our everyday way of living, whilst we wait for the bigger door to open.

Exercise 2:
Spiritual Practice – Releasing attachments that stop you from following your life's calling

Our attachments to ideas, people, material objects and groupthink can stop us from walking through the doors that life opens for us. Sometimes, even when we recognise these opportunities for the realisation of our life's calling, we shy away from them due to fear. We forget that life is an adventure and expect guarantees. Many times I have heard people say that they would like to follow their life's calling but they want to be 100% sure it is going to work out for them. What if I walk through a door and nothing happens? The alternative is to stay still, even if life remains unfulfilled.

In this practice, I invite you to work with Parvati, a representation of the Divine Mother, to release the luggage that hinders your life journey and concentrate on the essential qualities you need for the road.

Create sacred space by inviting Parvati, the Mother Goddess, to be with you. Ask her to guide you and help you release anything that prevents you from following your life's purpose.

Imagine you are standing in front of a flowing river. Use all your senses to take yourself into the visualisation: see the river in your mind's eye, hear, feel and smell the water. Put yourself firmly in this picture.

You need to cross the river. Your life purpose is waiting for you on the other side. You could use the narrow bridge or you could wade through the river as it's not too deep. However, you are carrying numerous bundles of things, some of which are very heavy. The bridge might not hold you and all you carry, and if you wade through the water you might lose your balance and fall.

Some of the things you are carrying are very precious to you, even though they are hindering your passage. However, you realise that to reach the other side you will need to leave most of your things behind, otherwise you will be stuck on the riverbank.

The Divine Mother asks you to choose five qualities, to take with you. To help you make a choice, the five elements of earth, water, air, fire and space, will offer you their advice. However, the final decision rests with you.

105

The first quality you will need relates to the element of earth. Earth is everything material, starting with your body, home, wealth, physical strength. The earth element is green in colour. Ask the earth to help you, if you do not already know, choose this first quality.

The second element is water, which is blue in colour. The water can advise you about choosing a quality associated with your emotions, your heart and love, your ability to feel joy and happiness. So ask the element of water for its advice about what this second quality could be.

The third element is related to air, which is white in colour. Air speaks to you about your mind and your thought processes. Do you wish an active mind, scientific, mathematical, logical, peaceful, daydreaming, discerning, or imaginary mind? Ask this element about the best quality for you in relation to your mind, for you'll need your mind to realise your life's calling.

Now invite in the fire element, which is red in colour. The fire element is about passion, drive and determination. What fire quality will you choose to help you achieve your life purpose?

The fifth element is the element of space, of consciousness, of spirit. It is golden in colour and is about awareness, psychic communication, clairvoyance, ability to meditate, inner knowing. There are many aspects of consciousness in your bundles and maybe you would like to take one of the aspects with you.

Once you have selected the five most important qualities, invite the Divine Mother Parvati to energise the qualities you have chosen. See these qualities as seeds of different colours: green, blue, white, red and gold. Your heart is like the fertile Earth. Imagine Parvati planting these seeds in your heart and blessing them so that they will grow strong, helping you fulfil your purpose. Now you are ready to start your journey across the river and maybe you would like to cross the bridge to the other side.

Your practice is now complete. Slowly become aware of your surroundings, focus on your breath and bring yourself back from the visualisation. Give thanks to the Divine Mother Parvati who has helped you with this exercise. Ask that she closes, protects and seals you and your room before she goes.

A Teaching from the Spirit of the West

A healer walked in the plains of the west,
looking for death who had taken her friends away;
snatched them from under her breath, without mercy.

She walked the path of the west,
to find a tree hit by thunder.
The tree had tried to grow.
Had pushed the stony ground away with its roots.
All in vain, burned at the end by the fire from the sky.

It must have been a great effort to grow through the stones,
to push the rocks aside.
But this did not stop the tree from trying.

When lightening came,
death took away the spirit of the tree.
Was it worth it? Or was it all for nothing?

Her friends were like the tree:
three of them, Gordon, Mhairi and Jo.
Dearly missed.

Like the tree, they pushed through the illness.
Embraced life, looking for ways to grow.
Their spirit strong, snatched by the cancer.

Death was there in the west.
He did not take her to join her friends.
Her life he says is not yet fulfilled.

One day it will be over.
But still death said she cannot die.
Her soul continues in eternity.

No lightening can burn her spirit.
No illness can harm her soul.
In the circle of life, there is no starting or ending point.

This is what death whispered in the west.
The spirit of the tree is always safe.
And so are her friends walking through eternity.

8

Destruction and Transformation

Spiritual Lesson 8: Emerging from the ashes of destruction,
the phoenix is birthing my new reality

Shedding skin: I am standing in front of the hot coals, ready to embrace myself as a keeper of the ancient tradition of firewalking, a ceremony that runs in the blood of my ancestors. I feel naked, as if the fire can see right through me and yet, her power is gentle and inviting. When I step onto the coals, the rain stops. I take it as a sign from heaven. I focus my attention on the end of the firewalk and step purposefully over the embers, completing the walk in three steps. I am aware that I do not walk alone. The fire has carried me, the ancient ones have held my hand, and my spirit answered a calling both old and familiar. At the end of the walk, I feel elated, having touched my very essence of infinite joy.

USING FIRE ENERGY

In Hindu philosophy, divine consciousness has three aspects: creator, sustainer, and destroyer (Jansen, 2001). The latter aspect brings transformation through destruction. Shiva, as the destroyer, is portrayed as an ascetic who renounces the comforts of life to follow a path of self-realisation. Through the taming of the ego, Shiva becomes master of himself and the universe. He is often depicted with his right foot standing on a demon, symbolising that he has overcome the conditioned mind. His left foot is raised in ecstatic dance. Unharmed within a circle of fire, Shiva teaches us that flames cannot burn those who shine the inner light of awareness.

In northern Greece where I was raised, the ancient tradition of firewalking, still practiced today, is called "Anastenaria" (Xygalatas, 2014). In 2008, I trained as an instructor of western firewalking, with the American company Sundoor. During a firewalk ceremony, we walk barefoot over hot coals and call out to helping spirits to aid a safe crossing.

Whilst in my own lineage we invoke the saints of Constantine and Helen, in the western firewalking course, we customarily invoke the power of Shiva—even though the ceremony is not Hindu. I found that the fire energy brings transformation at a deep level, and after someone firewalks, she is no longer the same. In both traditions, it takes courage and faith to surrender to the fire and overcome fear, to do what the mind believes is dangerous but the spirit knows is possible. Usually, the most daunting part of firewalking is the first step. As soon as we are on the hot embers, the Divine presence we invoked, either Shiva or the saints, can carry us through. We find determination to keep walking right to the end. There is no turning back.

Life is the same as firewalking. When the door to our path opens inviting us to leave our comfort zone, the hardest part is that first step. Once we take it, we usually find the momentum to keep going. The thought is usually more frightening than the act itself. Sometimes, in pursuit of our dreams, we create a safety net. By holding something in abeyance just in case we decide to turn back, our efforts do not bear fruit (or not the fruits we want). We are trying to firewalk with one foot, reserving the other lest we get burned. It is best to act decisively.

MOVING OUT OF OUR COMFORT ZONE

Many indigenous societies migrate according to the seasons in search of food and shelter. Sami shamans in Lapland smell the change in the air, and the tribe relocates, following the reindeer. Native American tribes used to follow the buffalo and move to different pastures. Similarly, my great-grandfather practiced "merominia," the reading of the stars each March, to divine the weather for the coming year. His reading directed the movement of sheep to higher ground and other agricultural activities. Like my grandfather's practice, the shaman's role was critical to the tribe because his interpretation of natural signs determined the survival of the group. Change was an integral part of their way of life, and accepting change with the seasons helped them survive.

In contrast, developed societies no longer need to undertake repeated displacements. When the weather grows cold, we turn up the heat. When our pantry runs low, we buy more food at the supermarket. With the ease of modern conveniences, we assume we can continue living the way we always have. We think we can control nature, expecting little change. Such conditioning, especially as we age, can make us resistant to change and reject the new.

Our autonomy from nature's cycles may not be the panacea we expected. We are slowly destroying the environment and depleting the Earth's natural resources. The resulting climate change is now a global concern. Even so, we find it difficult to consider alternative ways of life. Our comfort zone has become a prison that not only keeps us stuck, but also threatens us with extinction.

Swimming against the Current

The collective consciousness rarely welcomes change; it is easier to maintain status quo than change the direction of the river of life. When destruction comes into our life, the collective response towards us is often pity and fear. Even if we are able to embrace the change, others may continue to believe that what has happened to us is unfortunate. Whilst groupthink resists change and assumes the worst, it may be our door towards thriving.

Through personal work and self-reflection, a spiritual warrior can release her attachments to the collective consciousness. She understands that she does not have to be ill when everyone else is sick. She stays out of the emotional collective hole by remaining calm and present in the moment, and connected to her inner guidance. Like a ship, she can unfurl her sails and be carried by the fierce winds of transformation.

Welcoming Transformation

Birth and death define the cycles of nature. They are intertwined. Destruction is a natural force, like a fire that burns an old forest in order to regenerate. The soil, enriched by the flesh of the old trees, gives birth to new life. Change, the ebb and the flow, is a necessary blessing. We move to the next stage of our life confident in Earth's wisdom, rather than remain stuck in a status quo that no longer serves us.

Traditionally, Shiva is the protector of shamans and spiritual seekers. When a spiritual seeker is resisting change, Shiva arrives to remind her of her dedication to her spiritual path. Shiva encourages the seeker to continue her chosen journey—even if it means leaving behind the security of her everyday life. When Shiva the destroyer enters our life, we can welcome him and trust his fire as part of the cycle of life. Inner transformation may follow.

A Story: "Unleashing the Fire Spirit"

This is a meditative story I have channelled for this chapter, so I suggest you create a quiet, relaxing space for reflection.

Visualise a sixteenth century sailing ship. Before the journey, the captain charts the course and then sets sail. The wind carries the ship into shallow waters, and it beaches on a sandbank close to a beautiful island. The captain and crew disembark and live on the island. It is not where they are supposed to be, but they are warm, comfortable, and settled. There is not much to do on the island, and they soon get bored, but getting the ship back out to sea would require a lot of effort and hard work, and there is no guarantee they would reach their destination.

The crew is content to spend their days idle on the beach. Sometimes they talk about their intended destination, but the consensus is they are better off on the island.

"Being a sailor is hard."

"The seas can be treacherous."

"Let's stay safe, right where we are."

The captain, though, is still motivated to reach their destination, but cannot do much without his men. Eventually, he gives in as well and joins the chorus of torpor. The men become fat and lazy. They drink every night to numb themselves from any thoughts of home and where they expected to be. Months pass.

One day, the captain has had enough. He goes to speak to the shaman on the island, who in turn, consults with his helping spirits. The shaman returns and tells the captain that a solution exists, and the fire spirit wishes to help. The captain quickly accepts the help of the spirit, not knowing what else to do. The shaman warns the captain that the spirit will help him arrive at his destination, by whatever means. But first, the shaman must be certain of the captain's commitment. The captain again accepts the help of the fire spirit, and the shaman tells him there will be no going back. The captain agrees once more, for a third time. He is certain that this is the right decision for him and his crew.

The captain returns to the camp as his crew is preparing for their usual drunken feast. However, the fire spirit has other plans. With an explosion, the spirit erupts out of the island volcano. Fire pours down the mountain destroying everything in its path.

In a panic, the men turn and run to the sea as the flow of hot lava reaches their huts. They are in a living hell. Everything is burning, and smoke and dust rise all around them. The men have one option for survival: get back to the ship.

The captain re-charts the course, and the crew readies the ship. The sea helps, too, rising and falling to ease the hulking vessel off the sandbank. Now the ocean becomes their safe haven and the island, the treacherous land.

After months of neglect on the sandbank, the ship is in poor condition. The men work hard to make necessary restorations and keep her seaworthy. They manoeuvre in the rough seas and rest in the calm seas. They notice the beauty of each sunrise and sunset in the vastness of the ocean. Each night, they see the stars that light their way. With a renewed purpose in life, they are now excited about reaching their destination.

Sometimes, we need the fire spirit to put us back on course and move us out of the shallow waters where we have become beached. The power of destruction, the end of complacency, is essential so that transformation can come in. In Shiva's way, there is no growth without heat.

SUMMARY

In our society, destruction and renewal are often unwelcome and not fully understood. We prefer to stay in our comfort zone, tolerating fear and accepting compromise rather than follow our dream and life purpose. The power of Shiva the destroyer can help us burn through our conditioning and show us the way of change, through the glowing fire towards self-realisation. Throughout the process, we stay positive and listen to the voice of our heart, dance with the flames of destruction, and step on the conditioning of the mind.

Om Namah Shivaya. Destroyer, bringer of light and fire, may you dance over the remnants of my idle life! (Invocation to Shiva)

Exercise: Ceremony – Burning Obstacles with the Fire Spirit

If you feel stuck in your life, it may be time to ask for help from the fire spirit, the power of Shiva the destroyer. This ceremony will help relieve you of extra cargo and put you back on course. Remember, that like the captain in the story, once you engage the help of the fire spirit, there is no turning back, as fire destroys by its nature.

You will need an altar cloth, new white candle, sheet of blank paper, pen or pencil, matches or lighter, and flameproof dish.

Start your ceremony by creating the sacred space: welcome your higher self, and invoke the power of Shiva, the destroyer, the spirit of the fire. Then place the candle in the middle of the altar cloth. The candle represents the forces of nature, the fire spirit in the story above.

On the sheet of paper, make a list of the things you feel are stopping you from reaching your purpose. This is fuel for the fire, food for the fire spirit. If you are aware of the obstacles you can be specific; else, you can write down a general statement. For example, "My intention is to release whatever is stopping me, hindering me, and no longer serves me."

Light the candle. Say to your higher self, "I am ready to walk my path of life. I intend that my life is brought into alignment with my soul's calling." Ask the fire spirit to burn all obstacles that are preventing this.

Light the piece of paper and let it burn in the dish. The burning paper represents your commitment to spirit and yourself and your willingness to change.

Stay quiet for a few minutes, and ask if the fire spirit has any guidance for you. Finally, ask the light of the candle to fill you with strength and enliven your life purpose. Acknowledge that the fire spirit is working to bring you back on your life course.

Gently bring yourself back. Put out the candle flame. Do not use this candle for any other purpose. In the future, if you feel things are difficult for you, light the candle again and ask for the fire spirit to fill you with strength and a sense of purpose.

Close your ceremonial space by thanking your higher self and Shiva. Release Shiva and your higher self and ask that you and your space are completely protected and sealed.

PRAYER TO SHIVA

Shiva Om, destroyer
I call you in my life.
Through the fires of hell
I renew myself.

Shiva Om, power of fire,
Hear the voice of my soul,
It wants to speak,
but I am frightened.

I seek you through the night
when all hope has gone,
calling the fire spirit
to break through the life I have made for myself.

Once I had a dream,
but it soon fled.
When life became too comfortable,
I was trapped in a place of my own making.

You, who wore the ascetic gown
should know how it feels
to leave a warm comfortable bed
and seek your fortunes in the stormy night.

You whisper of trust in life.
Words that I do not know
but will soon have to discover their meaning
if I am ever to start the journey.

You say the journey is already made.
It began long ago
when I first agreed to walk it.
I have to let go of my fears.

Shiva says, life will support you
when you walk your golden path,
even if it feels unknown,
it is also strangely familiar.

Shiva says, trust in life.
Do not give up your dreams.
They will guide you through the night
into the new dawn.

Part II.
Into the Spirit–
The Flying Serpent

Having shed the skin, the renewed snake emerges to find that it is not made entirely from flesh and blood. The snake discovers its wings and heads for the sky, becoming a spiritual being, the flying serpent.

Part II takes us into a spiritual journey of self-discovery. A deep curiosity for the unseen world motivates us to uncover the spiritual realms. These worlds have their own rules; time runs differently and years may pass in self-exploration. Our light becomes brighter, enabling us to see in the realm beyond. We discover our spirit helpers and the nature spirits that surround us. We delve into the world of dreams. Our perception of life changes as we embrace an expanded view of reality. Initiation is a process of strengthening our wings and affirming our commitment to the embodiment of our spiritual self.

9

The Spirit World: Lifting the Veil

*Spiritual Lesson 9: To comprehend my life, I ally with
spirit entities of light*

*Into the spirit: Participating in the ancient ritual of the vision quest, I leave
my city life for the desert. I sit under the juniper tree for four days and four
nights waiting to hear the voice of spirit. Without food, the attachment to flesh
weakens and the spiritual light emerges. A sense of peace comes over me. No
longer occupied by the details of everyday life, I sit and listen. For two days,
nothing much happens. I watch two sunrises and sunsets, impressed by the
beauty of the natural world that I normally do not take the time to witness.
On the third day, I have a vision. Shiva hands me a rattle and reminds me
of my shamanic calling. He invites me to travel to Tibet and the Himalayas.
When the vision ends, I open my eyes and see two birds in front of me. They
make three perfect circles and fly away. Spirit has spoken.*

THERE IS MORE TO LIFE THAN MEETS THE EYE

Apart from the physical world, a spiritual dimension exists around us. This unseen
world can be accessed through our psychic, or sixth, sense, and experienced through

the five senses. Despite many credible accounts of spirit activity, out-of-body experiences, and unexplained presences, the general consensus is that the spirit world does not exist. The scientific approach of our age—"seeing is believing"—has skewed our attention to the physical world to the exclusion of any other.

Yet, some scientists have analysed psychic phenomena and found them to be real, even if they are unexplainable by the laws of physics. Radin (2010) examined the credible scientific research on psychic occurrences and he concluded that even if a large number of researchers had committed fraud, misconstrued, misapplied, and misunderstood the meta-analysis, the existence of telepathy, clairvoyance, precognition, psychokinesis, and other psychic phenomena is incontrovertible.

As the majority of people do not have psychic awareness, those who see spirits are often regarded as being mentally ill or odd in some way, and thus, have been marginalised, ridiculed, and even relegated to the world of entertainment. Due to the cultural tendency towards animosity, when people experience a phenomenon that defies a logical explanation, they, too, may be more likely to deny, dismiss, or attribute it to their imagination.

Conversely, indigenous traditions readily acknowledge that around our physical world exist other universes inhabited by spirit beings, beings with or without a tangible form. Just as our human bodies occupy a material dimension, spirit beings dwell in a spirit reality. These beings interact with the physical world, whether people acknowledge them or not. When we deny the existence of the spirit dimension, we cut ourselves off from a rich source of information, healing, and guidance. We also reject our own spiritual nature, as we too are multidimensional spiritual beings, temporarily occupying a body and inhabiting a physical environment. Consequently, we disown our true essence.

Our spirit has no beginning and no end in time, existing prior to incarnation in a human form and continuing life after the physical death. After death, our spirit may stay unseen around the Earth plane, or move to other spirit realms.

OUR DECEASED RELATIVES ARE PART OF THE SPIRIT WORLD

The most commonplace contact between physical beings and the spirit world occurs with our recently deceased relatives. My father, a typical pragmatic engineer, had a visitation from the spirit of his mother-in-law just after she died. My father dreamt he heard my grandmother's voice coming from her room downstairs in his home. (My terminally ill grandmother had recently been moved to the hospital.)

In his dream, my father went downstairs to her room and found her sitting in her armchair, dressed in her usual black clothes. She told him that she had just died and proceeded to tell my father what the future held for our family and what he must do as the head of the family. She was making sure she finished her business here before moving on. My grandmother then said, "I must go now as the hospital is phoning to tell you of my death." My father woke to the ringing telephone. My mother, who was closer to the phone, answered it, and was told of her mother's death.

Communication with the spirit world may engage any of the five senses and be direct or subtle—even barely perceptible. We may notice that a personal item is missing, a photograph of a loved one is lopsided, smell a perfume associated with the deceased, or notice ourselves singing a song the deceased relative liked. For example, one of my friends, who is psychic, would smell cigar smoke whenever his father's spirit was close. In such circumstances, we could visit a Spiritualist Church service, where a demonstration of mediumship takes place, or consult a psychic medium privately. Our loved one may wish to reassure us that their spirit is alive, happy and close to us.

We can find healing and closure by communicating with a deceased loved one. Some people die with unfinished business. They may have died suddenly or simply never had the opportunity to express their love or their wishes to their relatives or settle their affairs. Sometimes, too, people are reluctant to move on due to emotional attachments, their own or those of living relatives.

A friend Brian lost his father, who was in his fifties. Brian was distraught as they had been close. He was stuck in unending grief and anger about what had happened. He could not understand why his father died and blamed everyone, including his father for dying. I wanted to help Brian and introduced him to a friend Ian Shanes, who is a psychic medium. Brian invited Ian and me to his house so he could speak to his father. As Ian communicated a message of love and support to Brian from his father, I witnessed a huge transformation in Brian. The pain began leaving his face. Brian was still sad about his father's passing, but he was no longer incapacitated by grief. He started living again.

Types of Spirits: Helpers, Allies and Troublemakers

Spirit guides fall roughly into three categories: helpers, allies and troublemakers. Our deceased relatives may be in any of these categories, depending on their level of evolution.

The helpers include enlightened, highly evolved beings, such as angels and archangels, deities, saints, buddhas, and masters of light, whose sole aim is to help us on our life path, if we so wish. They have a "phalange," a team of spirit helpers that becomes available to us. The phalange may consist of beings who have incarnated on Earth before and were nuns, priests, doctors, or ordinary people who developed unconditional compassion and now wish to serve others. These beings offer their support wholeheartedly and always work for our highest good, never asking for anything in return.

The allies include beings who wish to unite with us because we may have a similar purpose. For example, some nature spirits may seek to form alliances with environmentalists. These spirits will progress in their soul's journey through us, as we will, through their advice. However, this is a co-dependent relationship that can sometimes go awry, if either party breaks the agreement. These beings may be more or less evolved. They have a personality, an egoic self, and thus, it is wise to be discerning about taking their advice and making agreements with them. They may show us other realities and try to appeal to our interests, so that we work with them. They need a human being through whom they can work and evolve.

Deceased relatives commonly belong to this category. However, sometimes they evolve in the spirit world and may become a helper, although not always so. Joan, a healer, had been contacted many times by her deceased mother, who was an alcoholic during her life. The mother was asking to be part of the daughter's spirit team. Joan always declined as she felt her mother's offer was not unconditional but based on self-interest. On a few occasions, I have worked with my great grandfather, who was a medicine man in Greece, as he has evolved since his death into a wise spirit helper.

When approached by allies, it is important to be discerning. In 2007, I visited the ancient pyramids in Mexico and Guatemala. Whilst there, I was approached by Aztec spirit priests, who showed me psychically their tradition and helped me clear heavy energies lingering in the sites, due to an ancient practice of human sacrifice. The spirits asked if they could come with me, saying they had information and knowledge to share. Naively, I said yes and then forgot about them. I did not realise these spirits had an agenda and wanted to join my spirit team. In my ignorance, I had let them in.

Two years later, they appeared to me in a psychic circle, expressing their disappointment at having been ignored, claiming I had agreed to work with them. My other guides came through and showed me how these spirits were looking for a human being to work with so they could evolve, and how I had been hoodwinked. Eventually, my guides and I persuaded them to leave. This was a big lesson for me, especially as their initial approach had been so subtle and seemingly innocuous.

The last category, the troublemakers, include spirits who range from mischievous to malevolent, and can cause havoc and illness in our life. These are spirits who entice us to have the extra glass of wine, to get angry with someone, or worse. They attach to humans and feed off negative energy. When people open themselves up energetically, for example through recreational drugs or when drunk, these spirit entities find fertile ground to play. They have no respect for people, and when they can no longer use someone, they will discard her without regret and move to the next person.

It is a misconception that all spirits are helpful or loving. We need to be aware that spirit beings are no different from human beings. Some will foster our development, and others will hinder it. We need to learn who is which.

WORKING WITH SPIRITS

When a spirit being approaches me, I ask three times if, in the name of the Divine Creator, they work fully and wholly for the light. According to universal law, they have to speak the truth and if I get even one negative answer, I will not work with them and so I ask my guardian angel or other helper to remove them. Usually, troublemakers flee when I repeat the question.

Working with Helpers. These spirits are there to assist us in our life journey. They can provide information, teachings, healing, and guidance for our lives and our personal development. Their aim is to help us progress. They assist us with what we need to learn in our life without interfering in our decisions. When we act out of ego, or make an unskilful choice, helping spirits generally stand back without judgement. They know this is part of our soul evolution. They may offer suggestions of what to do for our highest good, which we can choose to reject or follow. It is up to us to decide how we live our life.

Helping spirits work in a variety of ways. They may manifest in front of a person, to make their presence known and help her embrace a more spiritual life path (the role of proselytiser). They may arrange synchronicities, events where everything seems to fall into place, so a person can come into their own realisation of what their next step in life is (the role of spotlighter). When I started pursuing a spiritual path, I would see faces and shadows coming out of the bedroom wall towards me. At other times, all the electrical equipment, including the TV, would switch off. Eventually, I realised these were my helping spirits trying to attract my attention, so they could talk to me.

Sometimes people think very highly of their spirit guides, whilst putting themselves down. Our helping spirits have great respect for us, knowing that physical life can be challenging. It is important for us to realise that in this working relationship, we are all equals. A healthier approach is to see ourselves as part of a bigger spirit family, where everyone is appreciated and plays a valued role. At different times, some members of this spirit family incarnate, whilst others remain in the spiritual realms, to help the person fulfil their purpose for incarnating. Other evolved spirit entities associated with our team, may never incarnate.

Some helping spirits are more universal and look after the whole of life on Earth, as well as working with us individually. One of my main spirit guides is ISIS, a being of light who carries the Divine Mother energy in our world. She oversees the process of soul evolution on Earth and, at the same time, works with individuals such as myself, for their advancement on their spiritual journey.

Avoiding Unhelpful Spirits. Addictions in the physical world are notoriously linked with unhelpful spirit entities. These entities can take over a person when she is drunk or under the influence of recreational drugs. When a person takes hallucinogenic substances, their energy bodies open, making them more easily available to the spirit world. The ancient people may have used hallucinogenics to increase their spiritual awareness, but they also knew how to protect themselves psychically while under the influence of these substances.

Have you ever noticed how someone's nature changes and mental problems develop when a long-term alcoholic or drug addict? This transformation is often caused by spirit entities who have attached themselves to the person. They do not want the person to develop strength of character and be happy, as they are living off their negativity, forming a parasitic relationship. Fear and anger are strong emotions that create a lot of energy for these malevolent spirits. Violent outbursts are even more welcome, and more likely to occur.

Spiritually, we need to have compassion for these spirit beings. The malevolent spirit is trying to survive in a world that cannot sustain it on its own resources. These lost souls do not know another way of being. However, the person hosting the spirit is not a helpless victim either. At some level, she, too, is responsible. She is choosing to feed her own addictive, destructive behaviour, especially in the beginning.

However, addictions are linked to soul loss (chapter 5), and can be a symptom of overwhelming pain. The addictive substance, whether it is alcohol, drugs or chocolate, temporarily interrupts the circular cascade of recurrent nerve-to-nerve interaction, taking us out of the emotional and mental pain. It never addresses the underlying trauma (Paine, 2012). Our ego shadow chooses the substance as a quick fix, against our better judgment, even though the pain will return as soon as the substance is metabolised by the body. Addictions continue to create soul and power loss—until we are able to resist them. When we make a decision to decline the addictive substance, we start taking our power back. We place ourselves on the road to freedom.

The compassionate spirits will try and assist an addictive person by dissuading her from choosing destructive behaviour. The helping spirits cannot intervene to save someone who does not wish to be saved, but they can try their best to make her aware of her actions and show her another way.

When I was trying to get fit and give up sugar, I asked for help from my spirit guides. My spirit friends ensured there was no chocolate in the staff room, that all cakes were eaten by the time I got there, and when I went to the shops to buy chocolate, they pointed to the fresh satsumas. In the end, the decision was always mine. We lead our own lives and our choices are our responsibility.

In my work as a shamanic practitioner, I have helped many people who had entities attached to them, either knowingly or unknowingly. More often than not, possession followed large alcohol consumption or the use of recreational drugs, including plant substances such as Peyote and Ayahuasca. In two cases, after the healing, the entity kept coming back, even when the client was sober. I asked my spirit guides why this happens. They showed me how, in some cases, the person was allowing the entity to reattach through their continued negative behaviours and attitudes. In another situation, the spirit being had a karmic link with the client.

If the person does not take responsibility for her behaviour and attitude, and seek help to address the underlying causes attracting the entity, then it is difficult for the shamanic practitioner and her helping spirits to assist her. The host has to look deep within.

Few people are totally possessed. Those that are, usually refuse all offers of support, because it is not in the interest of the entity for the person to change. The person has little willpower left. She is an empty vessel. The spirit being inside her has taken over. However, a healing practitioner can bring the person's own energy and power back into her, through multiple soul retrievals (chapter 5) which, in time, push out the entity. The person could also consider addiction counselling to deal with the causes behind the compulsive behaviour.

Troublemakers are also attracted to spiritual practitioners, aiming to hinder our light work. Most of the time our helpers will protect us from their influence. Meditation and spiritual practice can assist us in understanding when troublemakers are around. A sudden change in disposition, or thoughts that do not have the ring of truth, may indicate their presence. One Friday evening in 2006, I was in the municipal office where I worked as a town planner, and started feeling tired, fed-up and generally dissatisfied. Many negative thoughts arose about my job. Then a thought said I should move back to Greece. I knew then these were not my thoughts. Immediately, the negative state cleared. The troublemaker was found out.

When dealing with the spirit world, we need to equip ourselves with discernment and common sense. One of my students channelled a troublemaker that pretended to be an ascended master. He was appealing to her ego. The advice of the "Master" was intrusive, disrespectful and dark. "Are these the words of a being of light?", we can ask ourselves.

I advise everyone to work solely with enlightened beings of the first category, the helpers. These highly evolved spirits will not promise you the world or appeal to your ego. They are teachers who are not there to do your bidding. They will only support your highest good; helping you on your life path with integrity and purpose, guiding you to experience your authentic nature and discover the beauty of your soul.

CONTACTING SPIRITS IN THREE STEPS

Spirit communication takes a certain amount of energy and if we are tired, we may compromise ourselves and our results. As a general rule, a person needs to be relaxed, physically well, in a good frame of mind, and free of long term health or severe mental problems to work independently with the spirit dimension. Otherwise, I recommend you find an experienced teacher to help you through the initial steps.

One can work safely with spirits in three steps: create a sacred space and, if you wish, an altar, engage with spirits, and release and seal the space. In each exercise of this book, we use the three steps as a standard protocol for working spiritually.

Create a Sacred Space and Altar. When we invite the spirits to come to our place, we wish to change the vibration and create our own temple. Preferably, a practitioner would have a dedicated room for her spiritual work. If this is not possible, she can clear the energies in a room used for other activities, with incense, toning, or using a singing bowl. For thousands of years, people have incorporated altars—from simple ones in nature made of twigs and flowers, to elaborate, even gilded, ones in churches and other places of worship. Regardless of its form, the purpose of an altar is to focus the spiritual energies into a specific space within the room and to centre our attention.

The exercise at the end of the chapter outlines how to create a sacred space and altar.

Engage with Spirit Beings. After establishing a sacred space, we welcome the spirit guides and teachers of the light into the room, and light the candle. If we do not know who our spirit guides are, it is important to find out by articulating our intention. The guide is our lighthouse showing us the way, the protector keeping all the sharks away. The next section includes ways of contacting and recognising our spirit guides.

Release the Spirits and Seal the Space. When we finish sacred work, it is important to disengage—with gratitude—and seal our space. When I was forgetting to seal myself and my space, I had a significant dream. The spirits showed me that in my healing space, the aura of the room had opened and a being with the body of a man and the head of a crocodile had sneaked through. I knew this being did not work for the light. The next day, I did an energetic clearing of my space, recreated the sacred space, and closed and sealed it afterwards.

We disengage from our work by thanking the spirits and asking them that before they leave, to completely seal ourselves and the room. We then put the candle out gently with our fingers or a snuffer, as if putting the fire to sleep. (I was asked by the spirits not to blow the candle out, as this would signify the death of the fire.)

WAYS OF SPIRIT COMMUNICATION

We can communicate with spirits in different ways: by journeying, overshadowing, and taking a medicine walk. Each technique is described below.

Journeying to Discover our Helping Spirits. Shamans refer to mysterious spiritual worlds that exist in different planes to our own. A paradigm that I use to explain the shamanic worlds is that of the tree of life.

Imagine a tree that is so large, it spans universes, star systems, and different dimensions. Engage all your senses, picturing the tree in your mind's eye. Feel its bark, smell the earth around it, hear the wind as it passes through the leaves, even taste its fruit. When you have a clear picture of it in your mind, focus on the tree.

When you sit next to this tree, you are in what is known as "the middle world." The tree is so big that you can travel down through its roots. As you do, you notice little openings through the dark roots, which take you into "the lower worlds." Each lower world is similar to our own, with animals, forests, and lakes. There are many such worlds. Some traditions say there is only one lower world; some say there are three and some, seven or nine. My shamanic helpers have shown me there are an infinite number.

You can explore these worlds on your own, or preferably, accompanied by your spirit guide. Maybe a guide awaits you there in one of the lower worlds. There could be more than one spirit guide, in the form of an animal, plant, human, or mythical being. Once you find them, you can start asking questions and have a conversation with them. Afterwards, you can trace your steps back into the middle world, back the way you came through the roots of the tree of life.

Similarly, you can decide to climb up into the branches of the tree. The branches reach across the clouds and beyond the stars and universes. As you ascend, you find different worlds, other realities, called the "upper worlds." I was shown by my spirit helpers that these upper worlds are infinite in number, too. Maybe, there is a being of light waiting for you there. At the end, you can, once again, find your way back by retracing your steps and climbing down the tree.

Overshadowing: Gaining a Physical Sense of One's Spirit Guide. "Overshadowing" is the process of learning how our spirit guide feels to us when he is present. Distinct from journeying through the tree of life, we notice the physical sensations in our body. We may feel as though we are being touched or sense a slight breeze.

To communicate with your guides through this medium, first bring yourself into a state of relaxation. Then, ask one of your spirit guides to step into your aura, as close to you as possible. Notice the physical sensations in your body in the here and now. Do you feel as if the spirit is touching you? Is there a breeze or change in temperature? Do you sense an electrical charge around you? Do you see, hear, or smell anything unusual? You are deepening your familiarity with your guide. Ask any questions you may have, and wait for the answer to pop into your head. You can repeat this exercise to become familiar with other guides who may be supporting you.

Medicine Walks. Not everyone is able to connect with their spirit guides by journeying and overshadowing. Sometimes we may prefer a more active approach. A third way to communicate with the spirit world, is to ask a question while walking in nature and notice any signs. Traditionally, this is called a "medicine walk," which includes fasting and starts at sunrise and ends at sundown. However, shorter walks can also be used as mediums for spirit communication, especially by people who are beginners.

I create sacred space around me by invoking my guides and then I say to them that I am doing a sacred walk to seek guidance from Mother Earth. I draw a line on the ground and step over the threshold. I then walk for a while and notice what happens. Maybe something on the ground is important, or a bird is whispering into my ear. Perhaps, I notice a tree with a peculiar shape that has a message for me.

During the walk, I use my peripheral vision to be aware of what is happening on either side of me rather than only looking ahead. By practising peripheral viewing, you will recognise your own aura and personal space and eventually, you may detect spirit presences around you and even behind you. I have found that peripheral viewing expands psychic awareness. At the end of the walk, I thank Mother Earth and release my guides and step back over the line of the threshold into ordinary life.

The ways to work with spirits are endless. Our helpers will use our own skills of perception to communicate with us. In 2006, when I was looking for guidance in my life, my helpers started communicating with me through songs. If there was something they wanted to tell me, I would find myself absentmindedly singing a song. Then, I would notice that the lyrics held meaning for me.

Some people are clairvoyant, while others are clairsentient (they have an inner knowing of spirit). Still others are clairaudient (they hear spirit). Being open and patient, and trusting your instincts will help ensure a successful and productive relationship with your spirit guides.

SUMMARY

Apart from our physical dimension, other dimensions exist parallel to our own, which we can access to communicate with the spirit beings who inhabit them. There are three categories of spirit entities, ranging from enlightened spirit helpers to unhelpful lost spirits. We can work safely with spirit guides by creating a protected sacred space and, once we have finished our work, by closing and sealing this space. We use different techniques to communicate with spirit guides. Journeying is a type of shamanic ceremony. Overshadowing monitors our visceral responses to spiritual realms, and medicine walks engage the natural world.

EXERCISE: CREATING A SACRED SPACE AND ALTAR

In this exercise you learn your first step in spirit communication: how to create a sacred space. Prepare the space by tidying the room and if possible, switch off and remove all technology, such as computers and mobile phones. Traditionally, indigenous people took days to prepare a space for ceremony, but in the modern era, we have time constraints.

Next, invite the protective powers in by drawing etherically a healing symbol or saying a prayer. I invite the Divine Creator to surround me and my work, which I dedicate to the highest good of all beings. I include my prayer for reference, but you may wish to use your own words.

I say, "Divine Creator I recognise myself as the Eternal Light, whose purpose is to embody a state of love. Please create around me a sacred space, protecting me and my work, for the next [number of] hours or until my work is complete. I give thanks for all the shining spirits of light who help me and protect me in your Name. I give thanks for my spiritual work, which I dedicate to the highest good of all beings."

You can also place symbols to further protect the room. My favourite is the rose cross, which predates Christianity. It includes the four directions, the centre of the cosmos, and the energies of the Divine Masculine and Feminine. Some people link the rose cross with Christ consciousness and Mary Magdalene. I draw the rose cross by first tracing the vertical line downwards, the horizontal line from left to right, and then, a circle enclosing the lines counterclockwise. Placing the symbol on the floor, I step into it and imagine that it is three-dimensional and completely surrounding me.

The Rose Cross

Within your sacred space, you may wish to create an altar. Your altar can take any form that expresses your inner world and helps you focus. It can be minimal and evocative with a single candle, or elaborate with a cloth, travel mementoes, crystals and pictures of deities or angels.

My altar represents the elements of the cosmos: water, wind (the feather and incense), earth (stone, crystals), and fire (the candle).

132

On the right side, I place the element of water representing flow. On the left, I place the element of wind/air, represented by incense or feathers that brings cleansing. In the middle, at the lower end, I place stones, crystals, or pieces of bark, symbolising the element of earth that brings grounding. The candle in the centre represents fire. Fire brings light. Light is in the centre of the altar mirroring its place in the centre of our being, the centre of our solar system and the centre of our universe.

You can then engage safely with your spirit guides. After your spiritual work is complete, thank the spirits, and release them. Ask them to seal and protect both the room and yourself before they go. Take your altar apart and only use these items for your spiritual work, allowing the spiritual energies to gradually build within them.

THE DANCE OF SPIRIT

Spiritdance, wild dance, dance of the consciousness.
The one who wishes to know more, to search and find.
There is nothing around me, my mind is closed to all possibilities.

Yet I cannot explain the shadows at night,
the slight breeze, the lights surrounding me.
The feeling that I am not alone.

Who is with me? Why are you here?
Are you going to frighten me?
I would rather not know you, even if you were once dear to me.

What is your purpose?
Are you here to scare me?
If you love me, leave me alone, helpless and wandering.

There is no proof you exist.
Yet I can feel you by me;
a comforting presence, until my mind questions my sanity.

If I was to accept you and dance with you,
will you show me the secrets of life?
Why are you here with me, I do not know your motivation.

But I feel you guiding me,
your hand pointing a way that I dare not walk.
It is dangerous to leave my comforts behind.

You don't always answer me,
you care not for my wishes and my dreams,
you only point a way back home giving me the choice.

If I come, my road will be filled by endless tears,
because my heart will break open,
and that I cannot allow.

If I could, it would be a big risk to take,
accepting you as my guide,
when you are not supposed to exist.

There is no proof you are here,
apart from the voice in my head.
And my heart's knowing.

I will walk with you.
I cannot do anything else.
I answer the call.

My heart aches in this world.
Taking refuge in the spiritual awakening,
is the only way for me to live.

10

Parallel Realities

Spiritual Lesson 10: My spirit knows of fantastical worlds—my mind is catching up with my inner reality

Into the Spirit: The Creator, who is formless consciousness, decided to build a place to manifest herself as physical life. Her light shone and created many universes and planets, full of physical and spiritual beings. None of these universes or beings are real, they are only her intention manifesting through light energy. Accordingly, all manifestations carry the Divine Consciousness, as nothing else exists. As she is infinite, an infinite number of worlds and dimensions have been projected, catering to an infinite number of life forms. The Creator continues to expand and grow and so does her creation. At the same time, worlds die, contract, and reunite with her.

In the last chapter, I wrote about the different categories of spirit beings and how we can contact them, including through journeying in the shamanic lower, middle, and upper worlds. I also explained that we are surrounded by spirit beings that belong to different categories, some of whom are our own dead relatives.

In this chapter, we will explore the worlds that spirits inhabit, including the places that we travel to when we die. My guides gave me this glimpse of creation that I share with you: They have said that what we perceive with our eyes as real, is in fact illusionary, a dream state. The physical form is temporary. Upon death, we transcend our body and wake up from this dream. The soul may eventually enter another dream and reincarnate into another life with a different form. The essential nature of every life form, as well as ourselves, is a void of nothingness, emptiness, consciousness without form.

The Earth reality is but one example of this Divine Creation. Since beings on Earth are mortal and die, other worlds are projected through the Creator's intention, accommodating those who have passed, allowing the souls to recuperate before reincarnating.

The Shamanic Worlds

Apart from the physical world we see with our eyes, there are other, parallel universes inhabited by different beings. These spirit worlds are of different dimensions or vibrational planes and exist alongside the physical universe. These are also known as the "shamanic worlds," the lower and upper worlds described in chapter nine. We can access these worlds in our meditation and dream state and through shamanic journeying.

In 2011, in my first visit to New Mexico, I connected with the Anasazi, an ancient people that inhabited North America until around the twelfth century AD (Stuart, 2014). After that, all traces of the Anasazi disappeared. They abandoned their settlements, without an apparent cause, such as natural disaster or war (Joseph, 2009). Various hypothesises exist as to their disappearance, from mainstream scientific sources proposing overpopulation or malnutrition and alternative suggestions that go as far as alien invasion.

During my shamanic teacher training, Sandra Ingerman organised visits to the ancient petroglyphs of the Anasazi. In her book, "Walking with Light" (2015), she speaks of these peoples' ascension into a higher realm, a different dimension. In this other world, they continue their existence. They can see us but unless we open psychically, we cannot see them. They were able to ascend to this plane due to their higher etheric energy levels and increased spiritual understanding.

In my call to the site of Tsankawi, a section of Bandelier National Monument, I found the Anasazi, in spirit. One of them came to me and guided me to various parts of the site. He showed me several energy points in the land. These were places where high vibrational energy was flowing from their dimension to ours. Connecting with these sites and receiving the light in our body, clears our energy fields. Some of these energy points had specific functions. For example, I remember one small womb-like cavity, where I was invited to lie inside as part of a re-birthing ritual.

My spirit guides showed me their perspective of these parallel dimensions and other worlds. They said that most people are so focused on the physical dimension that this is all they can perceive. When we open up spiritually, we may start to become aware of spirit beings around us. As we continue to expand our perception by entering an altered state of consciousness, through journeying, visualisation, and meditation, we may glimpse these different planes where evolved spirits live. We can only learn to observe these planes gradually. If we could see all dimensions simultaneously, we would be overwhelmed, or think we are insane. These spirit worlds appear ethereal to us, as if constructed by our imagination, unless we enter them through an out of body experience (see below). To my spirit guides, these worlds are as real as the Earth reality is to us. The enlightened beings who have full perception, see all dimensions as one. They do not differentiate between the physical and spirit realms.

My spirit guides have given me glimpses of parallel realities through out-of-body experiences. Whilst meditating receiving the Rays of Divine Consciousness (see chapter 19), I found myself rising quickly out of my body, as if I was going up in a fast elevator which then stopped suddenly. In my etheric body I entered a different reality, where my helpers put me in front of a television screen showing a film. As I watched the movie the guides told me which part had an insight for me. After the meditation I found the same film through an internet search. Whilst I was in the parallel world, everything was as real as everyday life. This was different to a journey, or visualisation. I truly was in another place and had no awareness of the Earth realm.

I once asked the helping spirits whether the spiritual planes they perceive are exactly as I see them in my shamanic journeys. They said that they use my points of reference, so I can easily understand what is happening. They also adjust my perception, so that I focus on the intention of the journey and see only what is of relevance to me. In a journey, we open a door into the place of creation, where everything is presented symbolically. Consequently, how I see these worlds may be different from your perception of them.

What happens in the spirit worlds affects the physical plane and vice versa. It is a symbiotic relationship. Arthur suffered from drug addiction and was in the process of rehabilitation. His energy system was weak, and he lacked life force and willpower. As a result, he was surrounded by negative spirit entities. In order to help him, I journeyed to the parallel realities and found a powerful spirit who volunteered to protect him. The spirit asked to be placed inside a pink, heart-shaped, quartz crystal, which Arthur was to wear constantly. I was sceptical that a macho man covered with tattoos, as Arthur was, would wear a pink crystal heart.

My spirit guides were bemused by my dilemma. To them, the physical plane and the spirit worlds I journey to are not separate. Upon their advice, I then travelled to a dark forest in the alternative reality and found Arthur. I placed the crystal heart beside him. He picked up the pink jewel and hung it around his neck. As the energy spread throughout his body, he cried. In real life, Arthur said he felt very emotional during the healing and a power spreading over his body. As a result of the intervention, he found the strength to make positive changes in his life. Due to the healing in the alternative world, Arthur received a healing in the physical reality. And he still wears an etheric crystal heart around his neck.

Healers and shamanic practitioners visit these parallel worlds to help their clients. Some of these worlds can be a paradise, whilst others may be dark and unpleasant. In chapter five (Soul Retrieval and Soul Reclamation), I wrote about how, sometimes, part of our soul dissociates from the body due to trauma. Our soul's parts can be found in alternative realities and usually, their location reflects our emotional state at the time of the soul loss. Soul parts that fled due to abuse, hopelessness, and depression may end up in places which appear arid, dark, and lifeless.

We may also visit these parallel worlds in our dreams. Sometimes during my sleep, my guides take my spirit to another plane where they can teach me about my soul's journey, or show me events that may happen in the future and affect my family. When I wake up, I realise that this was a significant dream. I also feel as if I had a very deep sleep, part of me knows that my spirit had been away. Chapter eleven explains different ways we can work with the dream reality.

The Worlds of the Dead:
Where Do We Go When We Die?

We live in a physical body, which eventually dies. As I explained in chapter four, around our physical body, exists the etheric body, which is an exact copy of its physical form. When most people die, they move out of their physical body and into their etheric body. This is why it can be difficult for some to grasp that they have passed, as they are seeing themselves exactly as they were in life. (Recall the example of the trapped souls around the graveyard in chapter four). In some Celtic traditions, after a person dies, all the mirrors in the house are covered. The deceased may not realise she has died, and if she looked in a mirror and saw no reflection, it may scare her.

Some people who die, especially those who die violently or who are very emotionally attached to their life and their loved ones, continue to stay around the Earth. They remain around us in the form of ghosts. Inhabiting their etheric body, they walk the same streets and live in their old homes. Some of them see the world as it was in their time, not as it is with repaved streets. They are caught in a parallel world, a time warp held in place by their state of consciousness. Other people who die in mental agony, stay behind in a lower astral plane, which is an in-between spirit place of lower vibration full of lost souls. Its inhabitants are kept there by their agitated state of consciousness. Mediums and shamanic practitioners can communicate with these souls to try and help them move on to the higher spirit realms.

Other deceased people are more aware and recognise that things have changed. Some people who die in peace move to the "other side," a parallel world, which looks similar to Earth and they continue to live consciously in this plane.

I visited my friend Jo in a dream about three months after her death. She wanted to show me her reality, the spirit world she now occupied. Her office looked like a modern office in our world. She spent her days there inputting data into a computer. Jo told me that she wanted to train as a protector, a spirit helper, of those living on Earth, but she had not yet been accepted for the training. She had to work her way up, as one does on Earth.

In my dream, this spirit world was similar to our own. There were even banks. Jo told me that some people had easy spirit lives. They had lived morally on Earth and thus had accumulated large deposits of money in these spirit banks, whilst others had been unskilful with either no deposits or debts that had to be paid off. Jo also said there were no job guarantees in the spirit world and thus, unemployment. She was lucky to have the office job. I then wanted to go out and walk around to see more, but a powerful guardian spirit brought me back into my body. As I found myself waking up from the dream, the guardian, who was an advanced being, said that I had gone far enough, my curiosity was inappropriate, and further access was denied.

Another time, I visited my grandmother, whom I called "Granny," in the spirit realm several months after she died. My mother had been very distressed by her mother's death and Granny kept visiting the Earth plane to try and help my mother be happy again, but there was nothing she could do to alleviate my mother's grief. When I visited Granny in the spirit world, she was living in a beautiful cottage in a little village. Other deceased relatives had small houses nearby. They told me they had been knocking on her door, but she would not come out. I went inside Granny's cottage and saw that she was depressed and energetically depleted. She could feel my mother's pain, but was helpless and had withdrawn into herself. I told Granny that her depression was helping no one, including herself, and that she had a life to live in the spirit realm. This spirit world was different from my friend Jo's, but what Granny would have preferred—a little village with her family nearby.

We do not all go to the same spirit world after we die. There are different planes for different people, depending on the spiritual development of the soul, the soul's karma and its awareness at the time of death. However, none of these planes is real. Like our own physical reality, these worlds are the projections of our state of consciousness at the time we die. Jo's office and my grandmother's cottage are the reflections of their beliefs of what they would find on the other side and how they wanted to continue living.

One of the most advantageous ways to die is to be at peace and aware of the process of moving from the physical into the spirit state. When my friend Frank Babcock, a spiritual healer, died in the United States, I received an e-mail two days later from a mutual friend informing me of Frank's passing. I was so sad, as Frank had been helpful to me during the early years of my spiritual development. Another friend, whose mother had received healings from Frank, called me. He was sad, too. As we were talking, Frank materialised in the room in front of me. I saw him with my physical eyes in his favourite light-coloured trousers and red jumper. He raised his hand to wave goodbye and left as suddenly as he had come. Frank moved to a higher spiritual plane for souls who had a high level of awareness and had purified their karma.

141

There are many different spirit worlds where we may go after our death. Most people are guided to a particular world by deceased friends and family or their angelic helpers. Other people, like Frank who have already advanced spiritually during their time on Earth, need less guidance, as they know where they are going.

Even when people pass into one of the spirit planes, they do not have to stay there all the time. They can visit the Earth plane and their relatives. From their world on the other side, deceased souls also have the opportunity to move further into the higher realms to advance spiritually. However, many choose to stay close to the Earth plane either to be reunited with their loved ones when they die or because they are still caught in their Earth identity and not ready to move on. This chapter's concluding exercise leads the reader through how to release deceased friends and relatives.

INCARNATION: A PHYSICAL EXPERIENCE

What is the point of incarnation, living in a physical body? The spirit, the eternal consciousness, is the only thing that exists. All the worlds we inhabit, the physical world, the world of dreams, the shamanic planes, the spirit worlds we move onto after death, are an illusion. None is real. These worlds are built by light, energy manifesting into matter, to provide an opportunity for the spirit to know itself and evolve through direct experience. When we die, our consciousness moves to the spirit realms. Accounts of near-death experiences describe going through a tunnel into a world of light, arriving at a place where people review their life events and meet their loved ones who have already passed. These worlds are equally illusionary, helping us to heal from our life experiences and remember our true nature.

My helping spirits provided a metaphor of the evolutionary journey of the soul. Imagine a chest with an infinite number of small drawers. Each drawer contains a theatre stage and a cast of souls acting in a play. Each drawer is another stage, another cast of actors, and another play—happening at once. As they are in different drawers, the souls are oblivious to neighbouring dramas or even that they are only actors and their life is simply a play. Each drawer represents a different life on Earth or elsewhere. The helping spirits are outside the chest of drawers. They can see all the plays taking place. They manifest inside the drawers at different times, trying to catch the attention of the actors, to make them aware that they are only enacting a play.

Being human, in a body has an advantage. It is a unique opportunity. Many souls look at the theatre on Earth and think, "That's a place I would like to be." However, there are limited places for incarnation as human beings. Many do not have the opportunity to incarnate. They stay around the Earth, hoping for their chance to take part in this theatre of life but remain in the wings, uncast.

Every human life is precious. During life, we have the opportunity to purify our negative karma and advance ourselves spiritually through direct experience. When we are in spirit form, we are swimming in a sea of innocence and light. We come to the world with that innocence. When we look at a baby, we can see the beauty of the pure spirit and its potential. Growing up is the process of separation from grace. We become aware of our own individuality and try to claim a place in the world for ourselves. We move from Oneness, to separation. We can stay in this state for a long time, often lifetimes. At some point, life opens a window in our heart and gives us a glimpse of our spiritual nature. We now have a choice to either stay in the life of our egoic mind, or to open our heart and take a step towards the rediscovery of our eternal spirit.

ISIS, the ancient Egyptian Goddess who manifests the Light of the Divine Mother, showed me how an ancient Egyptian myth portrays the human predicament. In the beginning, we were ruled by Osiris, the good king, who represents the innocence of the pure heart. He has no experience of the world and falls pray to his brother Seth. Seth represents the mind, the ego who wishes to become an individual. He kills Osiris, the innocent heart, in order to rule. Before the heart dies, it leaves a seed from which Horus is born. Horus represents the enlightened warrior, the strength of spirit. He has to live in difficult circumstances and battle the mind, that is, Seth.

In the struggle with the mind, Horus loses an eye, the ability to see from the conditioned perspective, but gains the all-seeing eye, the "utchat," the enlightened vision. Out of the battle with the ego-mind, Horus comes to rule with the wisdom and heart of the spirit that has grown through experience. The seasoned spirit is no longer lost and is aware of its strength and divine nature.

When we are born, we have the innocence of the heart, like Osiris. Then the world engulfs us and conditioning takes over. We lose our innocence and our divine connection and live in the world of Seth, dominated by individualism and separation. Eventually, through a lifetime or many lifetimes of experience, we rediscover our spiritual nature and Horus, the spiritual warrior, is awakened within us. Horus has to overcome the veils of conditioning and his perceptions of the world. In his journey, he sacrifices his human sight to gain the enlightened vision of his true nature.

When a soul incarnates on Earth, it does so for its development. The soul makes a commitment to learn and progress, to experience this new world, which is so different from any other. All these physical and spirit planes and the different experiences they manifest, exist for the soul to grow and learn from the consequences of its actions. The soul's aim is to become aware of its true nature, Divine, enlightened consciousness. In the bigger picture, the soul is not individual but part of the whole, the Creator that has manifested in trillions of beings. The journey of the soul through these different worlds informs and transforms the whole.

SUMMARY

Divine consciousness manifested the physical and spirit worlds and an infinite number of life forms, orchestrating a divine play to learn about itself. We take part in the Earth play, which is designed to help us realise that life is but a theatre and we have in fact, written the script. The physical world and dream states that we inhabit in life and those we move to after death, are all projections of our mind.

EXERCISE: CEREMONY – RELEASE YOUR DEAD FRIENDS AND RELATIVES

Archangel Michael, one of my spirit guides, showed me that due to the soul's attachment to its Earth family, a soul can remain around the spirit planes close to the Earth to be present at relatives' passing and reunite with them. The soul does not always take the opportunity to move into the higher planes and continue its journey. He said that our emotional attachment to the deceased also keeps us and them stuck. Archangel Michael gave me this practice to help release our loved ones.

Create a sacred space (see chapter 9). Invite your guides and teachers of the light, including Archangel Michael, to join you. Wait until you feel their vibration around you, or perceive them in your mind's eye.

Imagine your breath entering your heart as you inhale, and leaving your heart as you exhale. Breathe in love and breathe out love, to open your heart centre. Continue for a few minutes.

Intend that your consciousness is transported to the angelic realms of the light, a parallel world of high vibration inhabited by angels. Feel yourself relaxing into this expanded state. Immerse yourself in this world, by noticing the sounds, the smells, and the colours in your mind's eye. (Suggestion: I advise you not to visit the lower astral planes or the worlds of the dead unless you are experienced in working with your helping spirits.)

In the angelic realms, ask to merge with the consciousness of Archangel Michael. Feel yourself again being overshadowed by this angelic being of light (refer to "overshadowing," chapter 9).

In this state of connection, ask to know which deceased friends and relatives you are holding back from moving to higher realms due to emotional attachment or an agreement to meet after death. Do not judge yourself. This is a journey to increase awareness and heal both you and the deceased. Ask that they come to you in the form of their higher self.

Perceive the deceased in your mind's eye or have an inner knowing of them and even deceased pets who come close. When they come, thank them for knowing you in this life and for waiting for you. Say that you are now ready to let them go, as you are embracing your own spiritual nature. Say to your loved ones that, if they so wish, they can also move on. This is a time of forgiveness and release.

Before they go, you may wish to offer a healing with the angelic light, to any of the deceased that appear unwell or unhappy (remember my Granny's story above). If they accept the healing, you can proceed. In this state of being merged with the archangelic being, ask for the light energy of the angels to flow from your open hands into the spirit person or animal in front of you. Wait a few minutes whilst any healing takes place.

Ask Archangel Michael to fill you with this light, too. Receive the light in your body from the archangel for a few minutes, and then detach from him and intend to come back.

Finally, thank your spirit guides and Archangel Michael and release them, closing sacred space. Ask them to protect and seal you and the room you are working in, before they go.

Suggestion: After this exercise, you may feel emotional or find it difficult to detach from your memories of loved ones. It takes time to come to a place of acceptance, separation and detachment. When I teach this practice in The ISIS School, I give people a flower as a proxy for their love. They can fill the flower with their affection and positive words for the deceased and leave it somewhere in nature as a final goodbye and an expression of gratitude.

SEEKING THE TRUTH, I FIND MYSELF

Where am I, travelling in the distant lands of spirit,
pausing for a while to arrive on Earth?
Being caught by the needs of others,
I create a life for myself.

Who am I, the eternal traveller, jumping from life to life?
In many forms, sometimes a human, sometimes a bird or a plant,
sometimes an insect or a star?
I pause in the spirit realms for a while to look at my true self.

How can I find what I am, when I only know who I have become?
How can I be an individual, when I do not know my true nature?
I see my body as an extension of myself, some say this is all I am.
I feel the pain and suffering, the joy and ecstasy and a longing I cannot place.

I am fortunate, they say, because I seek,
even though little I find and even less I understand.
It has taken me a long time to come to this point of realisation;
before I was living blindly, sometimes happy, sometimes sad.

They say, there is a God in me,
but I cannot know for sure.
I am seeking to find Her,
somewhere inside me I know there is something more to life.

The opening of the heart
is filled with tears of grace and beauty.
They say this is what is inside me,
love waiting to come out and live again.

11

The Dream State

Spiritual Lesson 11: My dreams are a source of insight and direction. Observing the dream, I reflect on the illusion of life. What is real, and what is fake? Am I asleep, or am I awake?

Into the Spirit: I sit in amazement, listening to my spirit guide ISIS talk about the teachings she has given me. She calls these teachings the "hidden path to Ascension," "the missing link". For a while, I thought the channelled information was only for my benefit. Apparently not. These teachings are not meant to remain concealed in my notebooks. ISIS insists that my life purpose is to teach this wisdom around the world. I say that I do not know how or where to start. This seems a huge task. ISIS listens to my predicament.

Next day, I am having coffee with two women I met on a course. While one goes to the toilet, the other grabs my hand and tells me about her dream in which the ancient Egyptian Goddess ISIS invited her to work with the ISIS energy. When the woman asked ISIS how to accomplish this, ISIS showed her my face. The woman asks if I know anything about this energy.

The day after, another woman, Ann, who I knew from a psychic circle, phones me and asks if we could meet. I invite her to my flat. She asks me about my work, and I mention Reiki and shamanism but say nothing about the ISIS teachings. Ann, tells me about her dream, set in ancient Egypt. She was swimming in a pool inside a large, highly decorated room. There was a gate at the end of the room, which was opened by a man wearing a head mask of a jackal (the Egyptian god-form Anubis, opener of the hidden realms). As Ann approaches the gate, the masked man tells her to seek initiation into the ancient mysteries. She is shown my face and told I can offer this.

Now, I am unnerved. I do not feel ready. I am self-conscious, doubting, and insecure. I try to brush the information off as just dreams. But there is an inner knowing in Ann that will not give up. She knows the dream has to do with me and, no, she will not go elsewhere. I capitulate. We set a date. I teach my first ISIS course. Six years later I open The ISIS School of Holistic Health.

In the previous chapter, I wrote about the different shamanic worlds and explained where our soul travels when we die. In this chapter, I explore the dream states we visit in our sleep, from an esoteric, spiritual perspective.

A Legacy of Dream Interpretation

The world of dreams has been analysed by psychologists, doctors, and psychics alike. Are dreams the gateway to the soul, a way of accessing the archetypes we identify with (Jung, 2002)? Do they provide insight into the unconscious (Freud, 1994)? Popular psychology has found symbolism in dreams and interpreted their meanings (Debord, 2017). Dreams have both puzzled us and sparked our curiosity.

Through dreams, we can reach parts of our soul that we are either unaware of or have suppressed for various reasons. Those of us who do not wish or are unable to express our anger, emotions, and sexuality may do so safely in the dream state. I call these "healing dreams." They can be a benign way for the soul to release issues and regain emotional balance, as well as acknowledge problems that need to be dealt with.

Ancient people of many cultures paid attention to dreams, which were often seen as a doorway of communication with the Divine. Spiritually inspired dreams of Divine origin are sited in the Old Testament. Jacob's dream of the ladder to heaven was viewed as prophetic. Joseph's interpretation of the Pharaoh's dream of seven fat and seven lean cows was seen as a warning from God, predicting seven years of plenty followed by seven years of famine. The belief in the divinatory quality of dreams exists in our collective consciousness. In indigenous cultures, shamans and mystics continue to pay attention to "spiritual" dreams and interpret them for the community as a prophetic guide to direct collective action.

Sometimes, we do not remember our dreams. This may be due to quick changes in our perception and brain wave pattern as we move from the dream state to the wakened state. As we wake up and focus on the day ahead, we can quickly shift out of the dream space and forget the dream.

Some dreams are memorable. I call these "significant dreams," when we receive guidance about our life. Like my father's dream in chapter nine, significant dreams may also contain information about future events—positive and negative. Our spirit guides and teachers, as well as our own higher self, could be communicating this information to us. We may also wake up immediately after such a dream, so that we remember it. I recommend to my clients and students to keep a dream diary by their bed, as even significant dreams can quickly fade from our memory.

Our belief system influences how we perceive and record significant dreams. I always thought that significant dreams should come in the early morning so that I can remember them, and they do. A Himalayan shaman told me he pays particular attention to the dreams in the middle part of the night. This is when significant dreams appear to him.

My mother has inherited the ability from her mother and aunt to interpret dreams. Mum does this by using a system of reference where symbols have a meaning, for example a policeman denotes an angel, smelling flowers indicates a favourable outcome for an endeavour, whilst eating fried squid predicts a misfortune. This system of keyed symbols is common to her native area of Greece.

During one of my visits home, I dreamt a gang of men, dressed in black leather outfits, broke into my room and shot me. According to my mum's traditional interpretation, this was an auspicious dream. It denoted a visitation from angels who removed obstacles that no longer served my higher purpose, enabling a new beginning to take place. Her reading provided me with an explanation, which became more apparent when I resigned from my town planning post a few months later to follow my calling as a spiritual teacher.

Spiritual practitioners and healers often receive information through dreams about their clients and how they can help them. Before I do a shamanic soul retrieval healing, I usually have a dream that holds meaning for the client. In the dream, I am the client, and I see myself in various situations.

The first time this occurred, I described the dream to the client and he burst into tears. My dream explained beautifully how he was feeling and what his main issue was.

In dreams and spiritual work, we touch the essence of our soul. The exercise at the end of the chapter is an opportunity to engage in the experience of significant dreams. We can use this method to receive guidance from our dreams. At first, the messages may not always be clear. The more we practice, the clearer the symbolism can become.

Changing the Dream

Sometimes in dreams, I am aware that I am dreaming. Rather than observing the unfolding dream, I can participate actively and make decisions that influence the course of the dream. This, however, has repercussions in my everyday life. For example, in one dream, I was with a group of people on a leadership programme. We were welcoming a native teacher who had come to facilitate a sweat lodge ceremony, "to pour" a sweat lodge. The teacher was choosing two people to be trained as water pourers, ceremony facilitators. Knowing I was awake in the dream, I knew I could influence the dream in my favour. So, I changed the dream consciously and saw myself being chosen.

A few months later, a sweat lodge teacher came to a leadership programme I was on, and I was invited to train as a water pourer. Despite my earlier dream, it took me a long time to accept the invitation. Although, in the dream, I had changed the outcome so that I was selected for the training, I still had to follow through with the choice in the physical realm when the opportunity arose.

The decisions that I have taken while being awake in dreams have influenced the course of my life.

The Sleep Time

What do we do while asleep? Where do we go? In 2009, I attended a Spiritualist church service. The medium came to me and described the spirit guide who works with me while I am asleep. (The spirit guide, a deceased nun, said that she was willing to show me what I did during the sleep time. Before this, I had been told by some clients that I had visited them in their dreams and given them healing and information.)

That night, before sleeping, I sent some thoughts to the spirit nun, asking her to show me all that happened while I slept. The spirit nun took me to several situations where I was a spirit guide for other living people. In one case, I was the spirit guide of a man in Latin America who had once been involved in drug trafficking, but decided to change his life. He was attempting to leave the cartel, but was now being hunted by other gang members. I was trying to protect him by giving him courage and helping him find places to hide. As I was in spirit form, the man was unaware of my presence. And I was afraid the marauding members would see me, but they just walked through me. Eventually, the man had facial reconstruction and escaped.

What had happened in three hours of sleep time for me, lasted weeks for this man in the physical dimension. The spirit nun told me that time is flexible in these realms.

In another scenario, I was taken to houses, bars, theatres, and other places where people, unaware of their death, were still lingering. I appeared to them as someone who was working there so as not to alarm them, like the guardian spirit in the graveyard who masqueraded as a trapped soul (chapter 4). I eventually helped them realise that they had died and it was time to move to the spirit realms.

During the night, after each experience, I woke up, so that I could remember and record it. When morning came, I felt exhausted—as if I had never slept. After two nights, I learned why: being consciously aware in the sleep time takes a lot of energy, and the morning hangover was becoming stronger each day. Finally, I accepted that I needed to release my desire to be awake while asleep and simply enjoy sleeping and dreaming, knowing that I was helping others. Occasionally, I get one of these awake experiences, but not every night and not for the entire night.

The spirit nun taught me that we are multidimensional beings with many qualities and gifts. Whilst we live a physical life, which we are aware of, in the sleep state, we continue our soul's journey, unaware. Our spirit can travel in different dimensions and places. If we are healers, we may continue serving others while we sleep, even though we do not always know this consciously. Our body sleeps, but our spirit is awake and active.

Whilst our spirit is away when we sleep, another part of us, our soul that is still attached to the body, continues to dream, rest, and integrate the daily experiences. Not all of us leaves and travels to other situations—unless we have an out-of-body experience.

Out-of-Body Experiences

My grandmother passed down to many close relatives and cousins the ability to detach completely from their physical body as they fall into sleep. Their consciousness leaves the body, and they have an out-of-body experience. They see their body sleeping, whilst hovering as a spirit in the room. This is both a gift and a curse.

It is energetically disturbing for the etheric bodies to be separated from the physical body in this way. Even when they return to their body—and this takes effort, especially if they are afraid—they are left feeling tired, disorientated, light-headed and shaken. Out-of-body experiences can also leave the person energetically more open in their everyday life. For example, a cousin may feel empathetically what is happening to others and vulnerable to absorbing other people's energy. At those times, I recommend to family members to visit an energy healer, who can extract any foreign energy from their body, and balance and strengthen their etheric body. Cousins with this predicament found it helpful to abstain from alcohol.

In some out-of-body experiences, because the body is left as an empty vessel but not dead, the same as in a near-death experience, an outside spirit can come into it. A client told me that during one of her out-of-body experiences, she saw a shadow enter her body. When she eventually managed to get back into her body, the other spirit was still there. The spirit told her that he would be staying for a month, and there was nothing she could do about it. I advised her that she was much stronger than any spirit, as this was her body. I asked her to fill herself with the power of the Earth and sky, and then command this spirit to leave her body. Even though my client is not religious, I asked her also to invoke the power of the Creator and pray for the release of this spirit from her body and her environment. My client did, and the spirit left her body.

I have had out-of-body experiences, too, although not to the same extent as other family members. Interestingly, when one of my relatives has an out-of-body experience, she does not see her etheric body. She is consciousness with no body. Unlike her, in my out-of-body experiences, I find myself rising out of my physical body into my etheric body, the etheric replica of me. I can walk, levitate and travel in this etheric body. My spiritual practice and connection strengthens my etheric body and enables me to be more grounded, so it is a different experience.

Once during a self-hypnosis exercise, I noticed that I was floating above my body. I asked my spirit guide what I should do, but no advice came. I decided to float up to the ceiling. While there, I noticed all the cracks in the paint. Then, I decided to float back down. The process seemed to have taken mere minutes. When I was back in my body and looked at the clock, I had been gone over an hour. In this case time expanded. In other out-of-body experiences time contracted; events that would normally take hours, were completed in seconds.

Time perception is very different when we are not in the physical body. I can understand why mediums say that spirit people, who may have been dead for a long while, have no perception of time, as time is only a concept of our earthly realm.

For those who do spiritual work, out-of-body experiences demonstrate that we exist separately from the body, which may help us comprehend the magnificence of our spirit and access its wisdom. They can be a portal to awareness of our true selves and to the light and dark planes that exist around us. For most people, this would take years of meditation and spiritual work to accomplish.

For anyone who is new to having an out-of-body experience, spending time in nature, connecting with the trees and lying on the grass will be grounding. Working with a spirit guide, or mentor in the physical world, can help us manage what is happening and train us in the healing arts in order to better understand this gift. For example, when I have such an experience, it is due to my helping spirits' intervention. They are in control and once the healing work is complete, I find myself safely back in the body.

Out-of-body experiences are not a natural state. Regardless of our familiarity with them, we can train ourselves to only use part of our awareness to journey and enter alternative realities. This means we are aware of both the physical world and the spirit planes we journey into and we can bring ourselves back at will, and without disruption to our energy bodies.

Summary

Dreams can speak to us about our emotional needs, and hence, help heal our soul, relieve the pressures of everyday life, and resolve issues that may be too painful to deal with in the physical plane. Dreams can give us information about our life and soul's purpose, show us situations where we are out of balance, and enlighten us about the future. Spirit guides can help us remember our dreams and actions therein. In conscious dreaming, we become aware that we are in a dream and take charge of what is happening, which can influence our physical life.

When we sleep part of our consciousness leaves the body. Most of the time, we are unaware what our consciousness does when we sleep. For some people, all of their consciousness can leave the body, known as an "out-of-body experience." In this disembodied state, they are no longer asleep, but their body is completely inert. Their spirit can wander in different parts of the world or alternative realities. However, if they are in fear of this psychic gift, it can stop them from using it constructively for their spiritual development.

Exercise: Inviting Significant Dreams

This exercise will aid your transition to the dream state. You will need cleansing incense (such as white sage), a bowl of water, and an obsidian crystal.

Preparation. Create sacred space in the room you sleep in by cleansing the room with incense, such as white sage. As you waft the lighted incense around the room, known as "smudging," state your intention that all heavy, negative energy is carried away with the smoke. Let the element of wind remove everything stale, so fresh energy comes into the space.

Place a bowl of water somewhere in the room, and invite the helping spirits of dreaming to come. Dreaming is fluid, like water, and you wish to increase the flow of energy in the room and within yourself.

Place an obsidian crystal under your bed approximately at your feet, or nearby—but not under the pillow. Obsidian has the power to deflect any negative energy back to its source and open your psychic ability. At the same time, the crystal will ground you and keep you in touch with the Earth plane.

Ask for the element of fire to flow through you and for the highest vibration of light to come into your body through your heart. Then, once all four elements are thus engaged, go and lie down in your bed. Relax and quiet the mind by connecting with your breath.

Dream. To your guides and teachers, state your intention to have a significant guiding dream. Imagine a gate of fire through which you can enter the dream world. Go through the gate. Focus on your breathing. Allow yourself to drift into sleep, if possible, releasing all expectations lest they block your dreams.

Wake up. Allow yourself to awake naturally, without an alarm. Slowly focus on the dream. Do not think of the day ahead. When we attend to the everyday reality too quickly, we can lose touch with the dream world. In your mind, go through what you remember of the dream. Then write down the dream, even if you think you will remember it. Your recollection can be fleeting.

Close sacred space by thanking all your guides and teachers and release them. Say that your dream work is finished, and ask them to completely seal you and the room before they leave.

Finally, place the obsidian crystal on your altar or by a windowsill to charge it for another time. Thank the crystal being for its help. While showering, pour the water in the bowl over you as it has been blessed by the spirit guides throughout the night.

Suggestion: Even if you do not understand all that happened in your dream, write it down, and meditate upon it. Maybe there is a hidden meaning that will be revealed to you in time. Expectations of a significant dream, can actually block you from experiencing it. Accessing the dream world takes practice, and for some people, it may be a while before their dream channel is open.

THE SHAMAN'S DREAM

There was a dream
that began in a casino.
A man was looking at a woman dressed in black.

The man was dead, the woman asleep.
He did not know he was dead.
She did not know she was asleep.

She thought she looked nice in black,
Sexy and desirable,
until her grandmother appeared in the dream, out of the blue.

The man is dead,
he has nowhere to go.
It is your job to send him home, grandmother's words.

This the woman did.
The man did not know the woman was a shaman.
She could travel between the worlds in her sleep.

The woman did not know she did this either.
She thought it was just a dream at first.
But then she knew better.

The woman wanders in her sleep.
Like many souls finding a way for others.
Sometimes she knows she is asleep and sometimes she doesn't.

Yet what she does in her sleep
creates ripples in her life,
and the lives of others.

Is life a deep sleep from our true existence?
Are we asleep when we are awake?
Or is it the other way around?

To this day, the woman does not know for sure.

12

Connecting to Mother Earth

*Spiritual Lesson 12: I am a guest on Earth; I honour my host and
all other life forms*

*Into the spirit: I imagine a time when I could hear the sun greet me every day,
the trees speak to me, the fairies welcome me as I walk on the thick grass of
the forest. I imagine that I knew that there were animals waiting for me miles
away. In this vision, I speak to people telepathically, communicate directly
without words, even if they live on other continents. I hear the voice of spirit
through the birds, the clouds, and the rainbows. This age of connection with
all life is not a fantasy, but a distant memory.*

OPENING OUR SPIRITUAL CHANNEL THROUGH NATURE

My spirit guides have shown me that, long ago, humans knew they were
connected to everything alive, whether in spirit or physical form. We knew
we were part of all life, what the indigenous people describe as the "web of
life" or "silent knowledge." The sense of interconnection has been weakened
as we have shifted our attention from our heart centre to our logical mind.
We focus on the left side of the brain and a rational way of thinking to the

exclusion of our intuitive, creative right side of the brain. After thousands of years of neglect, our psychic centres have become dormant, but still exist and can be reawakened through spiritual practice and connection with nature.

Over the last few centuries, and more so since the Industrial Revolution, humans have alienated themselves from nature. We have moved from being part of the natural world to living in cities of concrete. This has led to a more self-centred approach to life. Disconnected from our heart, from nature, and from each other, many of us live predominantly in the materialism of our minds. One way to reclaim our spiritual nature is through connecting consciously with the Earth and other life-forms, through the web of life.

An Indigenous Story Explaining the Web of Life

In the Americas, the Mayan, Aztec, and some other Native American nations, describe the creator as an old grandmother spider, continually spinning a web through her song, sacred sound (Reichard, 2011). This massive web connects all life: the stars, planets, and universes, the plants, animals, stones, and human beings. All life forms, seen and unseen, are woven into and connect to the spider's web. The world continues to expand as the old grandmother spider keeps creating and recreating her web, connecting all. This is called the "web of life." By learning to connect to the web of life, we can communicate telepathically with everything around us.

Spending time in nature helps us develop our inner listening and spiritual awareness. We have always been part of the web of life, and we need to return to the natural environment to feel this belonging. When we are in nature we can start to relax and commune with the web. We can feel the soil with our bare feet and hands, breathe with the trees, and smell the perfumed air of the natural world. We come home to ourselves. We are nature.

One day walking in a public garden in the city of Glasgow, Scotland, I was drawn to a sycamore tree. I made an offering of oatmeal to the spirits of the tree, and asked to connect with the tree and the web of life that flows through it. The tree asked me to place my hands on her trunk and breathe deeply into my abdomen. With each breath, I felt myself relax and slow down. An energy vibration flowed from the tree into my hands and all the way down my body, into my back and feet and into the Earth. Then, something changed. I felt that the tree was breathing, too, with the same rhythm as my own. The tree and I were connecting deeply through the power of our synchronised breathing. My heart centre opened, and I felt the power of love flowing inside me for the tree. I saw her, the sycamore tree, as a living being, the same as I. All my worries and thoughts vanished as the tree and I connected through our breath. I understood I was one with the tree and everything around me.

Connecting with the trees and the Earth awakens and balances our energy bodies, chakras, and psychic centres, and revives the innate spiritual abilities that we lost when we disconnected from the right side of the brain. The first exercise below will guide you how to connect to the web of life through a tree.

We can also heal through the web of life. Just like a tree needs a good root system and a strong trunk to thrive, we, too, benefit from a strong connection with the Earth's prana to develop and maintain a healthy body. In holistic medicine practices, such as Ayurveda and Traditional Chinese Medicine (TCM), life force energy is referred to as "prana" and "chi," respectively. The flow of life force can become inhibited or blocked in our energy meridian channels. Stuck prana then gathers in those areas and creates imbalances in our system. Spiritually, energetic imbalances in the body reflect imbalances in our way of life that can lead to dis-ease and premature aging. It is imperative to maintain free-flowing life force energy in order to optimise our health (Kalipershad-Jethalal, 2015). The Earth's prana can help us unblock our energy centres.

The life force, prana, universal energy flowing inside our body is the same energy that flows within the web of life and around the Earth. Sometimes, our energy becomes disconnected from the web and forgets its origin. We are no longer attuned to the source of energy that created our body and everything that exists, instead it lies dormant within us. It is this disconnection and lack of attunement that, according to TCM, causes illness in our body and chaos in our life (Liao, 2009). Unless compromised by human activities and environmental pollution, nature always abounds with chi. Connecting regularly with the web of life through nature, like my experience with the sycamore tree, helps us maintain contact with the source of life force, awaken our dormant chi and heal the energy blockages in our body, (see exercise two below).

MOTHER EARTH

Indigenous people speak of the Earth as a living being, a being of consciousness. Many cultures view Earth as the mother who has created a wonderful world for her children to enjoy and play in. Below is a version of a story about the origin of human life on Earth that I was given at my sweat lodge training. It is based on the teachings of the late Native American Shaman Sun Bear (1929-1992).

Long ago, a group of spirits roamed the universe searching for a suitable locale to manifest in physical form. They searched for a long time, perhaps millions of years, but could not find anything. Most places were already inhabited or otherwise unsuitable. One day, the sun of this solar system attracted their attention, but when they approached it, they found it was too hot for physical life. "Do not give up!" said the sun. "The third planet down, the blue planet you can see from here, is soft and good-natured. She may welcome you, if you go and ask her. She is called "Earth." The spirits went to the blue planet, but despite her name, Earth, there was no earth to be seen. It was covered with water. They gathered around the Earth in despair. "Sweet Lady," they said to Earth, "We are looking for a home. Will you have us? We cannot all live in water." Earth responded. Out of the water came a red hot rock that created such steam, the atmosphere was formed. The rock cooled down and became an island. Many more rocks surfaced, creating more solid ground on which the spirits could live. In this way, life began on Earth and people honoured the red boulders by calling them "grandfathers" and "grandmothers."

According to the story, Earth has been our home ever since. Mother Earth has looked after us and manifested different environments and conditions so that all our needs are met. Some spirits in the story liked deserts and dry heat, and the Mother manifested such places for them. Other spirits preferred icy conditions, and Earth created these, too.

Mother Earth has provided us with a unique opportunity to experience the gift of physical life. Yet, disconnected from our own nature, we have taken life on Earth for granted. We have abused our host and ourselves and sullied our home. We have forgotten that we are part of the Earth.

A MESSAGE FROM MOTHER EARTH

As I was editing this chapter, Mother Earth came and spoke to me. These are her words:

The destruction that has taken place and continues to take place on the Earth causes much suffering and karmically binds together all the beings who cause the destruction and all those who are harmed by the devastation. All this karma has to be purified. Every time you harm the Earth, you cause suffering to yourselves and you tie yourselves tighter to this karma. You do not realise what you are doing.

There are many ways to clear this karma. Become aware, open your eyes to what you are doing. Change your ways, individually and collectively. Give back to the Earth what you have taken so that you complete a cycle of reciprocity. Finally, become aware of yourselves as multidimensional beings, as beings of light. Own your power to transmute the environmental pollution, and psychic pollution, such as the toxicity of your emotions and thoughts. Walk a spiritual path of service to All. As you serve the Earth and all beings, you serve yourselves.

Coming Home: Connecting to the Consciousness of the Earth

I had never felt a communion with the Earth until 2013, when I participated in my first four-day vision quest ceremony in Death Valley National Park in California. Participants go out into nature by themselves, without food for four days and four nights, returning to base camp on the fifth morning.

On my second day out, I heard the desert butterflies talking to me, as were the small bushes. I started seeing faces in the rocks. Everything was alive. I asked the rocks why they had not spoken to me before. They said they were always talking, but I had not stopped to listen. During that vision quest, the Earth became my friend. I would lie down on the ground each night and feel her heartbeat and her incredible love and support.

Leaving the desert, I felt very sad, as if I was leaving my spiritual home to return to my artificial, western life. Yet, this busy modern life soon engulfed me. I forgot about my connection with the Earth, but the Earth did not forget me. Six months later, I was in a sweat lodge in Scotland, and as I lay down on the ground, the Earth immediately welcomed me. I felt the familiar vibration of love that I had experienced in Death Valley. No matter where I am, I am always home, even when I forget the connection.

I encourage everyone to connect with the Earth at this deep level. This living mother is longing to hold our body once again. We can connect with the Earth through our bare feet and hands and talk to this wondrous living being. This is nature touching nature. The Earth is waiting for you.

Nature Spirits

During my vision quest, I realised that everything has a spirit and is conscious. The butterflies, rocks, and creosote bushes held conversations with me about life. The Earth herself has a voice, energy, and amazing story to share. In the natural environment, there are also spirits we cannot see with our physical eyes. They are the nature spirits, the spirits of the land, the caretakers of the Earth.

When we return to nature to reawaken our innate strength and unblock our prana, we are entering the domain of nature spirits. Ancient cultures speak of nature spirits as nymphs, gnomes, dwarves, little folk, the green people, and fairies. These beings cohabit our planet, but, most of the time, do not interact with humans. They look after the Earth, clean its energy, and support the continuation of life in the natural world.

I first saw nature spirits when I was on a 24-hour medicine walk ceremony, in Scotland. During this ceremony, participants fast and go out in nature, seeking spiritual guidance. My spirit guides asked me to sit in a particular spot and gaze at a group of trees. I did this for about an hour. Each time I looked away, the guides told me to look towards the trees. After a while, I saw them. On the branches of the trees were dwarves, similar to the hobbits of the Shire from the Lord of the Rings films.

Since then, I have been able to see and speak to nature spirits. I learned that they are not always helpful and sometimes play tricks on humans, because they find it funny. Some of them have a childlike sense of humour, and consider us to be too serious! After a ceremony in a circle of standing stones, in Kilmartin, Scotland, I was walking barefoot back to the car. A couple of nature spirits asked me to stand on a particular stone. They kept telling me it was a powerful stone and to connect with it. When I finally stepped onto the stone, I found, to my dismay, it was a cowpat. Luckily, I could wash my feet in a nearby stream. As I looked back, the fairy folk were rolling about on the grass laughing. I learned not to believe the fairy folk indiscriminately.

Another time, during a pilgrimage on the Isle of Lewis, I drove with some friends to one of the Callanish Stone circles to do a ceremony. It was a rainy day. As soon as we got out of the car, we were surrounded by nature spirits. They were waiting, they said, to take part in the ceremony, and posing seriously with their little drums ready. However, they could only keep the imposing demure for so long before they burst out laughing, and I knew then something was amiss. Nevertheless, we started walking towards the stone circle. As we approached, I had a revelation. I knew the stone circle had been flooded by the rain, and when it came into view, we saw it immersed in water. "So, what are you going to do now?" asked the little people laughing. They were testing us, to see if we would give up, or undertake the ceremony we came to do. We soon worked out we could do most of the ceremony on the outside of the circle and project our energy bodies into the circle for the final part. The nature spirits then stopped laughing. They recognised we were there for the highest good. They became solemn and participated in the whole ceremony. At the end of the ceremony, we thanked them for their help, even though they had been mischievous at first.

Not all nature spirits play tricks or test humans. Some are wise, enlightened, and helpful. When I was doing a water ceremony for a shamanic group, I merged with a water nymph called "Kalliroy," meaning the "good flow." Through me, this nature spirit carried out powerful shamanic healings for the participants.

On another occasion during a shamanic workshop in Santa Fe, New Mexico, we were asked to connect with the spirits of the land and seek their advice on healing the planet. A wise and humble nature spirit came to me and bowed, expressing gratitude for my spiritual work. Surprised by his gentle, loving presence, I confided that the nature spirits in Scotland were playing tricks on me. The wise fairy advised me to approach the nature spirits with reverence and make an offering to them each time I did a ceremony in nature, to acknowledge them and their work. The offering could be a piece of fruit or chocolate energised overnight on my altar. I followed his advice and since then, I have had no trouble from Scotland's fairy world.

The enlightened nature spirit from Santa Fe explained that we, the human beings, seem to take from nature, in an arrogant and self-centered way. By showing reverence and making an offering to the nature spirits, we are honouring all life. The nature spirits are under no obligation to assist us, especially as they observe human beings polluting the Earth and mistreating the natural world. By offering gratitude for their contribution, we recognise them as equal partners for the wellbeing of the planet.

CARETAKERS OF THE EARTH

Nature spirits are the caretakers of the Earth. They are responsible for looking after the wellbeing of the planet, and so are we. Indigenous cultures respect and still abide by this agreement, but we, modern westerners, are largely alienated from our responsibility.

The Tibetan Bön tradition believes that an ancient agreement exists between the nature spirits, whom they refer to as the "Lü" or the "Nagas," and human beings. A long time ago, nature spirits became suspicious of human behaviour and wreaked havoc. They watched as humans abused the Earth and then retaliated. They caused avalanches, tsunamis, and other natural disasters, bringing famine and illness, making life difficult and even dangerous for human beings. An enlightened Buddha, Tonpa Shenrab Miwoche, showed the spirits they were accumulating negative karma by their harmful behaviour. According to the universal law of cause and effect, "You reap what you sow"—which applies to humans and nature spirits. An agreement was then made between the humans and nature spirits that neither would harm the other, and both would respect and look after the Earth.

Since then, nature spirits perceive that we, collectively, have broken this agreement and we have been once more plundering and destroying the Earth. Consequently, some nature spirits feel saddened. They question if they are still bound by the agreement of the past since human beings have not kept their part of the bargain. The nature spirits can cause illness and famine and environmental disasters in a region, in an effort to defend themselves and the natural world from human greed. However, some enlightened nature spirits have said that they do not wish to cause harm, but prevent it.

In 2014, I attended a shamanic workshop in Cork, Ireland. Before the workshop began, I went for a walk in the old part of the town and found myself at Cork Cathedral. As I went inside to meditate, my mobile rang. A friend told me about an avalanche in Mount Everest. She had been to the base camp two years previously and was concerned for the wellbeing of friends there. She asked if I could send healing. I sat on a pew and connected with the living light of ISIS, asking for healing for the highest good. I felt the mountain spirit and the nature spirits of that land were not happy with all the human activity on the mountain. The mountain used to be revered as sacred land by the local people, who traditionally were very respectful. They recognised Everest as a place of pilgrimage. However, these days, vast numbers of people travel to the mountain with little respect for the sacredness of the area, leaving behind heaps of rubbish. The spirits told me there was too much pollution. I felt the avalanche was a warning from the spirit world to limit our activities in Everest and clean up after ourselves.

Wherever I travel, I try to establish a good relationship with the local nature spirits. I thank them for all they do to care for the Earth. I apologise for the environmental pollution. I say that most human beings are ignorant—we do not understand the damage our actions cause. We are so disconnected from the Earth and from ourselves that we do not know another way. Most of us do not deliberately pollute the Earth, but until the human collective consciousness is raised, ignorance and destruction will prevail. The solution to the Earth's environmental problems, rests with each one of us. As we, individually, connect with and respect the Earth, we create a wave of change in the collective consciousness. The nature spirits have said that they have been observing how more humans are becoming mindful of the effect their actions have on the environment and the wellbeing of the planet.

Honouring and Working with Nature Spirits

In ancient cultures, ceremonies would be performed to seek consent from the spirits of the land before any construction work began. If trees were felled, offerings would be made beforehand and other trees planted, to balance the scales. Like many other beings in the natural world, such as rocks, lakes, and seas, each tree is home to many nature spirits. When it is cut down, many beings are left homeless.

At one point in my career as a town planner, I was overseeing the creation of a new riverside walkway and public square in the south side of Glasgow. In order to implement the design, a number of trees had to be removed. I was saddened, but there was nothing I could do. I went to the site early to make offerings to the trees and explain the situation to the nature spirits.

When I arrived, the tree surgeon was already talking to the trees, explaining what was going to happen. He told me that once he had been called to a nunnery to fell three large oaks. As he was about to start, an old Irish nun came out and admonished him and his team. She told them that before they did anything, they had to sit and look at the trees and tell them what they were going to do. They did not dare disobey the elder nun. So, they looked at the trees and said it was necessary for them to be cut down due to the expansion of the convent. The tree surgeon sensed the trees understood this and accepted the situation. They told the surgeon that everything, including them, at some point has to die. The trees and the nature spirits gave their consent. Now, each time he has to cut a tree, he follows the wise nun's advice.

On another town planning assignment, I witnessed nature spirits intervening to prevent construction. I was planning a small garden on a public site coveted by an office developer. Arriving at work one day, I was told a decision was about to be made to sell the site. During my lunch break, I walked to the land and spoke to the nature spirits. I told them what was happening and that I had done all I could to create a garden, but could do no more. I asked for their help. When I returned to work, I met with my line manager who was in favour of the office high-rise and, out of the blue, a senior manager appeared. He was interested in the garden project. He said an office development would not work on the small plot and to proceed with the garden. I went back and thanked the nature spirits for their intervention and also asked them to look after the garden.

Most of the time, when we seek consent from nature, to undertake building work or make changes to the environment, the spirits agree to help—unless they see us acting out of greed. They may ask for something in return, for instance, planting other trees or taking better care of the land, but not always. In this way, we acknowledge and honour the nature spirits and the Earth.

We can heal the Earth by healing ourselves. When we address the traumas of our life and wounded self, we become more caring inwardly to ourselves and outwardly towards nature. Through spiritual practice, we understand that our actions have consequences. We have the opportunity to change our lifestyle and step into the shoes of the caretaker, allying with the nature spirits, rather than continuing as the planet's exploiter.

Becoming Earth's Healer through Spiritual Awakening

ISIS has said that we are living during a time of transition, between the legacy of individualism and separation and the forthcoming spiritual awakening. At this time, she suggests that we engage in healing both for ourselves and the Earth (for example, through the Earth retrieval exercise in chapter five).

ISIS offers us the following message.

At a global level, humanity is slowly but gradually awakening to the fact that the way the world is right now will only lead to its destruction. Rather than going into fear, this is the time to envisage the new reality on Earth, one that is based on harmony. Yet, how can harmony exist globally, when it is not present within? Doing the inner work is equally important. It is vital to view yourself and your life with compassion and self-love and, at the same time, with determination, so that you can make the changes these times are asking of you, personally and globally.

When many of you find that place of inner balance, a transformation can happen in the world. The Earth supports you during this time of upheaval and change, and holds you in your process, both individually and collectively. It is a great opportunity for you to walk past the fear of many generations, to embrace a new reality for yourself and the world.

Summary

Human beings were once highly evolved, psychically and spiritually. We lived in direct communication with our natural environment. We were connected to the right side of our brain and our intuition and creativity—and we still can be. When we stay connected to nature, we have access to the life force prana of Mother Earth and the universal energy that created all living forms, seen and unseen. All life is linked together through etheric energy lines called the "web of life," a rich source of healing, guidance, and wisdom.

We have also forgotten that we, too, are nature, that the Earth is our mother. The planet is a source of nourishment and love, both for our bodies and our soul. Communing with the spirit of the Earth, we connect deeply with ourselves.

Nature spirits are the caretakers of the Earth. They can sometimes be angered by our lack of consideration for the planet. It is advisable to honour and respect them, and live in harmony with them and all life.

EXERCISES: CONNECTING WITH THE WEB OF LIFE AND NATURE SPIRITS

Exercise 1.
Connect with the Web of Life – Breathe with the Trees

All life is the one energy manifested in different forms, and all life is connected through energy. In this exercise I share my experience with the sycamore tree and the connection to the Earth's prana.

The exercise takes place outdoors, in the natural environment. If possible, choose a place where you will not be interrupted. Open sacred space by inviting your guides and teachers of the light to support you. Dedicate your work to the highest good of all life. Honour the spirits of the land who live there. Make a small offering to them, asking for their permission to work spiritually there. An offering could be some oatmeal, juniper berries, tobacco, flowers, or chocolate. Preferably, the offerings would have been energised overnight on your altar. Stay quiet and feel with your body whether or not this place is good for you. If you feel anxious, or that something is wrong, thank the land and go to a different place. If it feels OK, move to the next step.

Set your intention to connect with the web of life through a tree. Ask for a tree to be your partner in this work. Keep walking around until you feel that a tree is calling you. When you find your tree partner, approach and make an offering to the spirits of the tree. Ask to place your hands on its trunk and connect to the web of life. Go ahead with the tree's permission.

Breathe deeply into your abdomen, connecting to the tree with each breath. Take your time. You may begin to feel more relaxed as energy flows through you. This is the energy of the web of life, the universal chi, entering your body.

Bring your focus into your heart. Intend for your heart centre to open. See the tree as a beautiful being, a life form the same as you. Let love flow from your heart to the tree. At the same time, receive love from the tree. Keep breathing slowly until you feel that you and the tree are breathing together, merging with each synchronised breath. This will deepen your connection and your auras will eventually unite.

Stay in this beautiful state for as long as you wish. If you feel lightheaded, due to the increased flow of chi that you may not be used to, disengage and place your palms on the ground. When you feel ready to leave, remove your hands from the tree. Thank your tree partner for the exchange of energy and thank your helping spirits and the spirits of the land. Release the spirits as your work has finished. Ask that you and the space are completely protected and sealed before they go.

Suggestion: Although I was taught this exercise from a tree, it is possible to connect and breathe together with the planet, the ocean, rocks, and other natural forms. It may be easier, however, to connect with the trees, as they are the conduits through which light and life force energy flows into the Earth and all beings.

Exercise 2:
Heal Energetic Imbalances in the Body by Connecting to the Web of Life

This exercise is a follow-up from the previous one.

The energy of the web of life is universal chi, life force energy. Chi will not only help you replenish your personal life force, but also help correct imbalances caused by blocked energy. You can do this by yourself, or with a friend.

Go out in nature and select your spot as per previous exercise and make an offering. State your intention to connect with the web of life through a tree for healing and the restoration of your life force. Ask for a tree to be your partner in this work. Keep walking around until you feel that a tree is calling you.

When you find your tree partner, approach the tree and make an offering to the spirits of the tree. With the tree's permission, sit with your back against the tree and ask that the energy of the web of life flows to you, restoring your life force energy and healing any imbalances in your body.

Wait patiently till you feel the energy running through you into the Earth. The energy is clearing out stagnant, heavier energy caused by blocks in your meridian channels, taking it into the Earth where it is cleansed. (For the Earth, this energy is akin to compost that can be broken up into its essence of light.) At the same time, your life force is being replenished. Stay in this state for a few minutes.

If you are working with a friend, ask her to stand in front of you. Ask for the web of life to flow through you to your partner and for her to receive healing for her highest good. Intend that your own energy does not flow to your partner. You can either hold your partner's hands or just open out your palms towards her. The life force energy will flow from the web of life inside the tree, to you and then to your friend.

Stay in this beautiful state for as long as you wish. If you feel lightheaded, due to the increased flow of chi, disengage and place your palms on the ground.

When you are ready to leave, remove your back from the tree to stop the connection. Thank the tree and your friend for this exchange of energy and thank your helping spirits and the spirits of the land. Release the spirits as your work has finished. Ask that you, your friend and the space are completely protected and sealed.

Exercise 3:
Create Harmony at Home with the Help of Nature Spirits

This exercise has been inspired by the work of Sandra Ingerman and the shamanic workshop "Medicine for the Earth and Healing with Spiritual Light" (Ingerman, 2001).

In the workshop Sandra invited the group to make contact with the nature spirits of their land, though ceremony or a shamanic journey. Even though you occupy the land, there are many beings in the unseen worlds who live around you. You can ally with nature to create harmony in your environment. When you work in amity with the spirits of the land, the energy will change and your home may become more welcoming and pleasant.

I realised the importance of creating a harmonious relationship with local nature spirits when my client Eric asked me to clear the energy of his flat in the west of Glasgow. I was told that every tenant who had lived there ended up sick. Even the landlord who had moved there briefly, became ill. After I

NATURE'S VOICE

I heard it in my heart,
nature's voice.
Was it the song of the waves,
or the voice of thunder and lighting,
hiding the beauty of the distant stars?

Where are you, child?
Whispered the Earth,
longing for the human heart to open.
You look above you, you look inside you,
you do not look down.

I am here, said the ancient mother,
welcoming you in my arms,
longing for your embrace.
Many generations have past,
since I felt your heartbeat next to mine.

Where are you, my child,
lost in your mind for so long,
seeking beauty,
even though it is abundant around you?
I made a beautiful home for you.

I built you a home as vast as the ocean,
As dense as the forest,
empty like the dessert, for you to fill.
I gave it to you, to look after,
to live here in happiness.

You have deserted me and hurt me;
my wounds lie open for you to see.
I see your pain is greater,
in this life you built for yourself.
How else could you ignore the wonders around you?

Let me heal your spirit;
take care of your body,
show you a better way.
So you can heal yourself through me,
deeply and profoundly.

I never left you.
How could I, I who bore you?
Through me, you grew in your mighty power.
Raised war against me and my children.
Killed yourself many times.

I called you with the song of the crickets,
the beauty of the blossoms,
the perfumed trees.
I called you in the dark of the night
with dreams of power.

Wake up, my child,
see what I have made for you.
Seek no more, all is here.
I have given you everything.
And all I ask for, is your love.

You have returned to me.
Back where you started.
In a circle of power,
you raised your voice
and sang me your heartsong.

13

Initiation: A Spiritual Life

Spiritual Lesson 13: Through initiation, I open the door to my authentic self

Into the spirit: I wake up in a dream. I am lying inside a coffin. I know I have been dead for years, many years. What happened to the little girl with the unprecedented zest for life? The wise self was gone, replaced by a mind-constructed reality in which I found little fulfilment. All that my mind had manifested: relationships, marriage, career, material goods, brought no lasting satisfaction. Any joy I had felt was ephemeral.

I know I need to get out of this coffin, but it is not easy. I make a fist with my hand and punch the lid with all my power. The wooden planks break apart. All I had to do was act purposefully. I claim my right to life and lift myself out of the grave.

I step out of the tomb onto a road to freedom, my hair and clothes covered in soil. I see my mother building a cairn, to support my new beginning. "I had been dead," I say, "Now I can walk in the world in my own way." This is my initiation into a spiritual life.

The Spiritual Calling

While many ignore the doors to walk a spiritual path that life presents, others choose to walk through them.

Life on Earth focuses on the practical and the physical and for most of us, spirituality is left to organised religions. Our current social systems are built on people working, paying taxes, and reproducing more people to take our place. Even though opportunities may present for us to develop our inner knowing, these are largely ignored, and life and our social systems roll on. For some, spirituality may even be regarded as a threat, leading a person to question her way of life. When someone opens up spiritually, she becomes more aware of who she is and of the world around her. This may impel her to make different choices in life, give up her old way of living and embrace a new approach, leave behind situations and people who no longer reflect how she feels. She may end unfulfilling relationships, resign from a job, sell her home, and travel in pursuit of spiritual wisdom.

Following a spiritual path is usually not easy and will challenge many things within us, as it attempts to wake us up from the illusions of our everyday world. We will be asked to face our fears and doubts and the inappropriateness of our pride and negative stereotyping, to overcome them and live more authentically. As we shed our old skin and familiar behavioural and mental patterns, the journey of self-discovery can be lonely; however, we may find support from spiritual teachers and like-minded people on a similar path.

I believe that moments of potential spiritual openings have been arranged by our soul before we incarnated. The soul comes to Earth for its development, to learn about itself through direct experience. And yet, the soul also knows that it will eventually lose sight of this higher understanding, due to the social conditioning of the planet. Life's demands can overtake the individual and cause her to forget her soul's purpose. As a result, the soul prearranges events to prompt potential spiritual awakenings during its current lifetime.

Initiation into a Spiritual Path

Since 2009, I have facilitated a shamanic group in Glasgow, Scotland, and witnessed the desire in people to follow a spiritual path. I have admired some people's dedication to their spiritual practice and calling, and also witnessed others' difficulty in taking time to study and thus reap the sweetest fruits of their efforts. The pivotal step is the sustained effort of conscious living. Some people however may read a book or attend a course with enthusiasm and then afterwards find their motivation waning.

During a shamanic journey, I was taken to the land of my ancestors in ancient Greece. I was met by a group of wise beings, the centaurs, who identified themselves as spiritual teachers. They said that for some people to progress on their spiritual path, an "initiation ritual," a rite of passage from everyday life to spiritual life, is helpful. Marking this change within them and the commitment to their calling, opens the doors of their heart and creates a flow of energy into their life, bringing them opportunities for spiritual growth (see exercise below).

The Way of the Ancients: Initiation as Empowerment. Ancient people recognised the spiritual dimension as an essential aspect of life. They also acknowledged that some people were predestined to follow a spiritual calling. Those called to the spiritual life were important people to their communities— people who abandoned normal life in search of the Divine. Accordingly, initiation rites were held to empower spiritual seekers and instil in them a sense of devotion, to help them follow the spiritual calling and serve their tribe.

ISIS told me that in early Egypt, those who did not seek spiritual truth, were thought of as the "living dead," souls living an aimless life. When someone chose to study the spiritual arts, they underwent a death and resurrection ritual to awaken from this torpor into the dynamism of a spiritual life. In ancient Greece, initiations took place as part of entering the Mysteries, the formal study of spirituality.

Indigenous Cultures: Initiation Rites. In traditional societies, the shaman is chosen through an initiation process whereby he is tested and embraced by spirit. These initiations are powerful ceremonies aimed at helping the spiritual seeker-cum-shaman prepare himself for this new step in life. Through rituals and trials, the initiate makes contact with his spiritual nature and learns to hear and trust his inner voice and the voice of spirit (Stephenson, 2006).

In these societies, initiation of the shaman is a way of life for the community of shamans, their followers, and every member of the tribe. Every stage of human life is honoured and celebrated through ceremonies and rituals that invoke the divine presence. These rites of passage mark important life transitions, which empower individuals to fulfil their role in their community. For example, there are initiations into adulthood, parenthood, and elderhood. The shaman is the facilitator of the divine plan on behalf of the people and leads these initiations for the tribe, hearing the voice of spirit (Eliade, 2004).

Similarly, in western societies during medieval times, when a person came of age for guild membership, he would be presented by his family. After a ceremony of initiation, he would learn the secrets of his new trade (Ralls, 2013).

Nowadays in the west, although we have lost much of the tradition of initiation and there is no formal recognition from the wider community of a person's choice to follow a spiritual path, life itself can be the initiator, providing the circumstances for growth. Life will seek out the person, bringing situations to her, where she is challenged to rely on inner strength to survive. In some cases, similar life experiences recur until the person finally learns the lesson. However, this can be a more difficult and slower process, as the person usually has to meet these confrontations without the community support and reassurance as in the tribal initiation.

Initiations through Dreams. Sometimes, spirit manifests an initiatory dream. These dreams can be incredibly powerful and life transforming, even more so than physical initiations. My first initiation came in this way, as I described at the start of the chapter. In the dream, when I broke out of the coffin, I was resurrected. Two months later, I understood the dream. Like the coffin, my marriage split apart and I emerged into a new life.

In 2014 in Kathmandu, Nepal, I had the opportunity to receive a healing from the egg shaman, who used to be a government employee with a successful career in finance. In his mid-forties, he was visited in a dream by a Hindu god who initiated him as a shaman and taught him how to extract heavy energies and disease from people. The man immediately left his job and became a healer for his community.

Such dreams and the life experiences that follow may constitute the initiation process for some people. The initiation can be a difficult and demanding transition or a smooth one. It is tailored to the individual, and help from the spiritual realms is always there. Initiation is also a process of self-discovery.

The Purpose of Initiation: Open the Heart

Entering a spiritual path brings a different focus to our life and affirms our willingness to awaken our consciousness and open our heart. As spiritual seekers, we may have many initiations, regardless of whether we follow a shamanic path. When we enter into different stages of our spiritual life, initiation is a way to prepare ourselves for the next phase and embrace our path at a deeper level.

The purpose of an initiation is to open a secret compartment inside our heart and to experience our soul's voice and our belonging. Initiation is a homecoming. It is a moving experience because we are touched by the Divine spirit, at the deepest level. It is a profound, graceful, and joyful gift. A spiritual initiation is also a process of attunement, where high etheric energies of light flow into our body, opening our spiritual channels and chakras and raising our vibration to increase our awareness. During an initiation, we become more aligned to the Universal Mind, the Divine Wisdom, and have thoughts and insights that do not originate from our egoic mind but from a higher source.

One of my initiations took place in the Great Pyramid of Giza in Egypt. I had travelled to Egypt following an invitation by my spirit guides. One morning, I took a taxi to the Giza plateau and went inside the Great Pyramid. A guard stood outside the pyramid, but nobody was inside, which was unusual. As I walked up the Grand Gallery towards the King's Chamber, I felt claustrophobic and trembled with fear. But I kept climbing. My spirit guides helped me continue when I was at the point of turning back. Inside the chamber, I sat on the floor and tried to chant some of the ISIS power chants and mantras I had learned, but they seemed to have no effect.

Then some people came and went. My spirit guides told me to centre myself and I tried hard, but was still anxious. After an hour, I decided to leave. Again, the place was empty. Climbing down the Grand Gallery, I heard sounds in my mind. I began chanting the sounds, and suddenly, my fear transformed into joy. The whole pyramid became alive. The chant echoed and vibrated off the walls, energy flowed into my body, and I felt the walls radiating light. My guides told me later that this chant unlocked the power of the Great Pyramid. I went out of the pyramid transformed, overwhelmed by joy and deep gratitude, and touched by the Divine.

As mentioned in chapter eleven, in 2006, my guide ISIS started instructing me into a spiritual teaching called the "Seven Gates of Awareness." The teaching begins with an initiation, where the initiate sits with me in sacred space. The enlightened being, ISIS, comes through me and performs the initiation. Afterwards, many people report feelings of gratitude and a sense of coming home.

I have also had the privilege to facilitate others' initiations inside the Great Pyramid. When I lead pilgrimages in Egypt, I notice in other people some of the elements of my initiation in the Great Pyramid. At first, there may be some apprehension, fear, or indecision, as well as an inner knowing of the importance of the process and a drive to continue. After the initiation, there is a deep sense of homecoming, an opening of the heart, and a transformation into gratitude.

LIFE AFTER INITIATION: DISMEMBERMENT

After an initiation, we may be called to reassess and change our way of living. This is called a "dismemberment" of our life, and it is an important part of the spiritual journey. When someone opens up spiritually, she may realise that her usual way of life may be at odds with her new values and understanding.

Some traditionally initiated shamans and healers undertake a journey-visualisation in an effort to change their material life, which is no longer aligned with their inner understanding. They imagine their body to be symbolically eaten by worms or ants, or in some other way consumed, so all that remains is a clean skeleton. The aim of the journey is to break free from what no longer serves them.

A dismemberment is also a way to detach from the egoic, material world. When we are freed symbolically from the flesh, the inner light of the soul shines through. In this way, we may gain a bigger perspective about life.

Dismemberment in a journey-visualisation is about creating space for changes in our life. Since I embarked on my spiritual journey, I have experienced multiple initiations and many dismemberments and changes in my life. The process is never-ending; the skeleton is continually polished. With each dismemberment, more of my inner light shines out. Like a forest fire, the old woods must die for the new life to begin.

A dismemberment in life takes courage and time. Change is not always easy, and for some people, it may take many years and much effort until they are able to align their life with their inner truth.

SUMMARY

Traditionally, the spiritual journey starts with initiation. Circumstances conspire to take the person through the life changes that must occur, to free her of the conditioning. In indigenous societies, the initiate would go through a series of ritual challenges designed to shed the ego, whilst in the western world, life is the teacher. Through these initiations, the person experiences a heart opening and a deepening of their spiritual process. The initiation is a door to coming home to the authentic self.

EXERCISE: AN INITIATION –THE CENTAUR'S CAVE

Throughout Europe, a tradition exists of the anthropomorphic shaman, where man takes the form of a beast or half beast, mates with the Earth and becomes one with nature. Cave paintings, dating from prehistoric times, depict men transforming into spirit animals, such as bison and deer.

The myth of the Centaurs speaks about a group of wise beings who were half man-half horse. They lived primarily in the mountain of Pelion, in Thessaly, a region known for its high vibrational energy. The Centaurs were reputed to have all the major Greek heroes under their tutelage. Their expertise was not warfare or swordsmanship, as one would expect from a hero's teacher, but inner knowledge about the soul and the world. They were respected throughout the classical world, and it was a great honour to have the opportunity to study with them.

These transcended beings can still teach us and initiate us into the spiritual path, through contact during a shamanic journey-visualisation. They gave me the initiation ritual below, to help people mark their own spiritual calling. You can carry out this ritual any time you wish to reaffirm your commitment to your life purpose. You will need an offering of wine or milk and honey, and maybe a drum or rattle (optional).

Stage 1: Purification. Start by creating the initiation space by welcoming your higher self and your helping spirits and building an altar, as in chapter nine.

Then set the intention: acknowledge your inner desire to follow a spiritual path and make a commitment to yourself and the world. You are making a pledge, a promise, that this is the path you will follow, respecting your inner guidance and the voice of spirit, instead of the ego and social conditioning. Ask for the spiritual initiation that will mark your commitment.

Imagine taking a knife and cutting all the cords that hold you to the world. With each cord, you release—with love—any person or situation that does not serve you, thanking her for all she has taught you about yourself. Doing this, you become a free spirit, dedicating your will to the will of the Creator. You are no longer accountable to the world, but to the highest good of all beings.

You may also wish to ask the helping spirits for a dismemberment, so all that is left of you is clean bones.

Stage 2: Initiation. Now invite the Centaurs of the light into your space and their leader Chiron. If you have a rattle or drum, you can use it at this time to welcome them. Wait until you feel their presence in your aura. You can make an offering of wine or milk and honey, which after the ritual, you can place by a tree in nature.

Once you feel or visualise the Centaurs near you, say that you wish to follow a spiritual path and ask to be initiated, as they initiated the heroes and shamans of the ancient times. Imagine galloping with them into their sacred cave, where the ancient Priestess of Persephone, embodying the lady of the underworld and the upperworld, also known as the Maiden of Life, daughter of the Earth Mother and the wife of Death, is waiting to meet you and initiate you into the path.

The Centaurs will watch over you whilst the initiation takes place. This is your own experience and it will be tailored by the Centaurs for you. They can teach you many things and show you the way, as they have done for many others throughout the ancient world.

At the end of the journey-visualisation, give thanks to the Centaurs and the Priestess. Imagine you are putting the offerings outside the cave; although at a later time, you can also place them by a tree near your home.

Stage 3: Release the Spirits. Slowly bring yourself back by becoming aware of your surroundings. Give thanks for all that has taken place. Say to the Centaurs and other helpers that you have finished your spiritual work, and you release them now. Ask that they protect you and the space before they go.

Suggestion: Following this ceremony, I suggest to keep a journal of any significant life experiences and dreams.

INITIATION

The Priestess holds the cup of knowledge
inviting you to look deep within.
What do you see in the flames of the fire?

The Horned One is gathering pace,
to break through the barriers of the mind,
inviting you to take part in the ancient ritual, personifying the Divine essence.

Who is the one who dares to cross the endless ocean?
Who screams the words of power in the midst of night?
Only the cave knows what they mean, for she has heard them since time
immemorial.

Find yourself, Traveller of no time, in the endless sea.
There is no destination, no place for you to go
other than inside yourself, where all roads will eventually lead you.

Find yourself through the ancient Priestess and the Horned One,
through the dance of the flames, the oil and the water,
through screams and laughter, joy and tears.

For all is you and you are nothing;
everything around you leads to within:
in the empty black void of surrender, in the bottomless pool of no beginning
and no end.

Find yourself before the end of time.
As you come back to finish the unfinished business,
turning one more leaf of the same book, completing the chapter before you
start anew.

Death the redeemer will take you away.
The endless circle of renewal will commence,
as if it had never ended, until it starts again.

Part III.
From the Spirit
to the Body:
The Ouroboros

In Part III, chapters fourteen through nineteen, the snake realises that spiritual awareness is only part of the puzzle of life. The flying serpent returns to Earth to complete the cycle and achieve its earthly purpose for incarnation. It lifts its head and plunges its fangs into its own tail, creating a perfect circle. Now, it is reborn as the Ouroboros, the infinite being that has no beginning and no end.

Becoming whole means straddling both realities, the physical and the spiritual. In these chapters, we now examine our path of countless lives, the eternal journey of the soul. On this voyage, we balance collective actions and individual responsibility. Our goal is to return once again to our inner self and stoke its fire, to discover our radiance. How does our life echo nature's cycles and the karmic choices we make? What can we learn from the stories and sequences of creation and destruction? Is there a cautionary tale about greed and the domination of others?

We discover that our genetic code, our DNA, still carries the seeds of Oneness. The journey takes us deeper into ourselves, anchoring us into the physical embodiment of our being, into our very body.

14

Nature's Seasons and Karmic Winds

Spiritual Lesson 14: I flow with the seasons of my life; by meeting winter's stillness, I spring into activity

Into the body: I sit and meditate, stilling the mind. "Where does the wind come from?" my spirit helper asks. I somehow know it is coming from my right side, I can feel its energy drifting towards me. This is the fresh wind of change, action and positivity, pushing me forward. "What about the other wind?" I enquire. There is no wind coming from my left side; the stale air that would bring a period of rest, integration, and peace. My guide smiles, and tells me to get back to work. One day, when the left wind comes, everything will stop. Will I then choose to rest and be at peace or continue to keep myself busy, running in circles?

NATURE'S SEASONS

Ancient and indigenous cultures lived according to the seasons, in order to survive. Whether they were agricultural societies as in classical Europe, hunter-gatherers in Africa, or migration peoples following the buffalo in the North American plains, the indigenous humans were attuned to the Earth's cyclical rhythms; otherwise, their tribes would starve. Animals and plants are naturally in harmony with the Earth's seasons, and so are humans, according to the indigenous tribes. Rather than adapting the environment to their needs, as we do in the west, native people, like the Australian aboriginals, adjust their life and behaviours to the calendar of the Earth, as shaped by changes in trees, the flowering of plants, the migration of birds. They have observed that Earth's seasons do not follow our western Gregorian calendar (Foster & Kreitzman, 2010).

Humans, like all other organisms, are affected by the seasons, even though modern technology shields us from the elements. The changing of the seasons influences us both physiologically and psychologically. However, being detached from nature and living inside our homes, we do not always observe that our body and moods are adapting to the external environment.

Ancient people aligned consciously with nature's seasons through festivals, ceremonies and celebrations. The cold winter was the time of rest, reflection and stories around the fire. Winter was personified by the Crone Cailleach in the Celtic world, or Demeter/Ceres in ancient Greece and Rome. In the beginning of spring, the Crone was reborn as the Maiden Bridget, Persephone or Proserpina who emerged from the underworld, like a plant coming out of the ground, and initiated a new beginning in peoples' lives. The death of the winter was followed by the rebirth of spring. People aligned with these cycles of nature by honouring their respective personifications, and adapting human activities to the demands and teachings of each season. The ancients tapped into the ebb and flow of the natural rhythm, recognising themselves as nature.

KARMIC SEASONS

At the same time, our life has its own seasons that, like the Earth's, are cyclical. We're affected by nature, the moon phases and change of seasons. Similarly, our karma creates an ebb and flow in our lives too. The karmic seasons mirror metaphorically the natural cycle, but they have a different duration. A karmic winter may last many years, or a couple of days. In my life, I have observed my own springs and winters, created by the forces of karma. Corresponding with nature, in karmic winter we hibernate quietly and nurture ourselves inside life's womb; in karmic spring, we blossom and display our colours. During karma's summer, we enjoy growth and vitality, the abundance we worked to create that will sustain us in the years to come. Throughout karmic autumn, we harvest what we sowed in previous years. Each season has its unique challenges, especially if we resist its gifts. We may find the winter slow and deathlike, sometimes feeling ill or deprived of energy. If we try to act, we experience difficulty, as if nothing seems to work. Similarly, we resist spring by refusing to change and act. Life may be pushing us in a certain direction, but we dig in our heels. Our rebirth could be painful as a result.

This is not a new philosophical concept. Through the power of observation, seekers can discover the karmic seasons of their lives, the quiet restorative years and busy productive times, the periods of plentiful harvest and the spells of famine. Like Earth's seasons, nothing stays the same and good and bad times alternate (Kouloukis, 2013). Others relate life seasons to a theological doctrine and argue that they are in God's plan for mankind and part of our evolution (Tournier, 2012).

THE TRAIN OF LIFE

Like Earth's seasons, our life is marked by periods of action and times of rest. If we were to swim continuously in the river of life, we would soon become exhausted. And so, we stop and sit quietly by the river's edge until the flow of life becomes strong again and moves us forward.

Imagine that you are on a train looking out at the scenery. You admire the vistas, a house on a hill, a distant cemetery, a row of trees. Suddenly, the scene changes and is replaced by another scene, and then another. So quick are the changes, you barely have time to register each successive landscape. When the train stops at a station, you wait. Now you can observe the ambience of the station. Some people leave the train, and others get on. And then, the train begins moving towards its next destination. This is like life, running fast like a train between stations. So many things come and go before our eyes. Life also has stops, railway stations, moments for relaxation, reflection, and integration.

To progress on our spiritual path, we need to understand and embrace the ebbs and flows of our life. There are times to put our foot on the accelerator and keep the car moving. Unfortunately, when we reach our destination, we may not hit the brake, having been socially conditioned to busyness. We drive our car in endless circles to keep moving, despite wasting energy. In the quiet times, we need to rest, switch off the engine, and stop. We need these pauses to review our journey, and reflect on its lessons. Then, with renewed energy and insights, we can get back into the car, restart the engine, and move again.

For many of us, life can appear more complicated than it actually is, as our perceptions can needlessly make things difficult. Amid our many responsibilities, we yearn for quiet time. The downtimes may seem out of reach, but will come eventually for everyone in the same way that winter follows autumn. And then, it is our choice to grasp the opportunity to stop.

How long are our quiet times supposed to last? It is different for each person and each stage of life. Using nature as an example: in the Gregorian western calendar, winter lasts three months but nature may have a different idea. Some years, winter's climate is mild and before we know it, the spring's shoots are coming out of the ground. Other years, winter is frigid and seems endless, encouraging us to stay indoors. Our life's winters are similar; they may be quick or last many years, depending on our karma and our ability to acknowledge it.

THE TWO KARMIC FORCES

The forces of karma create the seasons in our life, our winters of stillness and our springs of action. We live according to the law of karma. Our positive actions—the goodness we create in life—will have positive benefits. And, vice versa. Whatever we do today, we will receive back sooner or later. Our soul has accepted this universal law by incarnating on Earth.

Sometimes, people view karma only as suffering, a punishment for past misdeeds. Karma may be perceived as suffering when we experience the consequences of our negative actions, those actions that caused pain to others and ourselves. When an inner realisation makes us aware of the harm we have created and we change our attitudes, negative karma can be purified (chapter 6).

Karma can also be joyful. When we receive the positive effect of our actions, we collect the gifts we have given to others. Positive actions have positive results. The challenge can be to accept wholeheartedly and appreciate these gifts, to receive graciously the beauty we have created in the world externally. When we are able to accept the positive effect of our actions, positive karma is offset.

Eventually, through the process of inner awakening, we see the effect of our actions, both positive and negative. We have the potential to become mindful of our behaviours and their consequences. We may, in time, reach a state where we act intuitively, in accord with the highest good of all. Our wise actions, derived from the enlightened mind, do not create positive or negative karma.

In my professional life, I have witnessed many people in difficult situations, in the winter of their lives, experiencing serious illness or the loss of a job or home, due to the law of karma. Some had been deeply unhappy, caught in a rut, and were causing harm to themselves and others. Eventually, the law of karma gave them time to re-evaluate their life, so they could move towards spring. Some people take this opportunity to change their approach. Others remain emotionally stuck and continue to blame life and others for their predicament. Consequently, life may bring them the same lesson over and over and winter seems unending.

When I first met Bill he had been suffering for years with fibromyalgia syndrome (FMS), a long-term condition that caused pain all over his body. He had lived life hating himself, his job, and even his family. Bill had so much unresolved anger, from lost opportunities, but he was ignoring his feelings and choosing instead to direct his resentment towards others. It was everyone's fault but his. In his words, "People were not doing what they should do, or they were doing too much," which made Bill feel sidelined. When the karmic forces gathered, he had a serious accident. This was the first sign asking Bill to stop and re-evaluate his approach to life.

Bill ignored the accident, the lesson, and went back to work, immersing himself in the same behaviour patterns. Then the illness came, eventually making it impossible for him to work. Finally, he lost his home, as he had to move into a care facility. Bill and I worked for years sifting through all the negative thinking. Every time he blamed someone, we looked at similar situations where he was angry with himself. Through self-forgiveness, love and understanding of the bigger picture of the law of cause and effect, he started to get better. In time, he was able to walk unassisted outside his care home and then, around the block. After years of suffering, Bill was finding a new type of freedom, both mentally from all the blaming and resentment and physically from the restrictions placed upon him by the illness. Slowly, Bill started taking control of his life and experiencing the first signs of spring. His process is still unfolding.

Summary

As in nature, our life is cyclical rather than linear. Each season has a unique karmic opportunity—from the self-reflection of winter to the assimilation of summer, from the growth of spring to the gifts of autumn. Throughout our life, but especially in the stillness of winter, we can ponder the consequences of our behaviours and review our life's journey. Mystics and spiritual practitioners traditionally went into caves to reflect on their karmic actions with their spirit teachers. Following winter, they would emerge with renewed energy, into the springtime of their lives.

Exercise: Meditation Practice – The Cave of the Karmic Winds

Traditionally, mystics would withdraw into the stillness of a cave to access their inner wisdom, undisturbed in this womb of the Earth. In this exercise, you will create a cave, physical or imaginary, in which you withdraw to experience the two opposing karmic forces: the stale karmic air of winter and the fresh karmic wind of spring.

Before beginning, you may wish to simulate a cave in your home by constructing a small tent with a blanket and filling it with cushions.

Create sacred space by calling in your enlightened spirit teachers to help you with this practice. They could be your guardian angel, ancient gods, buddhas, or simply the Divine Source of All. Then set your intention to become aware of the karma you are carrying, symbolised by the negative forces of the stale air, and to create positive flow in your life through the fresh karmic wind.

Imagine yourself walking deep into a forest. You see a cave—your cave of self-realisation. Like the old mystics, you can go inside to withdraw from everyday life and listen to your spirit.

Before you enter your cave, intend to leave everything behind. At the side of the cave, visualise a fire. Imagine placing all your attachments into the fire: your clothes, car keys, home, job. In other words, put into the fire each thing you believe you cannot afford to lose, releasing all your attachments.

Naked, you enter the cave. Sit down and breathe slowly into your heart. With each inhale, ask your heart centre to open to receive the light of the world. With each exhale, imagine the light from your heart flowing to all beings.

In this space of the cave, ask to experience the stale air of karma, coming from your left. Feel the quiet surrounding you. What is the air trying to teach you? See the gifts the stale air is bringing to you. Insights about your life and your negative and positive karma may arise. To clear the negative karma, apologise for what has taken place. To clear the positive karma, express your appreciation for the gifts you have received. Acknowledge that you have created all of these situations for your own learning. Stay in this quiet space until you have received all the gifts of the stale air: the gift of going inward, the insight, and the clearing of the karma.

Filled with the gifts of self-realisation, ask to experience the fresh wind of karma, coming from your right, which creates action, movement, and flow. Feel the wind circling around you, revitalising you and your life. The positive flow creates new opportunities in your life, which will appear when you are ready.

You are mirroring these two karmic energies, the stale air and the fresh wind in your life. Both flow inside you. Ask that the two karmic forces merge. As the opposing powers unite, you are reborn into your own light. Feel your light expanding in your heart, consuming the whole of your body and everything around you. The cave is gone, and all that remains is the glow of your inner light. Remain in this space of realisation for as long as you wish.

Slowly, bring your awareness to the present by noticing your surroundings and in your mind, or reality, exit the cave, coming back into your everyday world. Thank your enlightened spirit teachers and release them. Ask them to completely seal and protect you and your space before they go.

INTO THE STILLNESS

I seek the quiet mind;
that which I cannot grasp,
filling my days with activity.

The quiet mind, the silent space.
Into the stillness I withdraw from the world.
The light is dim, so I can see the shadows.

The space opens for my soul to speak.
At first she whispers with a faint voice.
I am not sure I want to hear what she has to say.

The fruitless life I have been leading,
the many gifts I have received,
and what has been most fulfilling.

Do I continue on this road?
Fight the same battles with myself?
They have been rewarding in some way.

I had created an identity,
which was shattered on the damp walls of the cave;
drenched by the stream of my tears.

The light was dim, I realised,
because I had left the lamp unattended;
for many years I ran away from it.

It took courage to fill it again with oil.
To shine onto the walls of the cave,
the prison of my mind that kept me hidden.

The decaying smell of the stale air
showed me all that was rotten,
the rubbish heap I had to clean.

I took the lamp to the midden.
Shining on it a bright light.
Only I found many gems and made peace with life.

15

The Purpose of Incarnation

Spiritual Lesson 15: In spirit I understand my divine origin. In body I lose sight of my light. Playing the game of life I seek to find myself

Into the body: "I feel stuck. Day after day I take the train to and from work, come home, make dinner and vegetate in front of the television. Is this what I signed up for when I left the spirit world and incarnated?

I speak to a counsellor. I say to her I have to change my life, and I mean it. She reflects that it is sad. Yes, it is sad because my life does not serve me. The counsellor does not know this, but an inner knowing is arising within me that my life is supposed to have a purpose and I am not fulfilling it. I have fleeting ideas about what it could be but nothing concrete. Perhaps this is a journey in the dark until I switch on my inner light. I surrender and follow my intuition to reveal my calling.

FROM THE SPIRIT TO THE BODY

In the spirit realms of the light, there is no suffering. A spirit residing there—knowing it is the light of the Creator—exists in a state of peace. Moreover, a spirit does not think in the same way as an incarnated soul does. In the higher spirit realms, spirit thoughts are conscious intentions generated by the wisdom mind with no interference akin to the incarnated soul's monkey mind. Consequently, each spirit thought is a powerful action. It brings instant manifestation. For example, a spirit intends to visit a temple and immediately, is there. (The monkey mind is a term used within meditation teachings and Buddhism to describe the restless and easily distracted state of the conditioned mind, compared to the focussed quietness of the enlightened or wisdom mind (Wei-an, 2000)).

On Earth, souls are bound by the rules of the physical reality. They develop a personality that masks their true nature. In this realm, the mind generates tens of thousands of thoughts each day, most of them unconscious. These thoughts lack the power of pure intention, and consequently, may take years to manifest. This is good news and bad news. The good news is that since earthly thoughts derive from our conditioned self, they do not manifest instantly, thus protecting us from chaos and folly. Imagine having a genie that granted our every thought. The bad news is that this can make it difficult for the incarnated soul to see any link between her thoughts and her actions, and assume responsibility for the life events she created.

WHY SOULS INCARNATE

Souls choose to incarnate for many reasons and sometimes multiple reasons, but fall into two main interconnected categories: to gain perspective and to purify karma.

Incarnation to Gain Perspective. A soul may wish to experience physical life in all its diversity. It may choose to incarnate into any form, such as a tree, an animal, a human being, a stone, or a mountain. A soul can learn from its experience as any physical form.

A soul may also choose to expand its worldview by experiencing a particular human predicament. The soul can develop knowledge and understanding of what it is like to be blind, heterosexual, a child prodigy, an alcoholic, or an immigrant from a war-torn country. The possibilities, again, are endless.

A soul may also opt to balance its experiences by incarnating as rich in one life and poor in another, a woman in some lives and a man in others, the aggressor in one life and the victim in another life.

Incarnation to Purify Karma. All actions have consequences, and the soul is responsible for every action it initiates. All karmic debts, positive and negative, have to be repaid eventually by each soul. Therefore, a soul may be incarnating in a specific situation to pay back its karmic debt (chapter 6). The soul may incarnate to repeat a lesson that it was unable to learn in a previous incarnation. The soul may have become mired in social conditioning in a past life, lost its way, and never balanced its karmic scales.

A soul can also incarnate to help another soul. As an example, souls may choose to experience an earthquake in order to open the compassionate hearts of other souls, who are moved to come to their aid. A soul may choose to be born into a particular family to help them purify their karma. For instance, a more experienced soul could incarnate in a family with a pattern of alcohol abuse. The evolved soul with its love, compassion, forgiveness, and spiritual awareness may be able to show the other family members, stuck in the actions of the ancestors, a better way to live and help them break the cycle of alcohol abuse for future generations.

Incarnation for Multiple Reasons. Often in one lifetime, several of these intentions to gain perspective and to purify karma combine. Thus, a soul may be here to accomplish many lessons over a single incarnation.

A soul sometimes learns through joy or, more often, through adversity. The soul chooses to go through different events until it is able to fully acknowledge its Divinity. Consequently, we do not judge any soul we meet for who it is, what it is doing, or how it is experiencing life. Each soul is here to realise and work through its unique journey. We do not project our own opinions on someone else's path. Instead, we learn to develop compassion for their predicament. We may be in this soul's shoes in a different life.

Ultimately, each incarnation on Earth offers the soul the opportunity to become more aware of its brilliance, which is masked due to the conditioning of the mind, and to feel its essence as a radiant being.

THE GAME OF LIFE

Having made its choices in the spirit realms the soul then incarnates to play these out. However, life on Earth is not straightforward. We forget the choices we made in the spirit realms. We do not know that life is an illusion, a dream, a simulation game where we learn about ourselves through our reactions to predetermined events. Immersed in the conditioning, we no longer have full access to the wisdom mind.

Incarnation presents us with many possibilities. As we take part in the game of life, we meet different people who try to influence our decisions. It may be our parents, partners, teachers, the media, and our boss at work. Some, especially those who are part of our soul group, encourage us to achieve our life purpose, while others try to distract us and interfere for their own reasons. No matter what other people say or do, we are responsible for each decision we make and carry the allotted karma. The game of life is ours to play and each person is playing her own game.

In life, intuition too has a role. Intuition comes from the wisdom mind, but most of the time we dismiss it and follow the prescribed rules of social conditioning, which are more familiar and thus, usually more comfortable. Occasionally we may make a move quickly, because it feels right instinctively.

Like any game, the more we play, the better we become at playing it. Some people may repeat the same mistakes in life and develop a pattern until they experience a breakthrough. Others are quick learners. However, it does not matter how long it takes us to learn. There are potentially endless games, endless lives, for us to work things out. In the bigger perspective everything is a play, nothing bad happens if we make mistakes, suffer trauma, and die without fulfilling our life purpose. At some point, our soul finds the way home to spirit lands. Our immortal, Divine soul can never be harmed or perish. We will eventually learn to recognise an unhelpful move, what does not serve us in life. This is soul progress.

Our real opponent in the game of life is our ego shadow, conditioned self. We are playing to overcome our mentality about how life should be as well as all our doubts, fears, anger, and ignorance. We are also playing to appreciate our positive attributes, such as love, generosity, and kindness. The game of life reveals both our weaknesses and our talents. Depending on our conditioning, karma, and life purpose, the game may be challenging or easy.

The soul chooses the type of life, the particular events, and the characteristics of each incarnation. For instance, a soul may wish to come to Earth to learn about love. The soul chooses a life where it incarnates as a seventeenth-century aristocrat. The social conditioning of the aristocrat leads him to believe he is superior to the peasants, who he considers vulgar and barbaric. Then, he falls in love with a peasant and his beliefs are challenged. What will the soul do? Will it choose love?

Throughout our incarnations, we may play out thousands of different scenarios as chosen by our soul. Our first life may be easy, and subsequent ones harder—all to broaden our perspective and purify karma. Helpful choices are ones that are inspired by the Divine part inside each of us, our wise, enlightened self. Poor decisions are those generated by the egoic self. Through the incarnations, the soul aims to make better choices so that it can become, once more, a being of light and finally awaken out of the game.

Intervention: A Little Help from Paradise

The Garden of Eden. Shangri-la is not a faraway place. It is within us, mirrored by our enlightened mind. So, too, hell can be mirrored by the state of our conditioned consciousness.

Our life's journey is defined by our state of consciousness, our personal awareness and development, and our soul's goals for each of our incarnations—that is, what we are here to learn. Our karma designs each life based on our soul's goals for us. Some people may have difficult lives, incarnate in war zones or into places where they are being exploited, abused, and dehumanised. We would regard these places as a living hell. Others may have everything they desire: family, money, cars, and tropical vacations. We would perhaps say they live in paradise.

A luxurious material life, though, may not be heavenly to its actors. Heaven and hell are states of mind. We manifest a life in one or the other depending on our approach to life. The more conditioned we are, the more pain we live in. External circumstances can influence this, but inner happiness depends on our state of consciousness. Rich people endure suffering, and poor people experience joy. When my parents bought an old townhouse, they found the rope used by the previous tenants' son to hang himself. He was the son of a tobacco lord. The family hosted frequent parties on its cruise ship. At the end of every evening's soirée, as a display of their wealth, the parents tossed the grand piano overboard and into the sea. Many people may have envied the son's life of inherited wealth and leisure, yet he was apparently in a great deal of pain.

In 2008, during a trip to Nepal, I visited a Buddhist monastery along with other westerners. Prior to the rinpoche's lecture, we wandered around the grounds. We were conscious of the apparent poverty around us, the monks' threadbare robes and simple diets; however, the monks did not seem to care. Their most precious possession is their *mala* (prayer beads). During meditation and mantra chanting using their mala, the monks bring light energy into the body and feed the soul. Their life is one of continuous practice of developing inner happiness; clothes and food are secondary. According to author and meditation teacher Sharon Salzberg (2003), anything outside of us that we look to for inspiration is ephemeral. The inner wisdom, however, we can never lose.

The rinpoche I visited in Nepal in 2008, shared this way of life, based on Buddha's teaching of liberation from suffering and non-attachment (Bien, 2011). He taught in many places around Asia, where his students prepared beautiful meals and accommodated him comfortably to show their respect. But the rinpoche's heart preferred the simplicity of the monastery and the spiritual practices that brought him sustained joy.

At some point, a soul may incarnate in a place where authentic spiritual teachings, those that form a path to awakening, are available and can focus on its personal growth. This is a great gift, and usually the result of positive karma. Perhaps, the soul developed kindness and compassion in previous incarnations. Without this level of inner development, even if a soul incarnates in a place where spiritual teachings are readily available, or is the child of a shaman or spiritual teacher, it may not be able to follow the teachings due to its state of consciousness. Through past life regression, I know that I have studied Buddhism, shamanism, ancient Egyptian mystical teachings, and incarnated in the golden time of Atlantis. All these spiritual lives helped my soul grow and gather pearls of wisdom that I have brought into this life.

To experience our authentic self here on Earth, we can engage in a regular spiritual practice, such as meditation, prayer, contact with nature, yoga, and shamanic ceremony. Energy work that heightens our vibration and quietens the mind can bring us into contact with inner states of happiness through a genuine appreciation of life. The practices that lead us to these positive inner states may vary amongst us. I experience these inner states through working with the Path of ISIS and the Rays of Divine Consciousness, but other people may resonate with different spiritual teachings. The goal, however, is the same: to bring us closer to our Divine nature.

Some people claim that we do not need any practices, because we will all become enlightened one day—spontaneously. I agree that our natural state is the light of spirit, but I do not agree that illumination is automatic. We are all born with the wisdom mind, but whilst on Earth, we are rooted in the conditioned mind, which obscures our light and wisdom. It takes effort to lift the veil. It is very appealing to the conditioned mind to assume practice is superfluous, and enlightenment inevitable. The person can become complacent and further erode any awareness and peace she had. (Paradoxically, we will all become enlightened at some point, since this is each soul's ultimate purpose, but we engage in a journey to get there.)

The Divine Factor. Sometimes, in the game of life, there is Divine intervention; grace overcoming the law of karma. When all hope appears lost, our prayers are answered. The Creator, the amazing power of love, intervenes on our behalf and a miracle happens to change the soul's journey. Through this intervention, we may develop trust and faith in something unseen and outside of ourselves: the Divine.

Nikos was diagnosed with terminal cancer and given three months to live. The doctors told him that they could do nothing for him. Nikos travelled to Agion Oros, the Holy Mountain of the Orthodox church, in the peninsula of Khalkidhiki, Greece. He found an old ascetic living in a hermitage, and asked for help with his illness. The monk told Nikos he could not help him personally as only God had the power to save his life, but he would pray for him. Nikos stayed in the hermitage for two days whilst the monk prayed. Nikos prayed, too, for the first time in years. He realised he had wasted his life in the pursuit of material pleasure. He made a vow to live in a better way. At the end of the prayers, the monk turned to Nikos, "God has saved you."

When Nikos returned to Thessaloniki, his medical team confirmed that the cancer was in remission; in other words, it had disappeared. A year afterwards, Nikos had an aura reading. The psychic, who knew nothing about his story, told him he should have been dead according to his aura photograph.

Nikos' soul had chosen an early exit point, a quick game of life. However, through Divine intervention, the circumstances of his life were changed.

When I was a child, I could see, feel, and speak to God. And then, as I grew, I denied my psychic gifts and rejected God. Rediscovering my gifts in adulthood meant that I had to re-evaluate my belief system. When Jesus first appeared in my meditation room, I said to him: "You do not exist." But, he kept coming back, particularly when I was performing ISIS healings. After a couple of months of his repeated visits, we reached an understanding: "You are outside of religion. You are Christ Consciousness." (Jesus told me he had been an Initiate of ISIS, and spent 20 years in Egypt, immersed in the ancient teachings of light).

Three months later, God knocked on my door and shattered my identity as a non-believer. During a spiritual workshop, I was tasked with channelling my helping spirit while a fellow participant, Helen, took notes. A light being arrived and spoke through me. He manifested as an old man with a beard. He asked me to look into his eyes. I saw universes, stars, nebulas, and planets. I said to Helen that I did not know who this guy was—probably just another master of light!

Helen said I should ask the spirit his name. She said there was so much light when he came, she could see the pages in the notebook turning whiter. I reconnected with the spirit guide and asked the old man his name. "I am the one you called 'the father.' I am the one you prayed to at night." I burst into tears. There was so much love around me from this being. God said, "I never left you." I had walked away from God, but God was always around me. I was now ready to accept his love again, as I had with Jesus.

Some people believe it is impossible to talk to God, and that I must have channelled an angel and assumed it was God. In my experience, God talks to all who wish to listen. He is a thought away. The barrier between us and God is created by our mind and our upbringing. We may regard ourselves as small and unworthy, and God as too busy for us. But, his vast eternal spirit is always around each of us.

Being bathed in the love of the Creator is an ecstatic experience, an indescribable feeling of grace. Every time I have been touched by such love, something has changed within me. My heart opens with the overwhelming emotion. Seemingly insurmountable problems become manageable. I become happier and more aware.

In life, we may think we are alone in an uncaring world. We are always supported, but have volition. God walks with us, but we also have choices. Yet, we may ask: "Why did God have me fall in love with someone who hurt me? Why does God create hurricanes that cause so much destruction? Why did God give my child cancer?"

God does not make us do anything. We are the ones who fall in love; the ones who, collectively, are responsible for the conditions on this planet; the ones who choose our life circumstances. Our karma manifests the conditions for our soul's growth. We have decided the landmarks and landmines of our life journey prior to incarnation. Even with God's presence and love, we may still become embroiled in everyday dramas, at least until an inner realisation helps us make a different choice. God watches over us but it is our life to live.

At the same time, the Divine may intervene and change the circumstances of our life. We call this a miracle, as in Nikos' story.

BEING THE DIVINE INCARNATED

One of my soul's purpose is to help people discover their own light, to see themselves as the "Divine incarnated". To help me understand the journey of the soul my guides gave me a beautiful metaphor.

In a vision I was taken into the "halls of the Akashic records", where the chronicles of everyone's incarnations are kept. In the vision I saw a scribe who connected daily to the Divine through prayer. The scribe worked in a room filled with scrolls, each one carefully stored in a small niche in the wall. I saw the scribe take out one of the scrolls that already had some sacred symbols written on it, and walk down a narrow staircase that led deep underground. At the bottom of the stairwell was a cell, where a vicious gorilla was kept chained to the wall. When the scribe approached the animal, it bared its teeth. The scribe had a special amulet around his neck that acted as an etheric torch which he shone onto the gorilla. Immediately the animal transformed into a placid wise being. Sitting cross-legged, the creature spoke of the secrets of the cosmos and shared wisdom teachings. The scribe transcribed everything the gorilla said onto the papyrus. Then the scribe returned to his room and placed the papyrus in its niche within the halls of the Akashic records. I watched the scribe visit the gorilla several times, each time shining the light onto the animal and recording its wise words.

During the vision I began to feel sorry for the gorilla. I wondered if the scribe was using the animal to retrieve knowledge, and if the animal should be set free to roam in the jungle. My instinct was to free the captive gorilla, and I saw myself standing outside the cell with the intention of liberating the animal. Then, my guides intervened. They said the gorilla represented the basic instinct, the egoic self, and that it was dangerous to set it free as its nature was to destroy and create chaos. They told me that our world is in such a state because too many gorillas have been set free and allowed to roam unchecked. "What is going to happen to this gorilla," I asked? They showed me how the scribe would continue to shine the light onto the animal, who would, temporarily, become wise and placid. In time, the creature would grow old and gradually its wise Self would emerge fully and this state of mind would become permanent. They then shared a vision of an old gorilla with white hair, who had become the wise Self. "Now" they said, "this soul experiences ultimate freedom as the chains of the conditioning and the ego are no more."

EMBODYING OUR GIFTS

In this chapter, I have spoken about the reasons for our soul's incarnation; the purposeful mapping of why we are here; aligning our consciousness on the positive end of the paradise scale; and receiving a boost from Divine Grace. I have also shared a metaphor for the life journey of the soul. What remains is to reveal and develop our unique gifts, the talents we bring into each life. Each propels us that much closer to recovering our radiance.

Displaying our Gifts. In the material world, the mind can grow powerful and silence the voice of the heart. We may also believe that others are more capable and more gifted than ourselves. We feel diminished and ignore the talents we brought with us in this incarnation.

One powerful gift is the gift of service, to others and ourselves (Blavatsky, 1994). This is part of a spiritual path. In order to be of service we need to uncover, own, and share our talents. I used to feel embarrassed by my healing ability and spent many years hiding from it. A woman once said to me, "If God gave you this gift, why are you running away from it? By not accepting it, you are not only doing yourself a disservice, but also the Divine." I would add that in not owning our gifts, we are also depriving our community.

In indigenous societies, it is generally considered important for a person to develop his gifts, not just for himself, but so he can help the tribe (Marshall, 2002). Imagine if a hunter thought, "I should not shoot straight, in case others think I am showing off." The tribe would suffer. Walking our golden path and using our gifts to benefit others brings us peace and fulfilment.

A Story: "The Stonemason."

A stonemason was building a large church. As he worked,
he would sometimes find himself doing unusual things, such

as putting a stone in an odd place and carving an elaborate scene. Then, he would wonder how and why he did such things. People were moved by his skill, which he attributed to acting out of instinct. Then, the stonemason realised that God must be directing his actions because he was building a church. He was so humbled and grateful to be used as a tool for the Divine, that he paid more attention to these instincts and his work became exemplary.

Occasionally, he became disappointed with his work, and felt as if he took one step forward and two back. He was consoled, though, knowing that every day was an opportunity to apply and improve his craft. He became obsessed with creating more and more miracles with his hands. When a rich lord came from another land and asked the stonemason to build a mansion, he refused, saying he had to finish the church.

Eventually, the stonemason finished his masterpiece. As he laid the final stone, he felt happy and fulfilled. That night, God claimed his life. The stonemason died full of joy. With his hands, he had manifested God's love, and many people celebrated mass and learned about God in the church that the stonemason built.

In our life, we each have a purpose: to create God's love on Earth. This is not an easy task. First, we must discover our gifts and understand how to use them, and then, we must learn the art of surrender. When we work in alignment with our life's purpose, a sacred fire is lit within us and shows us the way for love to flow. The fire burns us from the inside until it consumes our whole being. The fire also rages against our conditioning, so at the end all that is left is happiness and contentment. There is nothing more for us to do, to deliver, or to hope for. Our work is complete, like the stonemason's church.

Sometimes, people seeing my level of joy and happiness assume that I have never had a difficult moment in life. At times, I have experienced painful challenges, and some situations, I would not want to relive—but each has made me who I am today. However, as in the story above, I have worked hard to learn the art of happiness, surrender to and embrace my path. Happiness became a state of mind, that does not have to do with the outside world. Happiness is developed through spiritual attunement to a higher understanding, which I share with you in this book.

I received a valuable lesson about just what it takes to step onto and claim one's path when I, with two friends, went though a sweat lodge apprenticeship. (A sweat lodge is ceremonial sweating in nature. It is designed as a place of sensory deprivation. In darkness and heat, we are given the opportunity to purify and cleanse the body and transcend the mind through ritual and prayer).

When we arrived at the site to begin our three solo lodges, a storm unleashed. The torrential rains hampered our efforts to light the fire. (In the fire, we heat the rocks that provide the warmth for the ceremonial sweating.) After many attempts, we managed to light the fire with our last piece of dry newspaper. The storm raged all day and night. Yet, none of us complained or stepped back. We each did our job: pouring the lodge, keeping the door, fetching wood and tending the fire. Having started at 8 a.m. the day before, we finished at 3 a.m. Our hearts were moving us and we had a task to do: to support each other and ourselves.

We can pray all we want to spirit. They are around us all the time. But we also have to show up, face our challenges, and claim our path. My deep sense of loyalty to my friends and community was the gift I relied on most. I said to myself, "Keep trying to kindle the fire, Fotoula. Do not give up. Do not let yourself and anyone down. If you are meant to go through this storm to become a water pourer so be it. Accept the challenge."

Accepting Others' Gifts. As we accept our own gifts, we can choose to release any judgments we hold towards others. If we judge another because of jealousy, insecurity, antipathy, a need to blame, then we are projecting negativity towards the other person. On the other hand, discernment is helpful, when our intuition is telling us that another person may cause us harm. I once met a woman who wanted to befriend me. My guides asked me not to give her my phone number. I did not know why, I merely had a feeling this stranger was not good for me. Later, I discovered she was a gossip and attention-seeker. My intuition had forewarned me. So, discernment is not negative, but judgement is. Had I blamed her and projected negative feelings towards her, this would be judgement.

Our conditioning can keep us from seeing the gifts others bring us. We may discriminate against someone because of her accent, her clothes, her occupation, or a myriad of other reasons, and as a result, miss learning opportunities. As we walk a spiritual path, we become more open. We realise we can learn something from everyone. We value everyone's contribution to the world, recognising we are all one.

One evening, I was walking in Sauchiehall Street, a busy Glasgow thoroughfare. Outside a music shop, a man in dishevelled clothes sat on the ground. He was quiet and had a little plate to collect alms from passers-by. I looked more closely and realised the man was an angel. He radiated immense light towards everyone who walked by. Most passed, unaware of his angelic presence. I placed a pound coin on his plate. He looked up at me and smiled. He could see I knew he was an angel. His gift was to shower everyone in the city with light, no matter who they were. The angel, with his act of unconditional service, was showing me something about myself. In my mind, I heard him ask me, "Would you have given me money if I was a devil?" "No," I admitted. My compassion had been conditional, whilst the angel offered light to all.

Summary

Souls incarnate and choose the predicaments they will face to gain perspective, to purify karma, or both. Our belief systems, emotions, and karma create the events of our life, and we choose how we will react. Our choices dictate how easy or difficult our life will be. Material wealth does not guarantee that our inner world will be equally rich. Happiness and contentment come through regular spiritual practice, which allows us to quiet the mind and develop the gifts our soul has brought to this incarnation. This creates an inner drive that places us firmly on our life path and opens us to see more clearly the gifts that others bring to us. We do not walk this path alone. Connecting with Divine Consciousness creates an inner bridge for attaining grace, happiness, and longstanding peace. This is the ultimate gift of life, realising the beauty of being love on Earth.

Exercises: Being the Vessel of Divine Love on Earth

In spirit form, we are aware that we are an aspect of Divine Love. In choosing physical life, the soul knows it will forget its origin as a being of light. Reuniting with the Divine flame within and manifesting the unique gifts of our soul, we heal both ourselves and the collective consciousness.

Exercise 1:
Meditation Practice to Unite with the Divine

This exercise is designed to help us experience the light of the Creator—the light that we are. You will need a representation of the Divine (optional), and materials to create your altar.

There are two stages in this exercise. First, we come into alignment and acknowledge our own power as a co-creator of the universe, the incarnated Divinity. Second, by surrendering our will to the Divine will, we open up to our life path, the reason we have incarnated.

Create sacred space and an altar with the four elements and other objects that have meaning for you (chapter 9, exercise). Place your representation of the Divine on the altar (optional). Then lie down with your head at the altar, or sit in front of it. Ask for the purest light to surround you and your altar. Ask that the light from the altar, the power of the Divine, be transferred into your body. If you have chosen to work with a representation of the Divine, feel that energy encompassing you and flowing into your body.

Stay in this space for a while, letting the presence of Divine Consciousness surround you and flow through you. If you become emotional, do not worry. Let the energy of any emotions arise and move through you in this safe place. Speak aloud all that is in your heart, including anything that stops you from embracing the Divine.

Then, imagine the flame of a candle appearing above your crown. This is the light of your Divine spirit. Intend to become the flame that shines in the darkness, become your own higher power. You are the power of the Divine Light.

You are a powerful being. Breathe out, and on the outbreath, if you wish, surrender to the Creator of all life, pledging to do her work for the highest good. As you surrender to the light of the world, dedicate your life to your soul's purpose.

Slowly bring yourself back from this meditation by becoming aware of your surroundings. Thank your spirit guides and helpers and the Divine presence and ask that they close, seal, and protect you and the space before they leave.

Exercise 2:
Visualisation to Connect with your Gifts

Create sacred space by calling your guides and teachers of the light to help you and wait until you feel their presence. (See overshadowing, chapter 9.) Create your altar (optional). Intend that you experience the gifts of your heart and integrate them into your everyday life. Imagine a door, open or shut, in front of your heart. See the door opening fully. Inside the door, lies an immense treasure—gold and jewels of many colours. The treasure has been kept inside your heart for a long time, gathering dust. Imagine rubbing the grime off and polishing the gold and jewels to a brilliant shine. Commit to show off the beauty of this treasure.

Imagine selecting one jewel, and look deeply into it. What does it represent to you? Let one word arise in your mind. The shining jewel symbolises your gift to the world. Put the jewel on a chain around your neck for all to see. Intend that this gift will manifest in your life. Whisper this gift to yourself a few times, and imagine the jewel becoming more radiant each time. As you use your gift, its brilliance increases.

Slowly bring yourself back from the visualisation by becoming aware of your breathing and your surroundings, and close sacred space. Give thanks to your guides and teachers of the light, and ask that they protect and seal you and the space before they go.

Suggestion: In the beginning, connect with the jewel every day, by imagining it hanging around your neck and becoming brighter as you whisper to yourself the gift it represents. In time, the jewel will grow so bright that it becomes one with your own brilliance. You are the jewel and the treasure manifested in human form.

A Kind Heart

A boy walked the streets.
He had nowhere to go.
In this grim world he thought he was alone.

Everyone seemed to want something from him.
The boy was suspicious,
looking for a motive behind every action.

A man called to him.
The boy turned around and looked at the man.
The man was smiling, but the boy was alert.

What do you want? He called
in a slightly aggressive tone.
So the man knew he was no pushover.

You dropped a penny, said the man
smiling to the boy.
The boy opened his hand and took it, knowing he had dropped nothing.

All day he wandered the streets.
Why did the man give him the stupid penny?
Part of him wished he hadn't.

His mind was shouting that it was right to take the penny,
so what if it wasn't his in the first place?
It is not as if the streets of London are paved in gold.

But there was also an awkward feeling,
reminding him of the smiling man,
so trusting, offering him the money, rather than taking it for himself.

Where did the penny come from?
Maybe whoever lost it had no use for it.
Otherwise they would have guarded their change.

The mind was making assumptions,
talking of a rich man who lost his penny because he had plenty.
Maybe the man who smiled at him also had an easy life.

The voice of the heart repeating, it was not his to take.
The boy got angry, shouting for the heart to shut up.
To stop talking, for he had enough.

For many years he had wandered the streets,
ran away from home to find another cruel world
with its rules of the jungle; the death of vulnerability.

He had come to believe this was life,
a hostile place where he had to fight like an animal,
with no mercy, for no one received any.

For a long time he had not cried,
but looking at the penny, this he did.
Sobbing for the first time in many years.

He thought of going back to find the man,
wandering to the same spot,
but nobody knew anything.

He wanted to throw the precious penny in the gutter.
To never see it again, it was too much trouble,
throw it away, like he had thrown away his life.

He made a choice to give the penny away.
To someone more needy,
for he could manage by himself.

A boy from the gutter
found an old lady singing with a crackling voice,
asking for pennies.

He went to her and offered her his own,
the old lady gave him a toothless smile.
She took the money and was gone.

The boy cried again,
the second time in many years.
What he had done, opened his heart.

He knew now he could choose another path,
Why did that man give him this blessed penny, he wondered.
The man was life's angel walking beside him.

16

Other Lives, Other Stories, One Light

Spiritual Lesson 16: As I track past and future lives, I heal myself in the present reality

Into the body: Wendy massages my feet and Pam my third eye simultaneously, so that I can be easily regressed into a past life. I find myself standing inside the portal of time and space, the place between lives. Soon, I will go through it into another life to meet a different version of myself.

In this place in-between lives, I pause. It is here that souls come to recuperate and review their life on Earth. The lords of karma encourage me onwards. I step through the portal. My voice changes and I become an Indian guru. Fascinated, Wendy asks me questions about my life, and I answer her with spiritual teachings that I did not know I possessed. Time passes, and I continue to speak. Pam takes me to the moment of death, and I see my body being swept away by the river Ganges. People are crying and mourning and I cannot understand why. I cannot imagine anything more preposterous. I am so alive, more so than I have ever been. I am going home.

THE DIFFERENT THEATRES OF LIFE

Part III's chapter sixteen "Other Lives, Other Stories, One Light" collapses the soul's timetable of the journey through different incarnations. It presents our connection to the Divine as fundamental to our interrelatedness with all beings across time and space. Past life regression is a dominant theme of this chapter.

Returning to chapter ten's metaphor of actors in infinite simultaneous plays in different drawers of a large bureau, I suggest that past, present, and future are illusory, and therefore, our lives and relationships also transcend time and place.

For example, what if the Romans never created their empire and Julius Caesar died as an infant? Different reality. Different outcome. Different play. Each possible scenario manifests a parallel world. Collectively, within these parallel worlds, souls play out their roles and are unaware they may be cast in multiple roles in different theatres of life simultaneously. An illustration of this hypothesis is explored by Paul Auster's novel "4 3 2 1", (2017).

In the Earth reality, we experience time as linear. For instance, we view the past as something that has already taken place and is fixed. This is part of the illusion of life on Earth. Time is true for the play we are in, the drawer of our reality. Time provides a crucial framework for the adventure of life on the planet. We believe past life, current life, and future life, and the spirit time in-between progress sequentially. This is not so, time is only an illusion of the physical world.

From the vantage point outside the chest of drawers, anyone soul's journey is beyond time and space. The spirits have shown me that a soul incarnates into multiple timescales of the Earth story. A soul may experience a life now, a life in ancient Rome, and another life in what we would call the future—each at the same time. Now. In the present. The possibilities and numbers of simultaneous incarnations are endless. The soul chooses its experiences, depending on its karma and its intentions.

Likewise, our current life has an infinite number of possible scenes. My friend Jamie told me how he regretted the many missed opportunities for growth in his life. When the doors life had opened for him appeared, Jamie was distracted and chose not to walk through. Then one night, a few days after we spoke, he had a psychic experience. He was visited by another part of himself who lived in a parallel reality. In this reality, his other self had taken all the opportunities that had come to Jamie and was enjoying a more affluent lifestyle.

In each life, there is a single golden path—the dream script for every actor in every drawer. On this optimal path towards self-realisation, we live in accordance with our life purpose throughout our lifetime. We follow our blueprint, and no parallel lives are created. However, in every life, there are many opportunities for us to realign with our blueprint—no matter how far off course we have gone. Nevertheless, as our life has a limited span, at some point all opportunities are exhausted.

Although it is a great joy to walk the golden path, it is also a brave and unconventional choice. By following our blueprint, life asks us to keep walking through our doubts and fears, trust our intuition and inner guidance, review our beliefs, and heal our ego shadow. This is everything the social conditioning tells us to avoid.

Each parallel life offers its own gifts. A soul may choose many different circumstances in the theatre of life through which it can experience the gift of awareness. The soul gains wisdom about itself from everything that it encounters. However, at some point, rather than living in endless life dramas, the soul may achieve inner contentment and seek to fully realise itself once more as a being of light.

The golden path opens the doors of the heart. Our vulnerability becomes our strength, and our true self is unmasked for all to see. Happiness arrives through shedding the layers of the conditioning, accepting ourselves, and rediscovering our own nature of unconditional love.

THE FUTURE HAS PASSED

In 2006, when I received my channeled guidance from my spirit helpers, ISIS said that my life had already been lived. What they installed in my body had already happened, even if I was still to experience it. When I pray for something, I often hear her voice telling me it has already taken place—even though to me, it is the future.

ISIS also showed me that this was not the first time I had walked this current life. In another play, due to its lack of awareness, humanity had destroyed itself in the twenty-first century and irrevocably harmed the planet. This had repercussions in the wider cosmos. The beings of light are giving us a second chance. They have changed some of the parameters of the play, for example by inviting spiritually advanced souls to incarnate. These souls are aware of our interconnection with the Earth and all life, and are actively seeking to protect the environment. At the same time, the light beings are bringing more spiritual energy into the Earth through transmissions and planetary alignments, giving us more opportunities to wake up from the illusion of the base consciousness and walk the collective golden path.

REINCARNATION

All lives take place at the same time, as in the analogy of the chest of drawers with all plays happening simultaneously. However, in our human experience, time is a critical factor for understanding life. In explaining incarnation and reincarnation, I have gone back to the lenses of the human world and the concept of time.

Incarnation is the act of the soul assuming a material body to experience physical life on Earth. Reincarnation is a hypothesis that following biological death, the soul starts a new life in a different physical body. Some scientists studied this phenomenon extensively by interviewing young children who still remember their past lives. Dr Tucker's (2009) explanation of reincarnation is based on quantum physics: He argues that consciousness is an energy or quantum at sub-atomic level, contained in the physical body but not part of it. At death, consciousness removes itself from the body and finds its way into another body.

After souls pass, they remain in the spiritual realms for varying amounts of time, although they do not experience the passing of time. They may then return to Earth, reincarnating in the same drawer or a different one. Sometimes, a soul returns to the same family unit, as a different family member, due to unfinished business. Forgiveness and love can heal karmic ties and release parties from sharing other lives in different roles.

My client Jennifer had lost her infant brother in a tragic accident. During our healing session, I was approached by a spirit being, who was bound in chains. The spirit said that he was Jennifer's brother and could not move on because he was tethered by the family karma. He asked for help. Jennifer performed a two-day Tibetan Bön karma purification ritual called "Dutri-Su Drib-Jong" to purify her brother's karma, and the whole family contributed offerings. A few months later, my client fell pregnant. During the pregnancy, Jennifer had a dream in which she was told by the soul of her deceased brother, that it was coming back as her daughter, the baby she was carrying. The soul was returning to the family as an act of gratitude. Freed from the family karma by the ceremony that everyone contributed to, the soul had chosen to return and share its love with the family. My client welcomed the gift of a beautiful, healthy, baby girl. The child is loved and has brought joy to everyone. Coincidentally, old grudges and petty jealousies amongst family members have disappeared. It is as if this soul's reincarnation has healed deeper issues within the family.

Other times, a soul may be able to choose a completely different life experience in another part of the world and never come into contact with its former family. One day, I was with my friend Carol, and her mother's spirit appeared. The spirit was radiating a beautiful, silver white light. When the mother died, Carol had performed a Bön practice called "Sur-ngo" for the smooth transference of her consciousness. The advanced spiritual practice helped purify her mother's karma. She was now shining the light of her spiritual nature. A lama had helped her mother's soul reincarnate into a place where she could learn spiritual wisdom. She was now living in New Zealand, and had no previous family karma to resolve, so Carol would not meet her in this new life.

In contrast to family relationships such as Carol's and her late mother's, we sometimes meet a stranger and experience déjà vu. We feel an instant recognition, either positive or negative, depending on the circumstances of our prior encounter. We may feel good in a place we have never been to, or distraught at the idea of going there. Memories may arise of events in another lifetime. People who are not open to these concepts may dismiss these visions as their imagination.

In 2011, I took an early morning flight from Glasgow to London. As I sat down, I felt an immediate outpouring of love for the man seated next to me. I could see he felt it, too. We were both surprised as we had never met before. We shared no sexual attraction, only a deep feeling of unconditional love. I closed my eyes and fell into a semi-sleep. The man made room for me, inviting me to lean against his shoulder, as the love continued to flow between us. We never met again. Our souls exchanged all they needed through the flow of love on the flight. I recognised we knew each other from a different life. My spiritual guide ISIS confirmed this. Our souls wanted to meet in this life and had orchestrated the rendezvous.

Past Life Regression

After town planning, I took a university post-graduate course in clinical hypnosis, which also covered the topic of past life regression. The module was included because people under hypnosis can spontaneously go into a past life. The person's unconscious mind connects with a past life situation where an unhealthy behavioural pattern may have originated. Usually, the soul has arranged this look back so it can heal.

In my practice, most people who wish to experience a past life regression do so out of curiosity, rather than an intention to heal a deep issue. However, if someone goes into a past life with the intention of bringing gifts and awareness to her current life, it can create a major shift within her.

This was the case for Sylvia who was feeling unhappy and unfulfilled in her life although she enjoyed a high standard of living. During a past life regression, she visited a life where she was immensely wealthy and lived in a grand, stately home in Europe. In that past life, she had made compromises to her happiness in order to retain her wealth. Sylvia decided that she did not want to waste her current life attaching to material comforts and relinquishing happiness. She recognised that clinging to wealth had been a distraction, which hindered her soul's journey and life purpose. The understanding gave her the strength to leave her unfulfilling job in her current life and claim her own life path.

In a different past life regression, Sylvia became aware of the reason she used to overeat. She saw herself as a lowly servant girl, collecting leftover crumbs from under the table, after the family had eaten. What a contrast to the wealthy matron, who lived in a grand estate. My guides showed her that a soul experiences both sides of the coin. We have the opportunity to learn different lessons from each life as well as rebalance our karma.

Past Life Soul Retrieval Therapy

Frailties of a past life can recur in a present life, and each is treatable. A soul part traumatised in a past life can be reunited in its present life, by a process I developed, called "past life soul retrieval." A physical injury suffered in a past life can present in a later life. Healing is possible by past life regression therapy. We can even change the course of a past life, and rewrite its trajectory.

Retrieving a Soul Part Stuck in a Past Life. After graduating as a clinical hypnotherapist, I worked in a small therapeutic centre in Glasgow, offering past life regression. After the regression, a few people reported still feeling stuck in the past life, even though they were trying to bring an end to what had happened. As I reflected on this, my shamanic training provided the answer. These people had lost part of their soul essence in the other life and needed to be reunited with it. This insight was confirmed on a spiritual pilgrimage to Nepal.

In Nepal, I visited Buddhist temples and monasteries. In one of the temples, there were many western people. We were all asked to sit at the back, as the monks would soon be commencing their daily *puja* (worship). I was sitting next to a middle-aged man named Charlie, who was becoming quite agitated, unsure if he should stay or go. Eventually, he decided to stay for the ceremony. As soon as the monks began chanting, Charlie felt sick. His whole body shook, and he burst out crying. I helped him leave the shrine room, and we sat outside on the steps of the temple. Charlie apologised profusely for taking me away from the ceremony, and did not understand his strong reaction.

My guides showed me that in another life, Charlie had lived in this monastery. His mother had taken him at age five, and left him there to become a Buddhist monk. His family believed this was a great honour, but Charlie felt abandoned and was devastated. Despite the monks' kindness, Charlie remained traumatised by the separation from his family and suffered a massive soul loss. Charlie died two years later. I told Charlie what I had been shown. As I was relaying the information about this life, Charlie felt goose bumps run up and down his spine and somehow knew the account to be true.

I then asked Charlie to close his eyes and ask for the soul part left in the temple from that life, to return. I felt the soul's energy return to Charlie's body. When the soul part came back, he immediately felt a charge in his body and began to relax. Soon, Charlie was happy again, and we both went back into the temple. He was now at peace and able to enjoy the rest of the puja.

This was not only a healing for Charlie, but also a profound lesson for me. For some people, knowing what has happened in another life is not enough. Therefore, I incorporated soul retrieval into my past life regression sessions. As a result, clients are able to sever ties with other lives and gain a sense of inner freedom by incorporating and welcoming home lost soul parts (chapter 5). I called these sessions "past life soul retrieval therapy."

221

Curing an Illness from a Past Life. We can carry a physical condition from another life into our current life. For instance, if we die of a heart condition, our energy body carries the physical illness and if the energy body is not healed in the spiritual realms, the heart condition could be taken into the next incarnation.

One evening in 2007, I was lying in bed with swollen ankles and giving myself a healing. For two years, my ankles would swell, especially during air travel. Even on a short domestic flight, I had to wear broad comfortable shoes to accommodate my feet.

During the healing, I had a vision of a past life. I was walking along a country lane and someone ran me over with his horse and cart. The wheels went over my feet and ankles. I then saw myself lying in my cottage, being attended to by a wise woman. Behind the woman, I saw my spirit guide ISIS channelling healing energy through the woman into my ankles. At the same time, I could feel the energy in my physical body in the present life. In a few hours, the swelling had disappeared. Now I am rarely troubled with swelling ankles, even though I travel frequently. I thanked ISIS for my healing.

Sometimes, healing conditions through past life regression is not simply a matter of healing the body. In most cases, there is a karmic reason for the illness (chapter 3). ISIS explained that through my healing work and personal development, I had purified the karma relating to my ankles, and through the grace of spirit, I could be healed. I learned a beautiful lesson, which has helped me facilitate karma purification for clients. Sometimes, past life karma keeps us stuck, especially if we do not wish to acknowledge our part in its creation and blame other people or life. Similar physical conditions and events may keep appearing until we stop and take notice.

Rewriting a Past Life. Magdalene had come to me for past life regression therapy. She was having trouble forming a meaningful relationship in her current life, having only attracted men who were disrespectful towards her. Even her father and brothers viewed her as subservient and treated her with contempt. In each of the past lives Magdalene went into, she experienced the same issue: she gave away her power to a man who treated her badly. In one life, her husband murdered her. After visiting her past lives, Magdalene could see her pattern of not standing up for herself. She was caught in the belief of needing a strong man, rather than the joy of a relationship based on equality and mutual respect. During the sessions, Magdalene forgave herself and the other

222

people involved and retrieved her lost soul parts from the past lives and her current life.

As Magdalene released herself from the unhealthy pattern, Archangel Michael appeared in the room. The archangel, who is one of my spirit helpers, asked me to call in the light of Grace and, through the archangel's guidance, change the ending of one of Magdalene's past lives. In my mind's eye I was being shown a different outcome to the past life, by the archangel, and I asked Magdalene to visualise it, too, based on my narrative. Soon, she was immersed in the visualisation and started describing the scenes herself, rather than me prompting her. In the visualisation, she was transported to India in the early nineteenth century. Magdalene now saw herself in a meaningful relationship with a man who loved her. She no longer felt subservient. Their beautiful partnership lasted until the end of her "past" life.

After Magdalene left, I asked Archangel Michael, "How is it possible to change a life that has already happened?" The archangel reaffirmed: "It is possible through the light of Divine Grace. You live all these lives simultaneously." What we consider a past life is happening now in another world, another drawer, in the chest of possibilities. A soul comes to Earth to gain awareness through its experiences. A script is written and the players take their positions in the theatre of life. However, the archangel said, "God can change the script, even for those lives we think we have already lived." The script is always open to rewrites.

HEALING OTHER LIVES THROUGH THE DIVINE MOTHER

Each of us may have the opportunity to experience multiple lives, unique situations of joy and sorrow, bliss and adversity. The fourth-century BC Taoist master Chang Tzû describes life as ten thousand joys and ten thousand sorrows (Bernhard, 2013). There are circumstances in every life where we can lose our soul essence, get stuck, and accumulate physical and emotional conditions, as well as situations where we have the chance to heal. My spiritual helpers have shown me how soul healing can take place through immersing ourselves in the pure energy of unconditional love. The exercise at the end of this chapter invokes the Divine Mother energy to help you on your healing journey.

The milk of the Divine Mother is offered to everyone, unconditionally. Her love embraces the world. Some early cultures , such as Celtic (Goddess Bridget), Hindu (Kamadhenu Devi), and Native American (White Buffalo Calf Woman) symbolised the Divine Mother as a cow who gives her milk and body to feed the people—asking nothing in return (Neumann, 2015). The ancient Egyptians called her "Hathor, the cosmic Mother," who nurtures her children with the milk of love and wisdom.

Unconditional love makes deep healing possible. We may wander from lifetime to lifetime, lost in the conditioned mind, making and obeying rules that restrict the heart. As a result, we become alienated from our Divine nature and find it hard to give and receive love. We confuse love with sex. We confuse Divine love with religion. Unconditional love is beyond sex and religion. It is the ultimate expression of human nature, the opening of the heart unbounded by any limitation.

In 2011, in Egypt, I visited a small temple in the west bank of Luxor, part of the artisans village. The temple is dedicated to Hathor. The carvings on its walls depict a woman with one breast exposed, out of which life energy flows to all. I facilitated a ceremony in the temple, and we left in awe—filled with the nurturing love of the Divine Mother.

Hathor's milk is the love that reminds us who we are. Her words to me were: "Those who are nurtured by my milk wake up, for my milk feeds the soul. I'm here to share the wisdom of unconditional love, though few have the courage to find it within them. I am the Living Gate of Love; the Gate of Awareness."

OUR RADIANT LIGHT CAN NEVER BE DIMMED

It is a spiritual paradox. Even though we may lose part of our soul in another life, carry over physical conditions due to past life trauma, and become stuck in behaviour patterns that span many life times, our authentic soul essence can never be harmed, diminished, or altered. It always is the perfect expression of the Divine within.

Shamans can journey to high dimensional realities, known collectively as the "upper world" in order to re-experience their soul essence and realign with their golden path for this life and all other incarnations that are taking place simultaneously in the different drawers. Through such a journey, they touch their primordial nature, which is pristine, untainted by life, karma, and trauma.

I was invited by the Dundee branch of the Theosophical Society in Scotland to give a lecture on shamanism and lead a workshop. My spirit helpers asked me to take the participants on a journey to the upper world. We travelled through the tree of life, climbing upwards through its trunk and branches. Shamanically, the tree of life connects all worlds and dimensions. We climbed past the sky, the stars, and the universes. We found ourselves in a golden room in an ethereal world, where all our spirit helpers had gathered. Each person in the circle had their own unique experience of their soul essence. I describe my own journey below. (Sometimes, my spirit helpers enable me to journey as well as lead the participants. I am then in two places at once. Other times, I do not journey and maintain awareness on behalf of each participant.)

My helpers had gathered in a circle, and asked me to step into the centre. I was invited to see myself beyond the body. Slowly, my body dissolved till only my soul remained. My soul took on a luminous form—like a jewel radiating light everywhere. The helpers invited my soul to shine its light to the cosmos, touching everything. I stayed in this space for a while, being the shining jewel. As I was radiating light, my life was being realigned, readjusting itself to its golden path. Just as it was time to come back from the journey, I saw the jewel that was me drop from the sky into my physical body that was drumming. I felt physically the weight of the jewel coming into my heart.

The light of the soul had been obscured by life's struggles and the cycle of reincarnation. After the journey, I invited participants to connect with their own light, their own radiating jewel, and imagine their soul shining brightly inside their body. I asked them to visualise inside their heart the light of one hundred thousand suns—each radiating simultaneously to every cell and organ of their body, and outside to the world.

No matter what happens to us in our lives and in our parallel realities, our luminosity and radiance always is. Constant. Unchanging. It is concealed by the physical body, but we can lift the veils and unmask it.

SUMMARY

In the Earth reality, we experience time as linear and our different life experiences as sequential. This is part of the illusion of life. We live parallel, past, present, and future lives simultaneously. We may meet people on our journey whom we knew in different incarnations. We may relive circumstances similar to those from other lives, until we gain awareness and address the issue. Past life regression can be a useful healing tool to bring back the wisdom and understanding from another life. Sometimes, we leave a part of ourselves in another life or carry physical conditions from one life to another. These, too, can be remedied. The journey through lifetimes is about the opening of the heart, learning about ourselves and awakening from the conditioning into our inner radiance.

EXERCISE: A HEALING FOR ALL YOUR INCARNATIONS THROUGH THE DIVINE MOTHER'S LOVE

In this practice, you heal through unconditional love from the Divine Mother, known as "Hathor" by the ancient Egyptians. You can rest from the journey of lifetimes in the Divine Mother's nurturing embrace.

Start by creating sacred space and inviting your spirit helpers of the light and the Divine Mother. Then, set your intention to go to the Divine Mother and surrender to the beauty of unconditional love. Follow the visualisation below:

Imagine you are in ancient Egypt, during a festival of light. Dressed in their best clothes, people have gathered to receive the love from Hathor, the Divine Mother. People are singing and dancing, and placing offerings of fruits and flowers outside the temple. After the ceremony, everyone will share the food, the abundance from the Earth, that will be blessed by Hathor's love.

As you approach the temple, the general excitement subdues. You hear female voices inside the courtyard singing an ancient chant. You smell the sweet perfume of frankincense, myrrh, white lotus and other essential oils wafting towards you.

You join the line to go inside the temple, behind the women, men, and children who have already gathered to receive the love of the Mother. Some of the children run around, until summoned by a parent to return to the line. Everyone accepts the children's playfulness and welcomes them. The adults know that the children still live in a state of unconditional love, the gift they are here to receive. The children are the living image of Hathor.

Your turn has come. A priestess offers you rosewater from a jug to wash your hands, face, and feet. You are carrying a white lotus flower, an offering to Hathor. The flower symbolises the purity and innocence of unconditional love. You make a commitment to receive and give love, to heal deeply and surrender to love.

As you pass through the courtyard, the chanting and incense cleanse you from any heavy energies you may be carrying. The harmonious chants speak to your soul. Allow the burdens from all your lifetimes to fall away. You do not need to carry them anymore. You can leave them at the door permanently, or pick them up as you come out. It is your choice.

You now enter the inner sanctum. The place is open to everyone today during the festival of light. The scent of lotus permeates the air, from the flowers that adorn the room and the oil burners in each corner. Everything speaks of the beauty of the heart, symbolised by the white lotus. The flower's splendour rises out of the murkiness of the swamp of life and greets the moon as it illuminates the night. (The white lotus only opens at night.)

In front of you stands the carving of the Mother, her exposed breasts are offered for all to drink the nectar of wisdom. As you approach the carving, you realise she is no longer a picture on the wall. The Mother is standing before you with outstretched arms, welcoming you. Go to her to receive her love that is beyond anything that you have experienced in your earthly life. Allow yourself to be nurtured by Hathor's milk and be initiated into the wisdom of the heart.

Stay in the Mother's embrace for as long as you wish. The Mother will always be with you in all your lifetimes. Invite her into your current life. Say to her that you offer her your heart, perfect and pure as well as hurt and closed by the conditioning. Ask her to help you be her emanation on this Earth, a being of love and light, as you were when born.

When you are ready to leave the temple, give thanks to the Mother and slowly turn back. Walk outside into the courtyard. You have given your offering to the Mother and now the priestess puts a garland of white lotuses around your neck. No matter if you are a man or a woman in this life, you are now transformed into Hathor, the power of love.

Slowly come back from the journey, becoming aware of your body and the surroundings of the room. Give thanks to Hathor and the helping spirits for all you received. Release your spirit helpers, asking them to protect and seal you and the space before they go.

Suggestion: Take time to rest and nurture yourself after the healing. May your first act of Divine love, be an act of love towards yourself.

Into the Light

I jump into the world and back into light.
I venture to Earth, being reborn into light.

What am I but a being of light?
In my human form I do not remember who I am.

I remember who I have been,
And can see what I have become, caught in the illusion.

And so it is meant to be.
Embracing my spiritual reality, I gain awareness.

Who am I but the light of God?
Who am I but a sun of the Universe?

This my soul must know
and creates many pathways of learning.

I meet people who help me.
They are another side of myself, another incarnation of the same essence.

I drink the water of the river of Lethe,
caught in the amnesia of the physical world.

I open my eyes into the unknown
trapped in the web of life, I cannot see beyond it.

Grandmother spider continues spinning and holds me stuck,
until I see I am the weaver and the web my own creation.

17

Earth: The Great Experiment

Spiritual Lesson 17: In the Earth school, I first lose and then find myself.
Clearing the heaviness from my cells, I shine the Divine light within

Into the body: I wake up in a dream, in a pharaonic tomb. I stand on the stone floor, looking at scenes on the walls from the ancient Egyptian Book of the Dead: Book of Coming Forth by Day. In one of the scenes, a woman holds a large, white feather in her hand. She is Ma'at, the personification of justice. She will ascertain what lies in my heart. I become aware of the continuous journey of reincarnation, many lives and many experiences. My spirit has been everything that I could imagine: a tree, a bird, a human being. During this last life, I had immense wealth and power. Did I use it wisely? Enclosed in the golden cage I created, did I care about the people I was responsible for? I thought I did. "Not so," said Ma'at. The only thing I cared about was filling this tomb with treasure, so that I could live comfortably in the afterlife. I recite the negative confessions to prove that I had been a moral man. Ma'at asks my heart to speak, and my heart denounces me. My heart talks about all the times I silenced it so that I could continue to live in the same way: all the times I selfishly looked after myself, my life, rather than take care of others; the times I sent soldiers to war and condemned those who opposed me. My heart denounces me with no pity, spelling out every incident I would rather forget.

Honouring All Life

On Earth, each soul can take any form: a plant, a stone, an animal, an insect, a fish, a human being. Although each life form has the same essence—that is, Divine Consciousness, all forms have their own advantages and drawbacks and different lessons to teach us. One of the main advantages of incarnating as a human being is our potential to advance at soul level due to our capacity to self-reflect, develop self-awareness and address our karma through spiritual practice (Ramachandran, 2012). At the same time, the conditioned mind, which can be so strong in humans, can take a soul deeper into separation through its attachment to pride and greed at the expense of selflessness, generosity, and loving kindness.

As a species, we arrogantly impose our dominance over all other life-forms. We cut down forests, drill into mountains, and put animals in cages. Despite our technology, our emotional intelligence is often primitive (Goleman, 1996). We do not realise that everything that exists is alive and has the same consciousness as us.

Plants, for instance, have the ability to communicate in their own way (Rajkotwala, 2017). In chapter twelve, I wrote about how I discovered, in my first vision quest, that all life forms had a spirit and a voice. Unlike humans, the natural world is aware of its interconnectedness through the web of life. However, their way of communication is intuitive and telepathic.

At the same time, a soul incarnating as an animal, may sometimes advance beyond a soul in a human form, for example by offering its life in service such as a guide dog or through the unconditional love of a pet. When I was a teenager, our family dog, a brown cocker spaniel we named "Hera," was an incarnated angel. She showed me her authentic light and how she came into my life to help me cope with the difficult teenage years. When I was sad or stressed, Hera always knew intuitively and would bang my bedroom door with her tail and come in and cheer me up. When I moved away from Greece to study in Paris and she could no longer be with me, Hera developed an illness and died, as her job in the physical world was complete. However, she stayed around me in spirit. The first time I sat in a psychic circle, in 2005, a woman saw a brown cocker spaniel with a big tail around me.

Most beings take different forms eventually. Our karma determines how our present life and other lives manifest. In the next life, we could be another human being, an animal, or fish. When I facilitate past life regressions, clients often remember lives where they were an insect, a tree, or a wild animal. Due to my psychic awareness, I have seen farm animals that had previous lives as human beings. I once looked into the eyes of a cow and understood that it was a man in its former life. This soul had reincarnated as a cow due to heavy karma from a past life.

It is wise to honour all life forms and treat everything with respect, rather than regard them as subservient, as objects to be used, or even separate from ourselves. Native American people consider animals and plants as brothers and sisters, attesting to the interconnectedness of all life forms. Buddhist philosophy instructs: revere every being as if it was your mother. The farm animals that we can be so cruel to, may have been a relative or even ourself in another life (Wangyal, 2002). By harming or mistreating another being, we cause harm to ourselves; we are all interrelated. The suffering we create— to the Earth, each other, animals, and plants, we blindly take on as karma for ourselves.

Cycles of Learning

When we incarnate, we can quickly forget who we are and all that we learned in other lives. Consequently, we have to consciously learn the physical and communication skills we will need for this new life with its particular life form. All these skills we will forget again. Regardless of our being, we come to this Earth school to learn wisdom, and we do not forget wisdom. We can take the pearls of wisdom we gather with us into our different lives. Wisdom is the light that shines through us.

All circumstances are learning opportunities. We learn through times of joy and times of sorrow. We learn from our mistakes, such as the child who burns a finger by touching a hot plate. We learn that our mindful and heartfelt choices lead to happiness. Other times, we are stubborn and do the same thing over and over until the pain is too much; we eventually try another tact.

Collectively, we also learn through joy and suffering. Our collective consciousness manifests what happens in the world globally. As a society, if we live in our egoic mind, we may manifest war, famine, disease, and other unhealthy situations. In ancient Sparta, mothers gave shields to their warrior sons, and said, "May you come back victorious bearing your shield, or may this shield carry your dead body home." This is how they were raised to behave towards their sons in time of war. This is what their social conditioning dictated, that they were proud of their sons being soldiers and going into battle. I wonder how many of them still believed in this principle when their son's body was brought back on his shield.

DIVINE JUSTICE: THE RULE OF MA'AT

Incarnation on Earth is a quest for harmony at an individual level and a collective level. When, as a society, we create disharmony, destruction follows. Empires fall. Sometimes, nature will manifest destruction to warn us or shake us up. A world that is based on unfairness, injustice, and misuse of the Earth's resources cannot be sustained. In time, such a world will always collapse; it does not have firm foundations. The only skilful way of being is to live globally in fairness, with respect for each other and all life, recognising we are all one.

The ancient Egyptians knew that we are all interconnected, sharing the same Divine Consciousness. In order to prosper, they sought to live according to the "rule of Ma'at" (Divine Justice). From the pharaoh to the peasant, everyone endeavoured to live according to the rule of Ma'at: respecting everything and harming nothing. The aim was to have an open heart, to be love in the world. Ma'at was personified as a woman with a white feather. After death, if the soul's heart was heavier than the feather, due to the karma accrued during its life, the rule of Ma'at had been broken. Corruption was the enemy of Ma'at and identified as a malevolent snake that first bites the hand that feeds it and then bites everyone else. The belief was that if Ma'at was not adhered to, chaos (known as "Set") would prevail.

The only way we can exit this cycle of suffering at a global level is through the elevation of our collective consciousness. Through spiritual practice, we develop a higher thinking that enables us to realise the futility of the reckless pursuit of power and the damage of the competitive nature of our world (Lorenz, 1989). In this endeavour of creation of global harmony, we all have our own unique gifts to contribute. This is the next state of human evolution, the Homo Spiritus, who exchanges the search for materialism with a spiritual perspective, living though the inner light of the heart. Through spiritual development and the growing of our inner wisdom, we can create a different way of being—individually and then, collectively.

The collective is made by all of us. We all have opportunities to live wisely, fairly, and responsibly; our choices influence the whole.

Applied Spirituality

In the West, an increasing number of us are questioning and changing the way we live, from materialism to mindful living. This is creating the possibility of a shift in the collective consciousness, towards the application of compassionate spirituality in everyday life. According to Roof (2003), this subtle change towards a personal spiritual wellbeing, which is outside religion, is evidenced by the spiritual influence in self-help groups, motivational trainings of corporations and businesses, hospitals and medical schools, as well as in social sciences. In Australia, for instance, the spiritual practices of mindfulness and meditation are slowly being introduced into education as a way to calm and relax children, build compassion and empathy for others, and reduce stress (Hobby & Jenkins, 2014).

The light is always stronger than the dark. The dark only exists when the light is hidden. When more of us feed our light instead of hiding it, the darkness and suffering of our world will recede. This is what is happening now in Earth's history.

At the same time, we live in cultures highly addicted to a certain way of operating, and many people cannot see any reason for change. Rather than judging those around us who may have a different perspective, it may be better to teach through example. Rather than attempting to convert others, it may be better to inspire them.

Anthony was pursuing a spiritual path and came to me for advice. He was passionate about his path. He had tried to convert his family and friends to his way of thinking, and was rebuffed. My guides gave him a message. They showed me a vision of Jesus sitting by a riverbank. He was just sitting, not preaching to anyone. People passed by and then would look back, awed by the man's inner radiance. Some stopped to ask him a question and sit by his feet. Jesus never raised his voice or said to anyone they must follow him. People were attracted by his light and the goodness of his heart.

By developing our inner light, we can show other people the benefits of a spiritual approach to life. Sometimes after a workshop, people have come to me, inspired by the radiance, and said, "I want to have the spiritual light that you have." I say, "We all have this light. We are all the same Divine Consciousness. But some of us choose to work to unmask our radiance by practicing and applying spirituality in every part of life."

If we wish to change the world, we can start with ourselves, doing our own inner work to develop our awareness and wisdom. Our personal journey to expand, strengthen, and grow our inner light can influence events globally.

THE DARK HELPS US KNOW THE LIGHT

The Earth school is a place of duality. Just as there is a benevolent force that works for the light creating goodness, a dark malevolent force also exists. Sometimes, souls are caught in this dark side. They may have had many incarnations where they misused power and tried to control others. Maybe they exercised black magic or teamed with malevolent spirits (chapter 9). Rather than working for the highest good of all, they chose to follow a path of the dark.

Sometimes, experiencing the dark is a conscious choice at soul level, prior to incarnation. In a meditation, my spiritual guide ISIS showed me the different gates of awareness that souls go through before enlightenment. At one of these gates, just prior to enlightenment, some spiritually advanced souls choose to forgo enlightenment to experience the darkness, the evil side of spirituality.

A soul may decide to work for the dark, to further realise the value of the gifts of the light and to gain a greater understanding of the allure and power of the dark. It is a noble choice that should not be condemned even if it is at great personal cost and causes suffering in the world. It is another path towards enlightenment. I have met people who have travelled this path before coming to an inner realisation to return to the light. They are spiritually gifted people who had chosen to experience the dark, and became trapped by it. They spent many incarnations in suffering until they found a way out to embrace the light once again.

The darkness is a snare. Black magic leaves traces in the etheric body that are carried over lifetimes. People who work with malevolent spirits that appeal to their ego, keep some of that evil force in their body. In addition, these spirits are not willing to release these people easily. I once did a series of healings for a client who had experienced several lives in the darkness. In one of these lives, she saw how the dark had ensnared her. After death, rather than going to the spiritual realms, her soul was taken into a dark realm by the entity. It could not escape. In this healing, my guide, ISIS, manifested in the past life. Immediately, all the dark entities fled and the soul was completely recovered and healed. The light of unconditional love of the Divine Mother is stronger than the darkness.

The light beings will not interfere in someone's life, unless they have the person's permission or that of her higher self. They will not manipulate, make promises to lure people into doing their bidding, or cause hurt to save others. However, the dark does not adhere to the same ethical code.

AN ALTERNATIVE CREATION STORY

ISIS has revealed to me how, long ago, she and other beings of light known as the "Council of Nine" created the conditions for physical life to be birthed on Earth.

First Phase: Testing Incarnation. In this first phase, Earth was populated by souls incarnating as different species to experience a physical adventure.

These first incarnating souls had tall, flexible bodies, and possessed many physical and spiritual gifts. Their bodies were lighter and more ethereal than ours. They could run, fly, and swim underwater great distances. They were telepathic and could communicate with every form of material life as well as the spiritual realms. They were advanced beings and relished the experience of physical form. They lived on universal energy, prana. Having experienced life, they left the Earth realm through the same inter-dimensional portal that allowed them to enter.

Second Phase: The Great Experiment. In time, the Council of Nine created an Earth school to help souls advance spiritually through what they called the "great experiment." Universal laws governing all life were introduced, such as the law of karma, the law of grace, and the law of free will. These laws were explained to all the beings that wished to take part in the experiment.

Twelve Star Systems, where life existed in different forms, decided to take part in the great experiment. There is also a thirteenth community of advanced spiritual beings, the angelic realm of the light. They are the helpers of the light, who look after all incarnated beings on Earth. The angelic beings work mostly from the ethereal realms, but some incarnate in various forms, including animals, like my dog Hera. They may also temporarily appear as human beings, to help us, like the beggar in chapter fifteen. However, not all of the angelic beings have been able to withstand the temptations of the Earth realm and some have been lured by the dark, like other souls, learning a karmic lesson through sorrow.

During this second phase, the world slowly began to change. Despite their advanced nature, souls became emotionally attached to the physical reality and found it increasingly difficult to sustain their high states of consciousness. Consequently, their vibration lowered and their attributes and abilities diminished. These souls gradually became earthbound.

The Council of Nine told the earthbound souls that they had to remain on the planet and work together in their communities, taking more classes in the Earth school to raise their collective consciousness and ascend to a higher Earth reality. Some communities achieved this, but most failed. When I visited ancient Mayan sites in Guatemala, I was shown that these communities had ascended into a higher dimension of the Earth reality. They live in a world parallel to our own and enjoy an Earth school of higher consciousness, with no pollution, war, or conflict.

As well as these higher Earth realities, inhabited by beings of evolved consciousness, lower vibrational Earth realities also exist (these are not the same as the lower and upper shamanic worlds I describe in chapter nine). These parallel worlds can, however, be visited by shamans through "journeying." The shaman's helping spirits may show the shaman a higher vibrational Earth reality, as this may be where they reside. Mythical creatures such as unicorns and dragons may also be found here. For the shaman, these higher realities could be places of healing, learning, and realisation of the possibility that exists for our own planet. The lower Earth realities are places of suffering, where a shaman may go to help souls understand their predicament.

The earthbound souls became trapped because they lost their ability to live in their heart. Some of the souls became arrogant, argumentative, and attached to desire, and tried to control others. Others became fearful. During a shamanic journey my guides showed me a scene where one of these earthbound souls felt compelled to kill another because he was frightened of him. When he did this, I saw him falling into an even lower vibration and losing his inherent spiritual gifts.

The light beings who were observing their creation had not expected these changes. The Earth was designed to be the most lush and beautiful of planets, filled with different environments, a true Garden of Eden. Yet, rather than being joyous in this place, the souls who occupied it were becoming increasingly unhappy through losing their heart connection. In an effort to help them, the light beings invented the death process, taking the souls into a spiritual realm where they could review their life without the limitations of the physical body.

If the existence of the planet was in jeopardy, the Council of Nine would step in and rescue the Earth, in whatever way it deemed appropriate. Since the beginning of the great experiment, our world has been destroyed four times due to the lowering of the collective consciousness caused by the attachment to the ego, competition, and separation from the heart. An example of global destruction is the great flood, recorded in many traditions, including the story of Noah in the Bible. Each subsequent world has been of a lower vibration, of lower light, than its predecessor.

SUMMARY

In the beginning of the Earth experiment, a beautiful planet was created to help souls experience physical life. All the beings who volunteered to live here carry the same Divine Consciousness and may choose to incarnate in different forms. From all the possible life forms, a human being is uniquely placed to raise his awareness through spiritual practice. However, after thousands of years of existence, we have forgotten that we are one with all life. In our current global environmental crisis, we are being asked to find the way back into our heart and to realise that we are not separate from, or more important, than any other life form. Only by adopting a new paradigm based on love and mutual respect, can we create harmony in ourselves and avoid further destruction.

EXERCISE: ACTIVATION – THE GOD PARTICLE

When we see ourselves as separate from other forms of life, we put our egoic mind and pride above love and wisdom. However, we are all the One Being, Divine Consciousness incarnating in a multitude of forms to gain awareness of itself. When we hurt someone, we hurt ourselves.

In this exercise, which consists of two parts, we first experience God's essence in ourselves and all life. We acknowledge and experience the Divine essence of all that resides on Earth, starting from the four elements and moving to different life forms. This is a way to energetically reunite with the Divine nature of all life.

Stage 1:
Alignment – The God Particle Manifesting in Earthly Life

As in all of the exercises in this book, start by creating your sacred space and welcoming your spirit guides. Set the intention to reunite with your Divine nature of Oneness.

Then imagine a bowl of water. Focus on the tiniest drop of water. Inside the drop of water, focus on a water molecule, the smallest particle of water. Now focus on the God particle within this. You may not know what that is, but ask to become the God particle of water. Part of you is water anyway. Notice how you feel being the God particle of water.

Repeat the exercise with the other three elements that make physical life: the air, lava/fire, and soil (earth). Each time, become the God particle of the element and notice how that feels.

Now repeat the exercise with a plant, and then with an animal of your choice. Notice how becoming the God particle of a plant and an animal feels.

Then bring your attention to yourself and to a tiny part of your skin. Focus on a molecule within that tiniest part of your skin. Ask to feel your own God particle. Consciously stay in this state of being the God particle, the Divine essence.

Being the God particle, radiate your light to the world. As you do so, become aware of the God particle in everything. As you radiate your light, all these other God particles radiate to you. Give and receive this Divine Light.

Stay in this space for a short while (ten to fifteen minutes). Then come back gently, becoming aware of your body and the room around you.

Close the sacred space, thanking your spirit guides and teachers of the light and asking that they seal and protect you and your room before they go.

Suggestion: Once you master this exercise, you can move to Stage 2.

Stage 2:
Activation – The God Particle in Our Star Seed

As part of the great experiment, the Twelve Star Systems agreed to bring their gifts to the Earth. However, through the process of incarnation, we have forgotten who we are and where we come from. Consequently, the gifts have also been forgotten. The gifts lie dormant within us until we reconnect to our star heritage.

Inside our etheric self, lies the star seed, the memory and gifts from our star system of origin.

Through the activation of the star seed within us, we open ourselves to be, once more, the ambassadors of our star worlds on Earth. We bring forward the energies and gifts of our star system, enriching life on the planet. When we know that we are part of a much bigger family within the universe, we can see ourselves as the honoured guests on Earth.

We thus fulfil an ancient contract between our soul, our star system of origin and the beings who invited us here. This also encourages other beings from our soul family to activate their own star seed, and embody their gifts.

In some people, a single activation may be life changing. ISIS showed me how my star seed was activated the first time I went inside the Great Pyramid. However, for some other people, I have found this is not always so. They may have to do more work to purify their karma and connect with their Divine nature, and go through multiple activations.

To connect with the God Particle in your star system of origin, create sacred space and welcome your spirit guides. Set the intention to reunite with your own Divine nature and activate your star seed.

Ask your guides and teachers of the light to take you back to your star system of origin, the time before you incarnated on Earth. You may find yourself looking at a star, planet, black hole, comet, or another celestial body you may have an affinity with. Visualise this place and engage all your senses in perceiving it.

Now ask to feel the God particle of that place and ask it to align with the God particle in you. Through this transmission, an alignment takes place between your vibration and the celestial body.

As you align to this celestial body, a light vibration is entering your body. This download of energy is enriching you and the Earth.

Become a vessel for this energy to flow to all. Staying in a quite place, intend for the energy to radiate from you to all beings. Stay in this space for a short while (ten to fifteen minutes).

Come back gently, becoming aware of your body and the room around you. Close the sacred space, thanking your spirit guides and teachers of the light and asking that they seal and protect you and your room before they go.

Suggestion: My guides have asked me to share this meditation to help you in this journey towards the activation of the star seed. In itself, the practice is very powerful. After I shared it in a meditation group, I realised that both the participants and I were astounded and slightly dazed from the high vibrations that were flowing through us.

This can be a single experience, or a practice you may wish to revisit. Each time you practice the two stages of this exercise, you dive deeper into your own Divine nature.

This is an important step in activating the star seed. A further activation can take place in sacred sites of high vibration. These sites were purposefully constructed by the ancestors as places where the universal energies could be harnessed and concentrated, as in the Great Pyramid, stone circles, and other prehistoric sites.

The Fall from Grace

People talk of a cruel God
who seeks vengeance,
to punish the children of man
who have forgotten him.

A God who raised the seas above the land,
who obliterated the sun,
who kept the winds unearthing all that was there before.
A God, who many times destroyed humanity.

This God, I ask you,
how can we look upon him?
He caused much suffering and
darkness to descend upon the Earth.

No, it was never us.
We humans are but the victims of God's wrath.
We forget how many times we killed each other and ourselves;
how we exploited the Earth for our own purposes.

The animals we locked in tiny cages,
feeding them their own flesh for our profits.
The Earth we polluted with poison,
caring not for the species that live on it.

Some of us enslaved others.
Brother killing brother
in the name of the same God.
This insane world we created.

We said we were the masters of nature,
the masters of others and the masters of ourselves.
In the day of reckoning,
waves engulfed everything.

Yet we did not die.
Just wiped the board clean,
to start again playing the same game.
Over thousands of years, nothing has changed.

We are still destroying the Earth,
killing the animals, hurting each other and ourselves.
Is it God's fault we choose to live in this way?
He has given us a paradise; we turned it into hell.

18

Lessons from the Fall of Atlantis for the Current World Situation

Spiritual Lesson 18: Humanity begins life in the garden of Oneness. Separation is the fall from Grace

Into the body: It is 2005, and I am attending a lecture about Atlantis in the Glasgow Royal Concert Hall. Over five hundred people are here to listen to a presentation on the mysterious world that preceded ours. The speaker discusses research that may reveal a lost continent. In the afternoon, we are encouraged to close our eyes and visualise what life in Atlantis may have been like. I shut my eyes and see myself in a lift. The door opens and I walk onto a cobbled street. I am in Atlantis. I know instantly I lived there. I remember the city layout. I see the temple where I used to work and the symbols projected onto the floor by the coloured crystals and glass ceiling. But then something happens. I find myself surrounded by water, in a river, and I surrender myself to the flow. Now I am in Egypt, and as I step out of the Nile, I see the golden top of a pyramid.

Traces of the utopian, golden time of Atlantis, survive in the collective memory. Through the veil of time, we can access a world reality that existed before our own. This society has much to teach us about our times and the direction we are taking.

243

Atlantis was conceived as a spiritual school for the souls who wished to evolve. It started its existence as a Garden of Eden. It was destroyed due to megalomania, ego, and unskilful use of technology. In its heyday, the Atlantis school taught respect for all life, that every being was connected to each other forming the one ecosystem. At the time of the fall, people's focus was on themselves and the group they belonged to. Separation between the "masters" and the "inferior" others led to the fall of that world.

Today, as in Atlantis, we are ruining our world, planet Earth, with our unsustainable lifestyle and greed. Believing ourselves to be the superior species, we are bound in a cycle of abuse and destruction. How can we find the door of the heart, the way back to full realisation?

Education: The School of Atlantis

According to Plato, as stated in his Socratic dialogues of Timaeus and Critias, written in 360 BC, Atlantis consisted of a group of islands in the Atlantic Ocean, with the main island being a vast mass of land, situated opposite the straits of Gibraltar (Gill, 2017).

Unlike the preceding worlds described in chapter seventeen, the denizens of Atlantis were less mature incarnated souls. A council of enlightened beings created a spiritual school in order to help the less spiritually aware inhabitants.

Most germane for our purposes about the legend of Atlantis is what led to its downfall. For hundreds of years, the School of Atlantis thrived. Faculty and students were fully engaged in the process of spiritual development and ceremonial practice. The students achieved a certain level of realisation before progressing to higher degrees of learning and perhaps to the running of the country, which was based on the principle of "enlightened government"; the wise Atlantean council of spiritual teachers were responsible for formulating and applying government policy.

At some point, the younger and less spiritually mature people rebelled against those who advocated a spiritual path. These defectors saw the process of spiritual engagement as tiresome and pointless, as enlightenment was not guaranteed. Instead, material wealth and status became their priority.

Coinciding with the resistance of some students towards spiritual education, the council of learned women and men was becoming increasingly distant from its young charges. They considered that by living close to less advanced souls their vibration would lower and they would lose some of their spiritual gifts and higher realisations. This would compromise the purity of their teachings. Consequently, they moved to isolated mountain temples to keep their energy pure.

The discontent that started within the spiritual school rippled throughout the community. Some young students, especially men, became disgruntled with the council's ceremonies and rituals. They did not understand the value of an enlightened government, especially one that ruled from afar. The Atlantean defectors argued that the government of Atlantis should be in their control, and the council should limit its purview to spirituality. For example, the defectors knew of rich lands that existed outside of Atlantis and wanted to conquer them and use their resources to make their lives more comfortable, with little regard to the indigenous people who inhabited them. Yet, in the government led by the council, a high priest could only consider such decisions, and this office took many years of learning and dedication. The students felt blocked by their elders, in their aggressive expansionist plans.

At first, the renegade ideas were condemned by the majority. Eventually, an individual, gifted in the art of public speaking and mass manipulation, changed the course of Atlantis. He lied and said that he had been divinely inspired to lead the people of Atlantis, the students, who were the majority. He also gave his followers privileges that were normally reserved for those who had achieved a high level of inner realisation. For instance, he wore a particular blue stone on his third eye, signifying the degree of divinely inspired, an office of the higher Atlantean council. He gave his followers a red stone called the "hands of God," which was another form of recognition. Neither he, nor his followers, had earned these degrees. Instead, he was stroking his ego and the ego of others, enticing people to follow him and sell their soul for a stone.

The renegade demanded the council step away from governance and adopt the secondary role of safeguarding the Divine connection of Atlantis. He told the council this was the wish of the people, who now had their own enlightened priesthood, comprising himself and his followers, to guide them.

The Atlantean council considered the petition and despite the audacity of its content, accepted it as the peoples' wish. The Council of Nine, the beings of light that created the circumstances for life on Earth, knew this was a mistake. The Atlantean council would be walking away from its responsibility to look after the people. The Council of Nine argued with the Atlantean council against relinquishing responsibility of governance to the students, but eventually accepted its decision since non-acceptance would interfere with the free will of incarnating souls.

The Atlantean council eventually became so marginalised that many of its members decided to leave the planet. However, this was not as straightforward as before. Even though they had kept themselves separate, to safeguard their vibration, by renouncing their responsibilities to the Atlantean people, the teachers had created karma that would have to be purified. Thus, through their decision, they entered the cycle of samsara: birth, death, and reincarnation. Previously, they had enjoyed an increased life span and were able to transform their bodies into rainbow light and ascend from the Earth realm, rather than relinquishing their body in the death process. Now, they too found themselves aging and unable to access the spiritual gift of ascension.

Some Atlantean teachers willingly chose to remain with the people. They had psychically seen the future destruction of Atlantis through a great flood and stayed to help. Prior to the flood they prepared sacred places in remote mountain ranges and in Egypt, as refuges for the surviving souls.

DOMINANCE: ATLANTIS, A SUPERPOWER

In the meantime, in the hands of the immature souls, the students who now had political power, Atlantis became a superpower. They misused the high-level technology, based on crystal energy, to colonise the lands of other people, exploiting their natural resources and enslaving the populations. These Atlanteans considered themselves the master race and regarded everyone else as inferior, primitive and uncivilised. They altered the DNA of the people under their rule, thus lowering the etheric light of the entire Earth. The Earth's vibration and frequency of light is a reflection of our collective spiritual understanding. When we live in harmony with each other, aligned with the rule of Ma'at, the energy of the Earth is of a higher resonance. The opposite is true at times of chaos.

The Atlanteans also placed energetic implants into people to manifest fear and anger and lower the general population's state of consciousness. These implants were small devices, like microchips, that influenced people's thoughts and emotions. The implants also affected their hosts' etheric body, which is an exact copy of the physical body, but made of energy. Although the implants no longer exist in our physical bodies, the memory of them still lives within some people today, who had been subjected to them in a past life in Atlantis. Through past life regression with a practitioner, we may return to the time when the implants were inserted in our body, and through an extraction process, remove the energy of these intrusions.

For example, my client Sheila was suffering from postpartum depression, also known as "baby blues." For over twenty-five years, she had found no relief from her condition. Past life regression was a major breakthrough for her. During our session, Sheila witnessed an implant being inserted into the right side of her brain in a previous life in Atlantis. My spirit guides and I were then able to remove it from her etheric body. The next day, Sheila phoned to tell me that she could not remember feeling so good.

These implants' discordant energies are still influencing the collective consciousness, having been unconsciously kept alive by the collective. In addition to past life regression, spiritual practice can neutralise their affect on individuals. To self-heal, I asked one of my guides, Archangel Michael, to cut the connection between my brain and the ancient machine that emitted discordant energies to the implant. I then saw in my mind's eye, the archangel using his sword of luminous light to sever the connection. He then placed a protective veil of golden light around my brain, and I am no longer affected by these energies.

RETRIBUTION: THE GREAT FLOOD

The myth of the great deluge that covered the entire Earth for several days is common in many cultures around the world. The bible, ancient Greek myths, Peruvian stories, Sanskrit teachings, and other ancient traditions present vivid accounts of the flood that ended the previous phase of human civilisation on Earth (Hancock, 2015).

What caused the deluge and how did the previous civilisation end up at the bottom of the sea? Eventually, the more aggressive Atlanteans engaged in a massive war with other Atlanteans who had fled with some of the council to what would later become Athens, Greece. The aggressive Atlanteans could not tolerate this division, branding those that left as traitors who had to be brought to justice. But the leader of this group was an advanced soul. Athena, a High Priestess named after the personification of Divine wisdom, knew how to thwart the power of the degenerate Atlanteans. She raised the sword against them, defending the city that would bear her name afterwards and saved its people from slavery. Plato gives an account about this war in the dialogue of Timaeus.

Atlantis was defeated and the Athenians decided to take over the main island to destroy the harmful technology. The surviving Atlanteans, tried to use the machinery to create chaos in the minds of the Athenians. The plan backfired. The forces they engaged caused a volcanic explosion, which sank the island and unleashed a global tsunami.

Not many survived the ensuing flood. And few places were unaffected—among them, the mountain ranges of the Himalayas and the Andes and Egypt. Eventually, members of the Atlantean council—now known as the "council of light"—visited these places to help survivors, who had regressed into a barbaric state, rebuild their communities. The council of light educated the remaining Earth population in the art of writing, agriculture, herbal medicine, and in places like Tibet and Egypt, in spiritual understanding.

In the case of Egypt, learning from the downfall of Atlantis, the council did not want to be isolated from the people and so, fostered a culture of spiritual study within their communities. Rather than separating themselves from the local population and retreating to mountain caves, these wise teachers lived nearby and some intermarried with the populace.

The few who were able to stay in an enlightened state ascended and are now working etherically with the Council of Nine to fulfil their commitment to humanity when Atlantis was first formed. The council's commitment to help souls on Earth ascend, created a karmic link. The Council of Nine are also bound by this karmic link to look after all the souls who take part in the Earth experiment. Our role in this karmic agreement, between us and the Council of Nine, is to awaken and to help others in our soul group awaken. We will then be able to ascend together and leave this Earth realm.

Lessons: The Karmic Consequences of Atlantis

We are still experiencing the karmic consequences of the Atlantean period. The lowering of the vibration of the Earth took place when the Atlanteans used implants and other etheric energy technology to alter people's brainwaves and their biological DNA. The original human DNA was a twelve-coded strand. This was shrunk to a single strand, and then animal DNA was introduced to create our present two-strand DNA.

Scientists have described the human DNA as the familiar two-strand double helix that is referenced in our schoolbooks. They are aware of the remaining ten strands, but many think of them as inactive and have labelled them the "junk DNA." Some alternative healers consider that the junk DNA holds information about our spiritual connection and has much to teach us about ourselves (J. R. Scogna & Scogna, 2014).

Apart from tampering with our DNA, the Atlanteans also tried to interfere with the Earth's natural rhythm and weather patterns. The abuse of energy ultimately caused the massive destruction and great flood. During the catastrophe, many souls who died suddenly were not able to pass to the light and even now remain around the Earth in lower realms of the astral plane. This has further reduced the vibration of the planet.

Prior to the flood, the immature Atlantean leaders aligned with dark powers in order to gain control. They called to the Earth discordant energies and bound themselves to dark entities and fallen angels through unskilful ceremonies involving human sacrifice and black magic. These entities and dark magicians appealed to the ego of the young, inexperienced souls. However, once these entities enter the Earth realm and a person's etheric body, it is difficult to expel them for they have their own agenda. These entities will keep attaching themselves to the same souls and their families, in other incarnations, creating a lot of damage and chaos. The short-term gains of their life in Atlantis has had grave consequences for these souls in future lifetimes. Through past life soul retrieval, karma purification and spiritual practice, healing for these souls is possible.

My spirit guides ask healing practitioners to have compassion for these souls. I was doing a past life healing for my client Dorothy, who had persistent headaches every time she tried to meditate. During the regression, Dorothy saw herself as a novice priestess in a past life in Atlantis. The high priest had persuaded her to go through the operation to have an implant in her brain. Even though she did not feel comfortable with this prospect, she naively accepted. As I was working with Dorothy, we could feel the presence of other spirits, heavy and unhappy, in the room. Dorothy identified them as the spirits of the high priest and his team. They were stuck in a lower vibration of the astral plane and asked for help. I tried to encourage them to apologise to

Dorothy, but the priests were reluctant to admit any wrongdoing.

Then, my spirit guides asked me to invite the priests to look into their own souls. The priests could see their souls were in pain, appearing shrivelled and filled with grey and black, heavy energy. They realised that the pain they had caused to others had affected them, too, at soul level. They were now kneeling in front of Dorothy, asking for forgiveness and release. Dorothy forgave the priests and released herself from the situation. Advanced spirit guides then came into the room and helped the priests move to the spiritual realms of the light where they could heal. After their departure, the healing room felt lighter. In other cases, such spirit release is not as straightforward. Some spirits do not wish to move on, choosing to hold onto their ego. The discordant beings they sold their soul to, may still have them under their control.

The Atlantean belief in race superiority and dominance of all other people and life-forms endures to this day. The Atlantean-style arrogance and resulting suffering keeps repeating. This is the personal lesson from the last world: surrender to life. Live harmoniously within ourselves, with others, and all nature.

When the council was closer to the community and led the people both spiritually and through enlightened governance, Atlantis prospered. When the council retreated to its ivory tower, due to the students' uprising and then abandoned its responsibility to the people, it forgot that the greatest gift is service to others. Thus, the collective lesson concerns the value of enlightened government. Be present. Be responsible. Serve others.

Clinical Implications: Practices to Heal Ourselves and the Collective Consciousness

Working with past life regression, as in the case above, I have found many people whose headaches and difficulties in meditating and spiritual and personal development were due to implants inserted by corrupt Atlantean priests. The reduction of our active DNA into two strands has also hindered us in our spiritual development as a species. Orientated towards separation, the animal strand continues to motivate us towards selfish behaviour, individually and collectively.

The enlightened beings have given me spiritual teachings that heal separation and gradually reveal our inherent state of Oneness. Not only do they address our spiritual DNA, but also provide a path towards reclaiming our inherent radiance.

The Path of ISIS: The Ascension Teachings of the Seven Gates of Awareness. I had a significant dream in which I was giving a lecture on the essence of God. I spoke about looking into "God's eyes" and seeing the cosmos and everything that exists, as one being. The state of Oneness is the state of the enlightened spirit. The way for us, on this planet, to reach this state is through the unconditional love of the Divine Mother.

However, our conditioned mind does not know what it means to be in a permanent state of unconditional love and live accordingly, although we may have glimpses of it. Embracing the unconditional love of the Divine Mother equips us with a powerful torch that allows us to expose and then integrate our shadow and light at ever deepening levels, until we become what we have always been: the Light of the One.

The teachings of the Divine Mother offer us access to high vibrational energies that reveal the magnificence of our inner being. These etheric energies, known in the ancient world as the "Living Light", bring healing and awareness.

This is the path of the ancient initiate of the mystery schools providing us with the tools to work on our soul's evolutionary process. This is the lost knowledge of the golden age that ISIS has reintroduced through the teachings of the Seven Gates of Awareness. These gates are energy fields within the body that, when opened, may activate an inner knowing which supports our soul's journey.

The teachings are offered by the Divine Mother through The ISIS School of Holistic Health. In 2006, ISIS and other beings of light installed, through an energy download, the ancient wisdom teachings into my body, as agreed with my higher self and purpose of incarnation. Since then, I have been channelling and teaching this high vibrational system of spiritual knowledge, which can be both life transformative and healing for some clients and students.

The ISIS Path Teachings are energy vibrations of the Living Light. However, in order to understand and experience the purity of the energy, we need structure. Therefore, the teachings are supported with meditations and chants in light language, so that we can work with different aspects of the same energy field. This allows us to increase our awareness of our world, our life, and the essence of our soul. The practices help us to grow spiritually, to open

251

our heart, access the state of the eternal spirit, and ascend into our own light.

Priestess/Priest of the Moon Ceremonies. These ceremonies, channelled from ISIS, aim to liberate us and our community from the separation that is instilled in our DNA and our world. They include moon ceremonies, a welcoming ceremony at birth, a naming rite, a releasing ceremony of the spirit at death, a marriage ceremony to our higher self, and an activation of the sacred sound and vibration of our etheric bodies, soul, and spirit.

The Twelve Rays of Divine Consciousness and DNA Activation. There are twelve Rays of Divine Consciousness, the same number as in the spiritual DNA code. Each ray is linked to a different strand of the twelve-stranded spiritual DNA. Six of the rays carry male energy (power and action), while six carry female energy (orientated towards being, stillness, and expansion). The practices associated with each of the rays strengthen our energy body and restructure our spiritual DNA. The rays are a gift, channelled from Archangel Gabriel and ISIS, enabling us to enter into higher states of consciousness and experience Oneness. (The Rays of Divine Consciousness are further explained in chapter nineteen).

It is not possible to heal our DNA and inner separation through reading books alone. The spirit guides have said that understanding can only be born within us through direct experience and spiritual practice. The above high vibrational teachings, which are the essence of the Divine light, are one way of achieving this. They have instructed me to teach these ways and share the practices, ceremonies, and tools that constitute the spiritual medicine of Oneness.

SUMMARY

Greed and corruption at a global level, and ignorance of its consequences, destroyed the world of Atlantis. A massive flood covered the Earth, recorded in many traditions, from the Quechuas in Peru to the Hebrews in the Old Testament. Despite having experienced a golden era under enlightened governance, the once great empire of Atlantis destroyed itself through its ignorance, expansionist policies, unskilful use of technology, and misuse of etheric energy. The legend of Atlantis teaches us to live in harmony and to serve others. Spiritual medicine, applied through practices, ceremonies, meditations and chants, can re-orientate us towards Oneness, at a personal and collective level.

THE HIGH PRIEST OF ATLANTIS

His knife covered in blood,
the blood of sacrifice, of the virgin on the ancient stone,
covered with symbols of darkness,
invoking an unearthly power.

Many young women had died on the black slate.
Many eyes, dilated from the drugs, had looked at him in amazement.
Many times he plunged his knife into innocent hearts.
Many words he chanted in the screeching voice of the dark spirit.

Many times he painted his hands in blood.
Covering himself with a cloak of power, fear and mystery.
Wearing the mask of the evil one.
Keeping the old order in place.

Not once did he think of his victims.
These innocent girls who gave their lives.
They were only there to serve his cause.
The cause of Atlantis, the cause of his god.

Until today, his hand never faltered,
his mind never questioned,
his heart unwavering, was never moved.
Until today, when the eyes of the girl seemed strangely familiar.

Emboldened by the unworldly chanting,
he raised his knife to take a life.
A life that never before mattered to him.
The voice of his conscience long silenced.

And the eyes, the beautiful hazel blue eyes,
the eyes that looked at him in amazement,
dilated through the drug and the poison;
the same eyes that stare back at him in the mirror.

In horror, recognition awakened inside him;
his daughter, beloved, lying on the stone,
dark magic weaving around her.
Staring at him, unable to speak.

After this sacrifice there is no more power.
No more fear and mystery, only regret.
The eyes of his girl haunting him,
bringing down the defences of his ego.

A broken man emerges.
For the first time in many years,
realising the price for power
is far too high to pay.

There is no way out of this.
No escape from the nightmare.
He can never leave, walk away, be a free man.
The price for power, far too high to pay.

19

The DNA Code and the
Rays of Divine Consciousness

*Spiritual Lesson 19: Through the Rays of Divine Consciousness, I discover
my ultimate potential, expressed by the divine sequence of the
twelve-strand DNA*

*Into the body: I scramble up the hill of Dunadd, rumoured to be the crowning
place of the ancient kings of Scotland, a place of high etheric power linked
with ley lines to the Great Pyramid. The stone-paved path is slippery from the
intermittent rain. Near the top, I fill the chalice carved in the rock with sacred
water. I place my bare foot on the hewn footprint, offering my prayers for the
land. After a while, I climb to the top: a plateau open to the elements. I lie
on the ground feeling the energy of the ancient power point streaming into my
body. I open my psychic centres and become aware of spirit people around
me. They are wearing white robes, and have long, elegant hands and bright
eyes. They talk about the golden time of Atlantis, when human life was about
celebration. They point to the sun and then to their chest. I look and see a sun
appearing inside every being. They radiate this light out, to all, including me.
"You are the sun, too," they say, "You do not know it."*

In chapter eighteen, I introduced the morality tale of Atlantis. Its rulers altered the DNA of their subjects in order to subjugate them. The genetic modifications affected people mentally and physically and lowered the Earth's vibration. Prior to the experiments, the human DNA consisted of twelve active strands, and the capacities of the human species were greater.

The Atlantean DNA Experiments

According to my spirit guides, at the time of Atlantis scientists used technology in the form of crystal energy to alter human brain waves and manipulate the DNA code of their subjects. Their goal was to mentally enslave inhabitants, creating a new race—the subservient underclass.

By tampering with the DNA, the Atlantean masters lowered their subjects' level of consciousness and increased their fertility. Subjects devolved from a higher state of inner knowing and connection to the self, the Divine, and others, to a baser state of programmed reasoning, strife for self-preservation and fear.

Genetics: The Divine Sequence

Atlantean scientists tampered with the genetic code by compressing the original, twelve-strand human DNA into a single strand. Through experimentation, they altered the DNA to the double helix that we associate with the DNA today—by using animal DNA with the compressed human strand. With each alteration, the underclass' access to the higher human abilities, linked to the awakened mind, was suppressed, and they became increasingly entrenched in the lower vibrations. Caught in the thought patterns and behaviours the scientists had literally hardwired into them, the people blindly trusted and obeyed their rulers.

This two-strand genetic code continues to limit us to a low vibrational, three-dimensional, physical reality, whereas the original, twelve-strand DNA linked everyone with their Divine Consciousness and enlightened state of mind. What today's science has branded as "junk DNA" is our ultimate potential. This potential still lies within us, but it is inactive in most people. Those who engage in meditation and spiritual practice with high vibrational energies, such as the Rays of Divine Consciousness, can gradually activate their whole DNA code. When the twelve-strand DNA is activated, we are assisted in our spiritual path. We come to understand spiritual truths at a deeper level, as if we always knew them.

Our genetically manipulated two-strand code reflects the duality that exists in our world—for instance, oneness and separation, positive and negative, light and dark. However, within the two-strand code, the twelve-strand DNA divine sequence still exists albeit in an inert state. Our DNA, even though it has been genetically manipulated, continues to carry the potential for Oneness, despite the fact that most of us are conditioned to manifest the strand of separation in our life.

Of the two, the animal DNA is the more powerful and pulls us towards separation. Our conditioned world further supports this disconnection, and it is reinforced in the media and by governments, corporations, and institutions. This world view feeds the ego mind and erodes harmony. Our inner core, though, remains aware of our interconnectedness with all living beings.

When the potential for Oneness within the DNA, is fully activated, we can experience the inner peace and wisdom enjoyed by our distant ancestors who lived on Earth before the Atlanteans. Accessing and maintaining this state requires our vigilance, as the link to fear and separation is still within us.

PHYSICAL COMPONENT: LABOUR AND CONSCRIPTION

To increase fertility and thus, the labour pool of menial workers and soldiers to fight the wars of expansion, the Atlantean scientists combined the human DNA with a monkey strand that was more aggressive and robust than the human DNA, further entrapping the new race in its baser instincts.

In contrast, the scientists and ruling masters isolated their own DNA by procreating only within their own community. The idea of a pure-blooded or blue-blooded race that we still carry in our cell memory, stems from these times.

The pre-Atlantean, original, twelve-strand DNA was characterised by low fertility. A woman could have one child or two children during her lifetime—but not more. Childbearing was seen as a precious gift and a woman's choice. There were no moral and social obligations for a woman to become a mother.

Women who chose to remain childless had roles within the community equal in importance to motherhood.

A woman who decided to conceive prepared herself spiritually for childbirth, and consciously chose a suitable partner from the community. She chose a man able to fulfil the role of a father, emotionally as well as physically. The couple would consult the star alignments to ensure that they were compatible and the time of conception was appropriate for the being incarnating. Through ritual and ceremony, similar to a wedding but without life long vows, the two people entered a sacred partnership, a sacred union to bring the child into the community. Each birth was considered a blessing and was rejoiced by all.

As well as enjoying a special relationship with their birth parents, each child was cared for by all the adults. A team of elders was also assigned to the children of the community. After the birth, the parents original "marriage" ceremony was dissolved, as the intention of the ritual was to bring a child into the world. People could choose freely to stay together or have different partners. Marriage, in the way we perceive it today, did not exist.

The Atlantean scientists' inclusion of animal DNA made multiple, successive births possible. Furthermore, each woman throughout the Atlantean kingdom, was assigned by the state to one man for life, to birth his children. She was now his property and it was an obligation to be a mother, not a choice. This increased the importance of men within the community. A man could now influence the children he sired. The more children a man had, the more privileges he was offered by the empire. The women's role was diminished to that of bearing and raising children. This was her duty in support of her man's wealth and the Atlantean empire.

The animal DNA manifested diseases within people, both men and women, as it was not fully compatible with the human body. These physical deficiencies were passed onto the children, and the life span of the new race began to decrease. The ability to regenerate and heal one's body had also been lost due to the interference with the DNA code.

In 2012, while on a spiritual pilgrimage in Sedona, Arizona, I had a vision of this era. The ancestors who lived before the Atlantean times showed me psychically, how human beings existed when the original, twelve-strand DNA was intact and fully active. The human body of these people had the ability to regenerate, which allowed a person to enjoy an average life span of 235 years. Aging still occurred, but only at the very end of life. People were aware of the subtle energy that flowed from the universe (the higher vibrations of light) and the light energy flowing from nature (through the web of life). They had developed practices to harness these energies, in order to heal their bodies and maintain their health. If they damaged their body, for example in an accident, they used these practices to self-heal.

The Atlantean empire's tinkering had several unintended consequences—disease, overpopulation, and the depletion of natural resources—that continue to plague our planet.

MENTAL COMPONENT: THE THORN OF SEPARATION

Through the Atlantean's energy manipulations, subjects were programmed to think and behave according to the will of the empire. This was a slavery of the mind. Although their rulers mistreated and exploited them, the subjects believed this was necessary for the good of the empire. They could not see that they were being used to further the objectives of a greedy elite. A residue of the Atlantean meddling is the conditioning of the mind towards fear and control we are experiencing today.

It may be difficult for us to imagine the ancient communities living on the planet pre-Atlantis, where everyone was a freethinker and moreover, was loved, valued, and lived in a state of Oneness. During a shamanic teachers' reunion in 2015, I was invited to journey into the past to meet these ancestors and ask them to share a sacred teaching that I could use to help heal myself, my clients, and the planet.

In the journey, I was taken to a camp of ancient, indigenous people. Women were cooking food over fires. A large, middle-aged woman welcomed me and said, "We all hunt together, cook together, and sing together. Every voice is valued." The feeling of unconditional love and joy that flowed from this tribe to me is indescribable. I was in tears, so touched by their love and acceptance. At the same time, I was aware of my own state of separation that prevented me from experiencing such a sense of community in my own life. A chasm seemed to exist between their state of being, orientated towards the highest good of all and Oneness, and the state of the western mind. They were wise elders to our current selfish teenage mentality.

The woman continued, "Like your contemporaries, you have been inflicted by the thorn of separation. And the thorn of separation is still stuck in your body." (Shamanically, external energies can take any form, which can then be extracted.) Another wise woman came out of one of the huts and removed the steel thorn from my right side. She said that I had to take the thorns out of my clients and students, so they can move to a higher state of consciousness. She pointed to a bucketful of thorns that I would extract from future clients.

The teaching of the thorn of separation helps us to understand the human predicament. Although we carry it in our bodies, separation, like the thorn, is not ours. It is inherited and inflicted. It is not our true nature.

RESTORING AND HEALING THE DNA WITH THE RAYS OF DIVINE CONSCIOUSNESS

We can undo the state of separation created by the Atlanteans and restore the divine sequence of Oneness using the Rays of Divine Consciousness. The rays generate energy fields within us—that promote compassion, bliss, forgiveness, and grace and take us on a profound inner journey to rediscover our true nature. At the same time, the rays show us where we hold negative karma and separation patterns, which can manifest as blocked energy in the body.

Each of the twelve Rays of Divine Consciousness is a specific field of high vibrational, etheric energy that emanates from the Divine. By immersing ourselves in these energy fields, we can foster:

a.   Awareness: increase our understanding of ourselves and the world around us by lifting the veil of the conditioning;

b.   Release from karma: reveal and purify our karma; and,

c.   Oneness: The Rays work to further activate the Divine sequence that we carry in the DNA. Each time we do the practice it take us closer to the state of Oneness that is inherent within our nature.

The keepers of the rays for our dimension are the archangelic realm of the light, specifically Archangel Gabriel and another being of light, which self-identified as the Mother and Father of the Divine Light. ISIS has said that the rays are now available to us because we are in a special time of transition, a time when more souls are looking for ways to free themselves from the heaviness of the earthly karma and the conditioning and programming. She said that our collective voice and prayer for self-realisation has gone out to the universe. The rays are one of the ways the enlightened beings have chosen to answer this prayer.

In 2012 on the spring equinox, I was gifted the Rays of Divine Consciousness teaching by Archangel Gabriel in order to help raise humanity's consciousness and restore our DNA to its full capacity and orientation towards Oneness. In Scotland, at the ancient ceremonial site of the hill of Dunadd, following the ritual described in the opening of this chapter, I became aware of a strong etheric presence around me. The presence identified itself as Archangel Gabriel.

The archangel asked me to open the crown chakra of the fellow participants through an attunement process that would link them to the first Ray of Divine Consciousness. At the time, I had no idea how to do this, but as soon as this thought entered my consciousness, I immediately became aware of the steps of the attunement. Afterwards, the archangel said that this process is related to the activation of the divine sequence, the twelve-strand DNA. A few months later, my spiritual guide ISIS gave me the meditation practice that would enable us to work consciously with the first ray. She encouraged me to practice the meditation daily.

The keepers of the rays have chosen me to be the teacher for this work. They ask that people who wish to learn to perform these ceremonies, first go through all the attunements and daily meditation practices for each of the twelve rays. The whole process takes years of dedicated, personal practice.

Since 2012, I have been meditating daily with the rays in many places—including sacred sites all over the globe; atop mountains; in deserts, ancient and modern temples, and hotel rooms; and at home. I have initiated numerous people through "the opening of the crown" attunement on the sacred site at Dunadd, during "The Rays of Divine Consciousness Retreat" that I ran in 2013 and subsequent years. During the attunement, each person feels the power coming into her body. Afterwards, I give her the meditation practice related to the ray so she can take this practice forward and work with it towards empowering her life. During the retreat, we practice the rays meditation and hold karma purification ceremonies for participants.

This way of working with high vibrational energies is profound and a gift to ourselves and the world. Each time the rays are channelled into a person's body, they also flow into the Earth, raising the vibration and consciousness of the planet and inviting everyone to work for the highest good of all beings.

Each ray brings its own fruits to the receiver, and it takes time to accumulate all the precious gifts they offer. The rays invite us to adopt a higher human expression, one of unconditional love and compassion, forgiveness, gratitude, joy, and bliss, and to see ourselves as the awakened being, the creator of all life. As we merge with these energy fields, we activate these higher qualities within us that have been dormant due to the programming of the mind. We slowly arrive at the understanding that no matter what happens in our everyday life, we are not our problems, but the one light that creates the cosmos. Archangel Gabriel has said, "What you are receiving through the rays is the essence of light."

In 2013, ISIS asked me to hold a monthly transmission of the Rays of Divine Consciousness to help lift the collective consciousness. ISIS then instructed me to invite anyone, throughout the world, who wished to receive a transmission of the rays to link with the energy. Everyone can take part in the monthly rays transmissions. One does not have to believe in the rays, Archangel Gabriel, ISIS, or the Divine, or have had the crown attunement to participate. People can still access and receive the energy. My parents were initially sceptical; however, when they realised how many people joined the transmissions and heard the benefits they accrued, they decided to try it. My parents now join every transmission.

The rays work for the highest good of all, and there is no way to know in advance what a participant in the transmission will experience. Sometimes, a participant will feel a gentle energy, whilst at other times, she may feel a strong flow of light, or even a little discomfort when the rays work on karma. Psychically, the teachers of The ISIS School are aware of a plethora of beings coming to receive this transmission: animals, plants, areas of the Earth, old and young people, beings from other planets, and babies in the womb. (For the dates of upcoming transmissions, refer to The ISIS School of Holistic Health website: http://www.theisisschoolofholistichealth.com/rays-transmissions.)

Summary

Towards the end of the Atlantean era, genetic engineering altered human brain waves and the DNA code, reducing it from its pure state of twelve strands and then combining it with animal DNA. Most of our innate, noble traits and higher abilities of Oneness were suppressed, which plunged people into a state of separation and fear. Further damage was unleashed when the scientists increased fertility. The genetic manipulation weakened the human body. The chaos and suffering caused by these interferences is still being experienced today—individually and collectively.

The original divine sequence of the twelve-strand DNA code still exists within us and can be activated through spiritual practice. The Rays of Divine Consciousness, radiating from the Divine heart into all dimensions, are powerful energy fields that awaken our dormant DNA codes, to help bring us back into a state of harmony and understanding of our true nature.

Exercise: Meditation – Experiencing the Rays of Divine Consciousness

In this practice, you bring the rays into your body to awaken your dormant potential of Oneness within the original DNA. (The monthly rays transmissions follow a similar intention. The rays retreat caters to individuals who wish to work with them consciously in meditation.)

You will need a glass of water for drinking.

Start your practice by creating sacred space: welcome your spirit guides and teachers of the light to be with you. Invite Archangel Gabriel, one of the keepers of the rays. Set your intention to experience the Rays of Divine Consciousness and a healing of your spiritual DNA. Place some water on your altar, or nearby, to drink after the practice. The water will also be imbued with the rays.

Bring yourself into a quiet, meditative state of mind, by focussing on your breath for a few minutes. Then, ask Archangel Gabriel for permission to engage in this practice. Only proceed if you receive a positive answer.

Ask Archangel Gabriel to help you experience the rays in your body, heal the separation, and ignite your potential for Oneness in your spiritual DNA. Affirm your intent to connect deeply with your primordial nature of unconditional love.

Focus your attention on the base of your spine inside the central meridian channel, where part of your vital energy resides. Imagine this as a ball of bright light. Breathe purposefully and rapidly, imagining that the in-breath engages the ball of light and the out-breath moves it higher up the central channel. Continue with this intense breathing until the ball of light moves up to your crown and then up to your eighth chakra (about a foot above your crown). If you suffer from a medical condition, proceed gently and with care and pace your breathing to suit your body.

Once your consciousness is in the eighth chakra, ask to receive the Rays of Divine Consciousness. Wait a few minutes. As the rays begin to flow through your crown, you may feel a slight pressure on the top of your head. You may also feel energy vibrations moving through you as the rays come down into your body. Imagine a line extending from your reproductive organs into the Earth, through which the energy will continue to flow to the planet during your practice. The sensations may be subtle or strong, depending on various factors such as fatigue, the condition of your energy body, and your ease with meditation practices and energy work. Over the practice, the energy may become stronger.

Meditate for at least twenty minutes and up to an hour, receiving the rays. Reaffirm your wish that your DNA heals from the state of separation into a state of wholeness. Visualise twelve strands of DNA inside your body interlinking and creating a beautiful mandala, a cyclical and colourful geometric pattern. Hold this image for a while.

Slowly come back. Breathe deeply, with the intention of bringing the ball of light from the eighth chakra back down into the base of your spine.

Finally, give thanks to Archangel Gabriel, keeper of the Rays of Divine Consciousness in our realm, for this gift to humanity and yourself. You may also wish to drink the water on the altar to help you ground, and you can offer some of the water to a river or the Earth, to share the merits of your practice with All.

Close the sacred space, thanking your spirit guides and teachers of the light and asking that they seal and protect you and your room before they go.

Advice: During this practice, you may feel the energy and power of the rays. This is not the same as having gone through the attunement of the opening of the crown. The attunement is another process altogether, which will help you connect with each ray in a much more profound way.

It is also tempting in our modern, fast-paced world to do a meditation only once, expecting miracles. The process of awakening is a journey that takes years if not lifetimes. This meditation should not be seen as a magic wand, but a regular practice.

RETURN TO SOURCE

There was a little light
floating in the universe,
looking at a world it never visited,
though it appeared beautiful.

Many lights had come together
to build what was once lost,
when the suffering had become unbearable
they joined hands to create a new Earth.

All they had to do was to join hands in a circle.
It appears so simple, so insignificant.
No machines involved, no technology.
Yet it was the most difficult undertaking.

They joined hands coming together,
hands of every colour, age and size.
A vibrant circle of black, red, yellow and white,
obliterating the darkness of thousands of years.

They built a new world;
with lights of every colour and size
and transparent bridges,
where they lived together in perfect harmony.

They only left one bit undone,
an old battlefield where nothing grew.
The smell of death and decay
that no man should choose to experience.

The old battlefield was there to remind them
what happened long ago
when the heart had been closed
and everyone felt alone.

From the sky the little light remembers
that terrible time on Earth.
Even from far in the universe
it could hear the voice of fear.

Now the Earth beings sing of love.
Joining their hands to create a massive circle,
a circle of different rainbow lights: black, red, yellow and white,
shining throughout the universe the golden radiance of their spirit.

Part IV.
The Rainbow Spirit

The snake transforms into a rainbow light, no longer bound by Earth and sky. This is our ticket to grace and the inner Garden of Eden, alongside the healing power of the sun, the psychic energy of the moon, and the benevolent influence of the distant stars. After many incarnations, lives and deaths, the soul awakens into its divinity. The monkey mind retreats to reveal the wisdom mind of the authentic Self. Touched by the Holy Spirit, the soul discovers the awakened state.

20

The Power of the Sun

Spiritual Lesson 20: I immerse myself in the sun's life force energy to discover the radiance of my spirit

The rainbow spirit: Standing on the flat roof of a house on the west bank of Luxor, Egypt, I greet the sunrise, bathing in the golden light. In the temples, the ancient ones have drawn the sun with rays that end as hands holding the ankh, the key of life. I understand this message from the old Egyptian scribes: the sun enables life on Earth. Can this being, this fire in the sky, help me with my spiritual connection?

The helping spirits say everything in nature has a spiritual side. It is the same with the sun. To manifest my spiritual light, they tell me to look to the sun for advice.

I turn to the sun once more, to ask how I can awaken into the light of my soul. On the day of the March equinox, I hear its voice. "I am the fire, the life force energy that creates the world, nurtures growth, and shines light so that you can see what is hidden and awake from the conditioned mind. Connect with me to receive these gifts and reveal your own radiance!"

The Sun Radiates the Light of Creation

Every sun in the universe is a conscious being of light that emanates energy. And every sun in the universe connects to every other sun, generating a network of life force energy, through etheric lines. The continuous radiance of the suns holds the network together.

The suns are connected to each other as well as to a single, central point—a central sun—from which all other suns are born.

The central sun is the point out of which all life manifests. In the beginning was the void, nothingness, pure Divine Consciousness. Out of the void, light first came into being—the central sun. The central sun birthed, and continues to birth and sustain, the physical world; the manifested world. Every sun in the cosmos, radiates the light of the central sun; the energy that creates and maintains the physical world.

The process of creation from light coming out of the void, or from an inert state of being to an active state of movement, is described in ancient scripture. Let there be light, out of which the world was born, says the bible (Genesis 1:3). In ancient Egyptian texts, a similar quotation exists. The creator Ra, identified as the sun, fashions the world through a divine soul that existed in an inert state. Prior to the creation, nothingness existed (Almond & Seddon, 2002). Similarly, the Toltec tradition talks about the unmanifested, formless consciousness Nagual, which gives birth to the manifested matter called "Tonal".

The sun in our solar system nurtures and sustains all life on Earth. The sun's heat makes all physical life possible. It is our own fire in the sky, our own point of creation. Ancient cultures from the Mayans, Toltecs, and Greeks to the Egyptians, Romans, Celts, and Mesopotamians, amongst others, revered the sun as a being of Divine Consciousness. I have connected psychically to many of these ancient civilisations and witnessed their rituals of connection with the sun of our solar system to harness the light of the central sun of creation.

The sun was seen as a father or grandfather, as it still is in indigenous spirituality. In ancient times, the sun was not viewed as a god in the way we may perceive god today. Our idea of god, a being outside of ourselves, far away in the sky, who is all powerful and judgemental, is based on our cultural conditioning and upbringing and is the remnant of an early, corrupted priesthood trying to control the masses.

Ancient communities realised that by connecting to the sun, they could absorb the life force energy of creation, heal their bodies, and direct the energy to the Earth to enable healthy growth, both physical and spiritual. In a daily ritual, people would turn their head towards the sun, extending their arms upwards in reverence to receive and be bathed in the etheric creative power of the sunlight. For example, "surya namaskar" (sun salutations) is a daily ritual prostration—a series of twelve movements, performed numerous times—by the Indian yogis. Swami Saraswati Satyananda explains that the sun is regarded as a powerful spiritual symbol in the ancient Vedas, helping practitioners to both purify and rejuvenate with its abundant prana–life force energy. As yogis salute the sun, they increase and ignite their internal life force and calm their conditioned mind. Sun salutations are a common opening sequence in western yoga studios (Saraswati Satyananda, 2008).

For the winter solstice 2012, I facilitated a morning ceremony in a sacred site in Scotland, which I describe in the opening of chapter 19. During our ritual, the sun appeared from behind the clouds. Psychically, I saw ancient people joining the ceremony. They were chanting and raising their hands towards the sun to bring the energy of the sun into their heart. Then, from their heart, they allowed the light to flow to all beings. I asked them to show me this practice and the chant, which I now include when I teach the Spiritual Path of ISIS course.

RITUALS TO HONOUR THE SUN

The sun's life force energy is intensified at specific times of the year, such as solstices and equinoxes. The ancients built ceremonial places to capture and further amplify the sun's energy, knowing it to be the light of creation. The etheric energy was then transferred, through ley lines, to other aligned sacred sites. One of the most well known is the Stonehenge stone circle in Wiltshire, England, which aligns to the summer solstice. The Sphinx and the Pyramids of Giza; the Fajada Butte spiral in Chaco Canyon, New Mexico; and Ahu Tongariki, Easter Island are among many such sacred sites believed to have been erected for use during the summer solstice. There are also sites aligned to the sun of the winter solstice, such as the Maeshowe Cairn in Orkney, Scotland, and the temple of Karnak in Egypt. Some of these sites also align with the sun at the equinoxes.

These sacred places act as etheric solar panels. They gather the subtle energy of the sun and direct it into the site, increasing its etheric power. At the same time, the energy flows into the Earth, raising its vibration. Meditating in these sites, especially at key dates of the year, such as during solstices and equinoxes, when the sites become more active, can help us calm our mind and align our chakras and etheric bodies with our purpose for incarnating. We may also experience an increase in perception of the invisible realms.

In some places, such as Egypt, a holy order of the sun emerged. Its members devoted their life to harnessing the solar energy for the benefit of all life and specifically, for their communities. They built temples of the sun—pyramids and sacred sites aligned to the solstices and equinoxes. Even today, during a visit to one of these sacred sites, we may be able to feel the sun's life force energy flowing into our body.

At sunrise during either solstices or equinoxes, the rays of the sun create a pathway of light into the sites. The energy remains high throughout the day, slowly reduces from dusk, and changes again to a different vibration after sunset. Although the energy of aligned sites peaks at these special times, for three days before and after, the energy is higher than usual.

In ancient times, during solstices and equinoxes, people would gather in the purposefully aligned sites, such as Stonehenge, to strengthen their vibration with the sun's energy. The rituals and ceremonies, often facilitated by the holy order of the sun, were also aimed at preparing the participants to receive the sun's light. Purifying the body and mind in different ways, for example through bathing at a spring or in herbal steam baths located in the vicinity, was a common practice prior to ceremonies. A four thousand-year-old ceremonial steam room was discovered in the Orkney Islands, known for its magnificent stone circles (Miller, 2015). Following preparatory, cleansing rites, people entered the sacred site from the early hours of the morning. They renewed their life force and gave thanks to the sun, which mirrored the light of their own essence.

Today, vast numbers of people are drawn to these ancient temples of the sun, especially at the times of the year when the energy peaks. According to conservation government body English Heritage, over 1.3 million people visited Stonehenge in 2016. What draws us to these sites? Could it be an inkling from a past life, an inner knowing that this is important, a cell memory looking for life force renewal, or simple curiosity?

THE DOWNFALL OF THE PRIESTHOOD: CORRUPTION AND GREED

In later times, as the collective consciousness became more entrenched in the conditioning, the holy order of the sun became corrupt in some cultures. In Egypt, the priesthood adopted the exclusive right to communicate with the sun being, who had been elevated to a creator god for the masses. One of the pharaohs, Akhenaten, realised that as the sun was shining for all beings, everyone was equal and able to receive its blessing directly—without the intervention of priests. The pharaoh closed most of the temples and disbanded the priesthood. After the pharaoh's mysterious death, the priesthood caste and its strictures re-emerged.

In other places in the Northern Hemisphere, the sun was transformed into a powerful male god who had to be appeased with sacrifices and substantial offerings, before giving his blessing. The Sun Temple of Apollo in Delphi, Greece, became one of the most successful financial enterprises in the classical world, by receiving fixed "donations" for hundreds of years in exchange for blessings and oracle guidance. While in Mexico, Aztec priests performed human sacrifices every fifty-two years, telling the people that without an offering of human life, the sun would stop rising. These practices and misuse of the etheric energies created a heavy karmic footprint in some of the Latin American pyramids. I advise people to invoke psychic protection if they wish to connect with them and align themselves with an earlier golden time at these sites; a time before human sacrificial practices were established.

LEY LINES

In ancient times, people were aware of the network of light, known as the "ley lines" or "dragon lines," which runs through and around the Earth. These etheric lines of power support the Earth's etheric body and the wellbeing of the planet. (Similar to a living organism, the Earth has an etheric body that protects the planet and all living beings on it.) The ley lines also support us spiritually, to connect to ourselves and open to other realms of light; mentally, to feel calmer and more content; emotionally, to open our heart and feel the love of the Divine; and physically, to heal our body.

Most of the ley lines are created by natural phenomena, such as chasms and fissures, and underground rivers and other water sources. Places where ley lines cross carry an even higher vibration. These junctions are often marked with ceremonial buildings, such as temples, churches, and cathedrals. According to some traditions, high vibration sites could be easily recognised when a specific type of animal travelled along ley lines. In Celtic lore, a horse, ox or mule identified the future location for St Mungo's tomb and the subsequent Glasgow Cathedral. When the animal stopped after walking on a straight line, the spot happened to be the crossing point of several ley lines, underground streams, and fissures. In Greek and Egyptian myths, these high energy points were identified by birds believed to be sent by the gods. Wherever the birds landed, a temple was subsequently built.

Nemetons: The Places where the Earth Breathes

Harnessing the etheric energy of the sun when standing on ley lines can be a very powerful experience. In the druidic lore, ley line crossings create power points on the Earth. These are also called "nemetons," or the places were the Earth breathes. My colleague Claudia Wolff took me to a sacred hill in Southern Germany. This hill has no temple to mark it. Claudia had found it by "accident." Yet, it is one of the most etherically powerful places on the planet. When we walked towards the etheric power point, I had a notion to take my shoes off and walk barefoot on the grass.

Unbeknownst to me, I was aligning myself with the ley lines that exist there and the power point they form. A few metres from the power point, I had an overwhelming sense of homecoming. I was so touched by the notion of being home to myself that I burst into tears. A few days later, Claudia, Fi Sutherland, and I held a ceremony of empowerment for a group of women on the same point. The energy and gifts from this power point were simply outstanding. This time, I was told to lie down with my arms outstretched, on the power point that forms, etherically, a star design. I was there for a few seconds when I felt myself expanding. I, too, was breathing with the Earth. My light soared and I was told by the spirits to sing. I had never felt my voice more powerful. I was experiencing the authentic Self, beyond the conditioning.

Harnessing the Energy of the Sun: The Omphalos Stone

Some ancients, including the Greeks and Egyptians, called the locations where numerous ley lines met the "navels of the Earth." On these spots, the energy of the sun was harnessed through the creation of a stone structure called an *omphalos* in Greek (navel). An omphalos stone is a rounded stone with a hole in the centre. It symbolises the point of creation, the light coming out of the void. The stone can hold an incredible amount of etheric energy. In ancient Greece, these stones were placed around oracle and healing centres.

Some healing practitioners create their own omphalos stone to produce a high energy point that is permanently charged by the sun and the ley line etheric network of the Earth (see second exercise below for instructions).

Healing the Collective Consciousness with Sunlight

As we step onto our spiritual path, we can turn to the sun to further ignite our awakening. The sun is a compassionate being of higher consciousness, which aids our soul during its earthly journey. Linked to the central sun, the point of creation, our sun mirrors the incredible light of our own soul—our internal sun. Thus, the sun is working with a bigger picture; radiating light to help our soul awake from the dream of the conditioning and find better ways of living. This is a process that started long ago, within the Earth experiment. In this way the sun assists us both individually and collectively.

It is no coincidence that, since the 1930s there has been a marked increase in solar activity, such as increased solar explosions and flares, radiation, sunspots and faculae (Friis-Christensen & Lassen, 1991). This is also a time when we are experiencing massive changes in our daily way of life. If we consider how our society was in the 1930s compared to our current time, we will realise that the outmoded structures of a feudal aristocratic system continue to be transformed towards a more democratic ideal that we are yet to reach.

For some, new ideas and ways of living are infused by a different type of spirituality. Practices from ancient Egyptian, Buddhist, and shamanic teachings, are re-emerging in the western world, to take us away from patriarchal dogma into an individual experience of the Divine connection in our heart. The sun is supporting this awakening of our individual and collective consciousness through explosions of solar energy, bathing the Earth in the etheric light of creation.

The beings of light who created Earth and physical life hold a picture of harmony and bliss for all beings. This utopian ideal that many of us long for can only occur in the Earth school if we wake up and understand our predicament. That is, recognise that the conditioned mind-sets and individualistic way of living have created a type of world that does not serve us at a fundamental, soul level. Our present world is based on structures that create and maintain injustice, poverty, and the abuse of power of fellow humans and other life forms, such as animals, plants, and the Earth itself. We dismiss the suffering of others, because, in our ignorance, we think what happens to someone else does not concern us. We have forgotten that, despite our separate physical bodies, we are all connected. We are the cells of the same one being. Someone else's suffering is our own. We also perpetuate our social systems by assuming that the way things are currently done is the only way our world can operate.

By increasing its activity, the sun as a conscious living being, is part of a larger awakening process that aims to show us the places where chaos exists and how unhealthy our world is. Unskilful policies and behaviours that have been hidden for a long time, are being exposed. At the same time, more people are questioning the collective way of living and feeling propelled to make changes. This shift towards conscious and mindful living can create a change in our global reality.

At some point, when enough people change their perception of our world, a critical mass will be reached, which will initiate change at a global level. However, it is important to realise that these changes need to take place peacefully, rather than through revolution and violent upheavals, which would only create more karmic debt.

Summary

The sun, the bringer of life and nurturer of all existence on Earth, is helping us awaken spiritually from the illusionary dream of the conditioned mind and reach a higher level of awareness. The ultimate goal is to create shifts in the collective consciousness and return to a state of wholeness when we, too, become conscious of our inner sun. Like the ancient races that built Stonehenge and the pyramids, we can acknowledge this Divine being and harness its creative energy through ceremony and spiritual practice, to heal ourselves and the collective.

EXERCISES: THE SUN AND THE STONE

Exercise 1:
Visualisation – Immersing Yourself in the Sun's Subtle Energy

This exercise is best practiced during the day and weather permitting, outdoors. We can harness the sun's rays and channel its energy into our body, every day of our life. It does not need to be sunny, as the sun is always present even if masked by clouds. The exercise may be especially beneficial to those who live in climates where days can be shorter and darker at certain times of the year. For example, I have found this exercise helpful for people in the west of Scotland.

Although the sun is a physical manifestation of light, its force is not solely directed to the physical bodies. All of our being—our etheric energy bodies, chakras, and inner knowing—is enhanced and strengthened by the light of the sun. Our soul rejoices in the sunlight. Awakened by the sun's rays, our soul remembers its own brilliance.

Start the exercise by creating sacred space. Take some time to acknowledge and welcome your spirit guides and teachers of the light into your room or space.

Invoke the sun, as if you are talking to a living being, asking to be filled by its energy. You can use a sacred text, such as "Ādityah-dayam," a Sanskrit hymn to the sun, your own words, or the invocation I have channelled below.

"Sun, eternal fire in the sky, being of light, I welcome you. I
see your brilliance and thank you for nurturing all physical life
on this planet, including my own. When I eat food, I eat that
which you have sustained. I eat your light. When I drink
water, I drink that which you have purified. I drink your light.
I am born on this Earth because of your light and sustained

by your light. My body and soul seek you. I ask now that the
light of creation, the life force energy you radiate to all beings,
fills every cell of my body, healing me at all levels."

Close your eyes, and imagine that the sun is radiating above your head. The rays of the sun penetrate your crown and flow down balancing and activating your third eye and down into your central channel, expanding throughout your entire meridian system. Every cell and organ in your body is filled with the rays of the sun. The sunlight flows into all your etheric bodies. Your chakras expand, opening and coming into a state of balance. Every part of your being, physical and etheric, is filled with the power of sunlight.

If you have any pain, physical or emotional, direct the sunlight to this area. Ask the sunlight to open and heal everything that is out of balance. Experience the light streaming inside you.

Let the sunlight flow inside your heart. Let the power that creates life, deeply heal and open the etheric spiritual heart centre.

Imagine that the sunlight activates the light inside your heart, your own brilliance that has lain hidden. Inside us, the light of the central sun exists. Picture radiant light streaming from your heart to all the cells in your body and to the world around you. Surrender to the flow of light inside your heart. Stay in this space for a few minutes, as your light transforms and heals everything, like a sun that creates and nurtures life.

Slowly come back from the visualisation. Give thanks to the sun for its gift of life and for reminding you that you, too, are a brilliant sun.

Thank your guides and teachers for holding sacred space during your practice. Release them, asking them to close, seal and protect you and the place before they go.

Practice 2:
Creating Your Own Omphalos Stone

An omphalos stone can be created in any place you wish to harness the energy of the sun, such as a meditation room, a peace garden, a healing sanctuary. It can be a large or small stone, but it must be permanently placed on the ground. You can erect it both inside or outside the house. In ancient Greece, the stone was either square or rounded, purposefully cut with a hole drilled manually into it. Over it, a rounded dome was placed. The circular dome can be a terracotta pot from a garden centre, which you may wish to decorate.

After you have prepared your stone and pot and chosen where you will place it, it is time to ceremoniously create your own sun temple.

Place your stone at the place you have chosen, preferably towards the east, and remove the pot so the stone is unveiled. Ask your spirit guides, teachers of the light, and ancestors who worked with the omphalos stone for the highest good, to hold a sacred space for this ceremony and guide you to create a powerful etheric field over the land.

Invite the power of the sun to come into the stone, to feed the Earth and all beings. Ask the stone to align with the sun. Feel the rays of the sun feeding the stone, like the nourishment of the mother for an embryo. The light flows into the stone and into the Earth. You may wish to rattle, sing, or just feel what is happening. The light in the stone will start to increase and radiate out. Etherically, a star form will take shape and align with the sun. At some point, you may feel the sun's transmission is complete.

There are powerful ley lines and etheric nodes all over the Earth. Ask for your omphalos to align with a ley line that will support your work. An energy line will form, connecting your stone to the ley lines network, coming from whichever direction supports you. It could be a local ley line or one from far away. Wait until you feel the energy flowing into the stone. Once this is done, place the pot over the stone.

Then give thanks to all the beings who helped you create the omphalos stone as a daily support for your work. Release your spirit helpers, asking that before they go, they seal and protect you and the space.

Suggestions: There are numerous ways you can work with your omphalos stone. You now have a charged, etheric light bulb in your sacred space, which can help you meditate, connect with yourself, charge your crystals, and aid your healing practice. Also, I would not recommend placing this stone in rooms where you socialise or sleep, unless specifically guided to do so. At key points in the year, such as solstices and equinoxes, or whenever you are guided, you can repeat this ceremony to recharge the omphalos stone with sunlight.

Hymn to the Sun

You are the light eternal,
manifested as fire in the sky.
Rising from sleep, I seek your rays,
the light of day, the light of awareness.

Life bringer, nurturer,
your warmth caresses every soul.
You touch us in different ways;
some we can see, others we do not know.

Sun in the sky, Sun in the universe,
radiant star of the day.
Abundance of heat and light;
like flowers, we turn our heads towards you.

You radiate light into the empty space,
chasing the night, clearing the mind.
Unhindered, you shine;
all darkness flees before you.

May your power find my sacred centre;
unlocking the doors of my heart.
So I can shine with you across the universes.
Overcoming the long night of my mind.

21

The Guiding Light of the Moon and the Great Cosmic Mother

Spiritual Lesson 21: The moonlight shines into my unconscious, revealing a pool of hidden wisdom and feminine power

The rainbow spirit: I offer here, my adaptation of a Celtic myth.

Three men were searching for treasure, a woman called "Moon" with hair made of silver, and thinking of the money her hair would bring them. Deep into the forest they went to look for her. After many nights, a maiden with silver hair appeared. They asked her for her hair, but she would not give it to them. "Go to my mother," she said, "for I am still young and my mother's hair shines much brighter." For fourteen days, the men walked in the forest. And then, they came across a woman who was heavily pregnant. Her hair shone so brightly that they could see her in the midst of night in the dark forest. Her hair outshone the stars in the sky. They asked her for one single hair—worth a whole treasure. "Go to my mother," she said, "for she is the lady of wisdom, to give you what you seek."

The men thought that if this woman's hair shone so brightly, her mother's would be like the sun. But, they were sorely disappointed. After another fourteen days of walking in the forest, they came across an old, smelly crone with hardly any hair. So dirty was her hair, it seemed worthless. Yet, in desperation, they asked for one of her hairs. The hag looked at them and said she would give her treasure to the one who made love to her! She looked hungrily towards the three men, spittle drooling from her lower lip, revealing the one rotten tooth she had left.

As she stepped forward, the stench overpowered two of the men. Each ran away. The third remained. Lovingly, he took the crone into his arms. He wanted to give this gift to the old lady, and kissed her mouth and sagging breasts, taking care to ignite within her the fire of longing. Making love to her was an act of kindness that turned into shared bliss. Exhausted, he fell asleep in her arms.

The next day, the man awoke in the arms of the maiden with the silver hair, the first woman the three men had found in the dark forest. Moon, seeing his confusion said, "I am the Great Cosmic Mother in triple form. I am all three women: born in the new moon, I become the maiden in the waxing moon, mother in the full moon, and crone in the waning moon, to die in the dark moon and be reborn again. My treasure, I have given you, is the light of wisdom, the light of the heart. And, I will also grant your wish for a single hair, even though it will continue to change like I do, growing brighter and dimmer and renewing itself." The man understood this was a spiritual gift and thanking Moon, he took the hair. In his life, he came to treasure the gift from Moon, for it taught him many things about himself.

THE FEMININE POWER OF THE MOON

The Celtic myth demonstrates the link among the Great Cosmic Mother, a personification of the Creator who births the world from her womb, the Divine feminine, and the moon. The Great Cosmic Mother is sometimes called the "Triple Goddess," for the three phases linked to the moon: the maiden in the waxing moon, the mother of the full moon and the crone in the waning moon.

Both the sun and moon are beings of consciousness, so old that they are often called "grandfather and grandmother" respectively, by indigenous cultures.

Unlike the sun, whose powerful light is evident for all to see, creating life through heat, the moon's light is subtle and mysterious. Whereas the sun relates to the element of fire and active transformation, the moon, with its gravitational pull, governs the element of water and evolution through its continuous cycle of birth (new moon), life (full moon), and death (dark moon).

Closer to the Earth than the sun, the moon affects its inhabitants differently and cyclically. It moves the waters, creating tides in the seas and mood swings in human beings. In many cultures, the moon is a symbol of feminine energy, whereas the sun represents the masculine.

The moon follows the Earth like a constant companion recording and witnessing all that happens on the planet and being a catalyst for change.

THE EFFECT OF THE MOON

Ancient people recognised the effect of the moon on human life, knowledge that has been systemised into what we now know as astrology. Shamanic and indigenous cultures worked in alignment with the energy of the moon, performing certain ceremonies to coincide with the moon phases. Healing modalities such as Ayurveda take cognisance of the moon's power in the different phases. Ancient religions and spiritual traditions still use a lunar, or lunisolar calendar. The Tibetan year contains either twelve or thirteen lunar months. Each month starts and ends with a new moon. All the details of the calendar are calculated on the basis of the lunar cycle (Henning, 2007).

During my 2008 travels in Nepal, I met a rinpoche of the Nyingma tradition, one of the oldest of the schools of Tibetan Buddhism. On a day with an auspicious full moon, he took us to the Swayambhunath stupa (a Buddhist sacred building), for a spiritual practice. Due to the high vibrational energy of that day's particular full moon, the benefits of our practice would be compounded by three million. So, one prayer had the effect of three million prayers. These auspicious dates, related to the moon, are noted every year in the Tibetan Buddhist calendar, so that practitioners can benefit from the high energy through meditation and spiritual practice.

Before the establishment of our western, twelve-month, solar Gregorian calendar, ancient people used to work with the energy of the moon through a lunar or lunisolar calendar. Our current calendar does not take the phases of the moon into account. In contrast, the ancient calendars used the definition of the lunar months, and some made adjustments, to create a 365-day calendar year.

Over thousands of years, people observed how the moon's energy assisted, guided, and discouraged certain activities on Earth—from the conception of a child to the sowing of seeds and the harvesting of crops. In medieval England, different moons were given names based on agricultural activities, such as the harvest moon, seed moon, flower moon, planting moon. Rudolf Steiner's system of organic farming has lunar, astral, and esoteric associations that were known to the ancient Indo-European priesthood and are still observed by indigenous cultures (Smith, 2009).

A woman's most fertile reproductive circle has the same length as a lunar cycle of 29.5 days (Cutler, Schleidt, Friedmann, Preti, & Stine, 1987). Some indigenous Native American cultures call the menstrual cycle, the "moon time."

The influence of the moon is not always positive. It is a force that needs to be harnessed and integrated. Mood swings have traditionally been blamed on the full moon. Crime in general is also higher on the full moon, according to a psychological study of criminal behaviour in metropolitan areas (Tasso & Miller, 2010).

Such traditional ideas of the moon's influence, that western logic has until recently rejected as mere superstition, are now being investigated scientifically. For example, Chakraborty (2013) suggests that there is an association between the phases of the moon, their impact on the Earth's electromagnetic field, and human reproduction, as well as mental and physical illness. The lunar gravitational force, Chakraborty concludes, impacts on human physiology, specifically the cardiovascular and autonomic neural systems.

THE FIVE PHASES OF THE MOON

Each of the five moon phases—new, waxing, full, waning, and dark—has a different quality and potential for spiritual work.

New. The new moon, a mere sliver of light in the sky, is a call for beginnings and physical action. The influence of this phase covers the time of the new moon and the following twenty-four hours. Out of the dark waters of the womb, a baby, small and vulnerable, is born. The new moon is a time to form new ideas, create positive change, and plant the seeds for new projects. It is a good time to perform ceremonies to launch a new project and take steps towards its realisation.

A baby is born fresh from spirit. Likewise, the new moon provides an opportunity to ride on a wave of expansive, positive energy. We look for ways to walk towards a new reality and away from what has kept us small and stuck in the past. Everything to do with activity, the human body, and nature, is favoured during this time.

New Moon Meditation. On the night of the new moon, we invite the moon's energy to flow into our aura and body. Focusing within, we ask the moon to energise our potential and the birth of new life. This could be a project we are already working on, or something else that the moon may wish to show us. We are open to receiving guidance from the moon about any action we need to take in the physical reality to help our baby grow.

New Moon Affirmation: "The light is borne within me."

Waxing. The waxing moon, growing in illumination, supports growth. As the energy of the new moon increases to its full phase, so does the energy of the physical body. This is the time of the maiden. The influence of this phase lasts from the day after the new moon to the day before the full moon.

Waxing Moon Meditation. During the nights of the waxing moon, we invite the moon's energy to flow into our aura and body. Focusing within, we visualise the rays of the moon touching the baby who now grows steadily into the maiden. Our projects and ideas may receive a positive boost. Our body, too, is filled with the energy. At the same time, this energy may reveal areas of imbalance. We let the light of the moon heal our physical and etheric bodies.

Waxing Moon Affirmation. "Each day, I grow into my potential."

Full. The full moon at its peak roundness and luminosity, is also at its peak energy. This is the time of the pregnant mother, abundant with life. The effect of the full moon lasts three days, the day of the full moon, the day before, and the day after.

The expansive energy of a full moon can be both positive and unsettling. It is a time for us to remain focused and abstain from alcohol and chemicals. If we are out of balance, the moon energy may trigger an accident; otherwise, it will flow through us and support and energise us.

Full Moon Rituals. There are many rituals to honour and harness the energy of the full moon. A simple way for us to take in the light of the moon is to step outside at night and ask the full moon to bless us. Witnessing the full moon change, expand, and vibrate during this practice, we may feel the light coming into the body.

Another ritual is to create moon waters; water being an element governed by the moon. Place a glass of water before you and in a meditation, slowly see the moon descending into your body through your crown, your third eye, and your throat—until it merges with your heart. You and the moon are now one. From your heart, imagine light flowing to the water. Then, imagine the moon flowing out of your body through the crown, back into the sky. You can then pour the water into a river or stream or anywhere on the land, knowing that it will flow around the Earth, bringing the healing from the moon to all. The moon influences the waters without human intervention, but the healing and wellbeing of the Earth is our job. By allying with the moon, through the power of our intention and our own light, we create radiance within us and the potential for healing of the planet.

If you are working with a specific project, you could visualise it filled with the light of the full moon.

Full Moon Affirmation: "I am the light of my heart, shining brightly over the Earth."

Waning. The waning moon, decreasing in intensity following a full moon, is a time when energy contracts, taking with it all that is unhelpful. This phase lasts around fourteen days, from the second day after the full moon to the day before the dark moon. It is characterised by the actions of surrender and release. Rather than working in the physical world, the waning moon supports everything that is an expression of our inner being. This is the time of the crone, the wise elder. Spirituality, channelling, psychic development, and artistic endeavours are generally favoured during this time.

Meditation with the Waning Moon. The veil lifts between the worlds, inviting us to go deeper within. We ask the void that is opening in the sky, to take away all that is unhelpful or unnecessary in our life. If we are working on a project, it is time to clear obstacles, either externally or within ourselves. The waning moon can free us from any unnecessary burdens, clearing our path. We can visualise the void as a dark hole sucking out what we no longer need.

Affirmation of the Waning Moon: "I surrender to the void. By letting go, I am free."

Dark. The dark moon, invisible in the sky, is the time when the void is wide open, and simultaneously, the womb is about to burst forth with new life. It is an auspicious time to honour our ancestors, those who walked before us, and whose cells gave us our body. In Celtic lore, this is the last day of the crone, who has been aging during the waning of the moon. During the dark moon, the aged crone becomes the lady of death called "Cailleach Bheur".

She walks the Earth carrying the bones of our ancestors. She places the bones in her cauldron to cleanse them of their karma, so that they can be healed and reborn with the new moon. The dark moon phase lasts twenty-four hours before the new moon appears in the sky.

Meditation with the Dark Moon. In the cave of the old crone, a fire is lit and a cauldron is bubbling with the dark waters. The crone is waiting for us. She will help us purify our ancestral karma. We give her the bones of our ancestors. We pray for their highest good. We forgive them for anything we have held against them. This is a time to make peace, whilst thanking them for the gift of life. If anyone comes to mind, we speak to the crone about our specific grievances with that person and ask that all may be settled between us. The crone may give us advice about that ancestor or our life. At the end, we pay the crone what she asks. The visualisation can be done by anyone, even one who does not know her ancestors, including an adoptee. We all carry our parental genetic makeup in our cells.

Affirmation of the Dark Moon: "Healing the past of those who came before me, I walk the path of my life."

PRIESTESSES OF THE MOON

The moon is linked with the feminine and known, in some cultures, as the "moon Goddess" or the "grandmother." Its subtle light ignites an inner treasure of intuition, psychic ability, soul knowing, and wisdom. To harness the gifts of the moon, indigenous people perform ritual and ceremony.

From 2010, for five consecutive years, I took part in a Mayan ceremony called the "moondance." The week-long ceremony ends on the night of the full moon. The women perform the dance of the serpent from sunset to sunrise, to the sound of drums played by men, and sacred song that both men and women sing together. The ceremony aims to bring the Divine feminine energy of grandmother moon into the Earth and balance the masculine and feminine powers. Harmony, flow, healing, and transformation are seen as the gifts of the moon to all beings, including participants and observers, both male and female.

Through channelling, I was also introduced to an ancient sect of women priestesses, who called themselves the "priestesses of the moon." These women lived in small communities and were given wisdom teachings by the enlightened spirit beings to help their people live in a mindful and moral way. The first time I encountered these women, they told me. "We are the old grandmothers, before Atlantis and everything that came after. We are from the time of the Great Cosmic Mother. Our tradition is as old as humanity."

During each full moon, these priestesses would gather and use their drums and voices to harness the energy of the moon. They were there to celebrate the moon and seek guidance for their tribe, enabling the flow of energy to continue gracing the land. (In the moondance ceremony, at intervals during the night, the women dancers smoke a sacred pipe made of obsidian. This is called the "vision time," when the moon may offer guidance to the women, to share with others. Perhaps the moondance ceremony is a remnant from the times of the priestesses of the moon.) These priestesses were the caretakers of the community, and their word was absolute. In times of crisis, they delivered the moon's message, and wise were the people who listened and heeded their words.

The role of the priestess was not easy, as it carried a great deal of responsibility. A woman was invited to participate in the ceremonies only if she was willing to always work for the light and uphold the guidance of the enlightened beings—even if at personal cost. Sacrifices may mean having the inner strength to do the right thing for the tribe, such as go to war when her heart ached for peace, or going against the popular view. These wise women lead an impeccable moral life through continuous personal work for inner growth, and the tribe trusted them to deliver the word of the Great Mystery, Divine guidance from the unseen worlds.

The being of light who assisted the priestesses, the Great Cosmic Mother, a personification of the Creator who births the world from her Divine womb, had an unbending will. She was wild and untamed and worked solely for the light. The moon was her symbol. At the same time, despite her wild disposition, she was warm and nurturing. She helped children to be birthed and crops grow. Through her, the tribe was connected to a continuous pool of love and support, in the same way a child is connected to her mother. However, a time came when the children rebelled. People began questioning the absolute authority of the priestesses. They no longer wanted to listen to these women, even though they spoke the words of the Great Cosmic Mother.

A new male warrior mentality emerged, lacking in compassion, wisdom, and deeper understanding; it sought to take land and chattels for its own. Women were seen as weak and the moon was obscured by the sun, which became the symbol of a male God; the masculine triumphing over the feminine. People did not realise that we need both powers, sun and moon, masculine and feminine, to be in balance. At the time of the patriarchy, the law of the strongest was celebrated and violence and chaos prevailed in the land. The time of the priestesses of the moon was no more, Ma'at was violated and humanity fell into darkness.

REVIVING THE PRIESTHOOD

In 2011, in Kilmichael Glen in Scotland, I climbed a sacred hill with Fi Sutherland. We were following a buzzard through marshland and bogs. Eventually, we arrived at the top of the hill where three stones stood. We meditated by the stones, and guidance came to me. In the old days, this was a fire hill—where ceremonial fires were lit at key times of the year, such as the Celtic festivals. The veils between our world and the world of spirit lifted, and a wild, old spirit woman appeared. She introduced herself as the "spirit of the land." She talked about a time long ago when the land had flourished and priestesses of the moon had gathered on the hill and danced under the light of the full moon, supported by the tribe.

The spirit of the Celtic land then showed me teams of women, around the globe, gathering under the light of the full moon. She said Fi and I had done this, too, in a past life. She asked me to remember these ways and share them again with people, bringing them back into the arms of the Great Cosmic Mother, the Divine feminine. She showed me how unhappy people can be when they are disconnected from the Great Cosmic Mother's love, the moon, and the feminine power.

In place of the loving Great Cosmic Mother, we have created a patriarchal force that is always pushing us forward, telling us we are undeserving and that we must keep striving, work harder, and repent for our misdeeds. A mother does not judge her children. She accepts her children, no matter what they have done. Bathed in her love, the children can grow into a state of wholeness.

From 2012-14, I facilitated a two-year, part-time training called "The Priestess and Priest of the Moon." I welcomed men and women to join the training, as both genders have a female side, which needs to be integrated. The training can be challenging. In order to embody the priesthood, a person is called to work on their ego-shadow. Anything that is out of balance within us will show up during the training to be recognised and worked through.

During the first week of the training, I was guided to do a ceremony in an ancient stone circle called the "circle of the moon," in another glen, Kilmartin Glen, Scotland. Barefoot, we walked in a spiral path into the centre of the circle. We felt this light come into our bodies, aligning us with the ancient priesthood of the moon. It was a time of initiation into a new path that we were called to embody.

As we progressed, the gifts of the training also became apparent. We were performing ancient rituals for ourselves and on behalf of others with the moon as our guide. We cleared the land, helped the dead, and went through ceremonial rebirthing, welcoming ourselves into life. We walked the time of the Mother at the full moon—expansion, love, and nourishment; the Maiden at the waxing moon—initiation; and the Crone in the waning and dark moons—healing and wisdom. We hailed our own spirit, activated our sacred sound and married our higher self. We travelled the Celtic land and the land of Egypt, connecting to a time beyond our own, bringing the gifts of the Great Cosmic Mother, the Divine feminine, into ourselves and the Earth.

SUMMARY

The light of the moon is an invisible yet powerful vibrational ray that moves the waters of the oceans and exposes our ego. In the night, the moon shines deep into our soul to reveal a well of wisdom that we have hidden from ourselves and the world. The light of the moon brings flow into our life, which we can either accept or resist.

The moon's etheric energy has five phases. The vibration grows during the waxing period and peaks monthly at the full moon. In tandem with the moon, we enter a time of growth and renewal. After the full moon, the energy withdraws during the waning phase, slowly opening to a void that absorbs energy. The void opens fully in the dark moon, when there is no visible moon in the sky and removes stagnant energy. In a moment, everything changes as the void gives birth to the new moon and the cycle begins anew.

During the era of the matriarchy, ancient people embraced the etheric influence of the moon in supporting life. A priesthood of the moon was formed, initially by women, who dedicated their lives to the wellbeing of their tribe and to the planet. The priesthood brought to the people the guidance and the blessing of the Great Cosmic Mother, a female personification of the Creator (Sjoo & Mor, 2013). The Mother helped people live harmoniously with each other and the land. Although the patriarchy vanquished the Mother, she still walks the Earth, her arms open wide, ready to receive her children. Slowly, with the help of the moon, we rediscover the light of the Mother and realise she never left us.

EXERCISE: JOURNEY – ALIGNING WITH THE MOON AND THE MOTHER

In this journey, I guide you back into the arms of the Great Cosmic Mother, which you may wish to welcome as a supporting force in your life. The best time to do this journey is on the night of the full moon, indoors or outside. For part of it, it is good if you are able to see the full moon. If this is not possible, you can visualise the full moon in your mind's eye.

For this journey you will need materials for an altar, and fresh or blessed water to drink afterwards.

Start the journey by creating a sacred space, welcoming your guides and teachers of the light. Put together an altar on which you place some fresh or blessed water that you can drink later.

Leave your space and go outside to a place where you can see the full moon (if this is not possible, visualise the moon in your mind's eye). Looking at the moon, ask that she blesses you with her light. Ask the moon to bring you into the wisdom of the inner feminine. Wait to feel the light of the moon in your body. The moon may also whisper in your ear further guidance, welcoming you back.

Return to and sit near your altar. Filled with the light of the moon, go into a journey: imagine walking deep into a forest. Even though the forest is dark, your path is clearly marked by the light of the full moon. Follow the path that takes you to a ceremonial place in nature. It could be a circle of standing stones, a circle of trees, or an ancient temple.

Imagine sitting at the edge of this ceremonial place. Everything is quiet until suddenly, the wind starts to blow. The breeze moves through the trees, rustling leaves. You hear an owl hooting in the distance, and you smell incense. You feel safe and comfortable there.

Slowly, you become aware of a line of men and women coming into the space and chanting in an ancient language. One of the women carries a drum, and a man plays the flute. They form a circle and connect with the energy of the moon, invoking the Great Cosmic Mother. An etheric light spreads out from their circle in all directions, flowing around the Earth.

You may become aware of other people, like yourself, sitting outside the circle. The woman carrying the drum smiles and beckons you and any others to come into the circle. You can participate or come back another time. If you choose to stay, step into their circle. A woman carrying incense comes and clears your aura. A beautiful perfume permeates the air.

You and any others are now asked to sit in the middle. The priestesses and priests continue to chant and move counter clockwise around you, raising the etheric energy of the space. The drumming quickens, and then suddenly, it stops. A luminous being, a radiant woman walks into the circle.

This lady is not of this world; she is of the world of spirit. She is the Great Cosmic Mother. She flows among the people, radiating her light, bringing everyone home. The Great Cosmic Mother appears in different forms to different people. Notice how she appears to you. She is here to welcome you back, so that you no longer wander alone in life.

The Great Cosmic Mother may hold you in her arms, whisper in your ear, give advice about your life, and offer healing. Whatever she does, receive what is meant for you.

The Great Cosmic Mother now stands at the edge of the circle. She raises her arms and waves of light sweep through the circle. The energy builds and flows to everyone there.

Slowly, the luminous being fades away. Like the moon, she can disappear from our sight, but she is always around the Earth, following the planet day and night.

The sound of the man's flute begins again and slowly, a chant comes from the priests and priestesses as they extend gratitude to the moon and the Great Cosmic Mother. As the song fades, the rhythmic drumming starts. The priesthood leave the circle to return at the next full moon.

It is now time for you to slowly leave the circle, too. As you walk back through the forest, the light of the moon fades as dawn approaches. A new day, a new sun will soon be born in the horizon. With the promise of new life to come, slowly bring yourself back, becoming aware of your space.

When you are back, give thanks to the Great Cosmic Mother and the moon, and drink some of the water from your altar, which is imbued with the energies you worked with during the journey. Later, offer the rest of the water to the Earth and the spirits of the land.

Thank your guides and teachers of the light for holding space for you and now release them, closing the space. Ask that they protect and seal the space and yourself before they go.

Suggestion: In the nights following this exercise, you may have powerful dreams and may wish to write them down. You can repeat this journey each full moon to work with the light of the Great Cosmic Mother. If, during this time, the Great Cosmic Mother calls you to her priesthood, ask yourself if you are ready to embody this path, making sure that it is an inner calling rather than a wish of the egoic mind. The way to the hill of wisdom is steep, for it goes through the tunnel of the underworld of the soul.

The Gifts of the Mother

Deep into antiquity
there was a light, now dimmed.
A time of joy and harmony,
for everything was birthed from the womb of the Mother.

In the full moon, circles were joined,
taking everyone deep into their heart,
to feel wanted and cherished;
all over the Earth, people came together.

The light of the moon flowed into the land,
bringing growth, hope, and surrender,
a knowing that everyone was cared for;
the Great Cosmic Mother walked the Earth.

Subtle ways had the moon
to show its light through the clouds.
Sometimes dark, impenetrable.
Other times, visible and bright.

A mirror to the human soul,
the moon brought gifts of wisdom.
Visions of all that is to come,
visions of what we wish to forget.

The maiden of fresh insight;
the mother of abundant life;
the crone that puts the dead to sleep,
each appearing in times of need.

My voice travels back in time,
seeking the forsaken mother.
Looking for her at the top of hills,
in the dark springs, in a well of fire.

She answers a call I was unaware of,
she weaves around me a new way:
to walk back into the land of the living,
crossing wastelands of my own existence.

22

Star Alignments

Spiritual Lesson 22: On sacred sites, I meet the legacy of the ancient ones and walk through star gates of power

The rainbow spirit: I gather the courage to enter The Sanctuary, another name that my spirit guide uses to describe the Place of Ascension, the Great Pyramid of Giza. This time, I do not venture up the ladder to heaven, the staircase to the King's Chamber in the Great Gallery. Instead, I continue along a corridor that takes me into another chamber, a place of healing. The Queen's Chamber has been prepared for me; abundant energies of high vibration are evident. I have left the Earth's normal vibration and entered another energy field that my soul recognises. I am within the field of Sirinian energy.

Etheric beings from Sirius Star invite me to sit and meditate: "Daughter of ISET-SOTHIS, you have come here to be realigned with your etheric blueprint. We will offer you the keys to ascension so that you and others can find the way back to higher states of consciousness." I sit in silence, but I do not feel anything extraordinary or see any visions. After half an hour, I am told the process is complete.

I stand up, and my head spins. I feel as if my body shifts forwards and backwards, only I have not moved. I know that something profound has just happened, which I am yet to discover.

Connect: The Sirinian Portal

The Sirius star is the brightest star in the night sky visible from Earth with the naked eye. According to astronomers, Sirius is a binary constellation of two celestial bodies, called "Sirius A" and "Sirius B." Esoteric sources and the Dogon tribe from Mali, West Africa, argue the existence of a third celestial body, named "Sirius C" (Temple, 1998).

According to Thoth, the ancient Egyptian God of wisdom and learning, this star and its inhabitants hold the key for unlocking life on Earth. When I channel his words, Thoth calls these star people "the Sirinians," to differentiate from inhabitants of the country we call Syria. I will continue using his term in the book.

Alongside the Council of Nine, Sirinian light beings, known as "life engineers," were instrumental in creating the conditions for physical life to exist on Earth, as part of the Earth experiment. Prior to their intervention, there was no physical life on the planet, only water. They re-modelled the Earth, creating land masses and an atmosphere that would support the wide variety of physical life forms that would inhabit it. Their intervention was an act of unconditional love towards all living beings who incarnate on Earth.

The Sirinians and the Council of Nine saw an opportunity for a planetary school on Earth. Through the process of incarnation, souls from different solar systems, could come together to study. They asked ISIS, a being of light embodying the Divine Mother energy, to support the school. ISIS agreed. The Council of Nine planned the school and brought in the students. The Sirinians built it. ISIS became the school's principal, and created a spiritual path for those students who wished to graduate and return home.

Although the Sirinians are the engineers of the school, their remit did not finish after construction. They have always cared for humanity and life on Earth, assisting ISIS's work. In ancient Egypt, ISIS's connection with Sirius was so interlinked that she was called ISIS of Sirius, or to use the ancient words, ISET-SOTHIS. In times of planetary crisis, the Sirinians, with the agreement of the Council of Nine and an invitation from human beings, have helped. In the past, they have sent their people, wise teachers, to incarnate—even if it meant they, too, may be stranded here for many lives due to the law of karma. These teachers offered people various practical skills from agriculture and animal husbandry to advanced engineering, as well as spiritual awareness.

ISIS has shown me that the Sirinians created an interdimensional portal in their star system, which continuously beams etheric light of a specific high vibration towards the Earth. This portal is linked to our evolution; when our collective consciousness increases, so does the energy vibration beamed towards the planet. Although the Sirinians cannot interfere with the law of karma and we reap what we have individually and collectively sown, they assist us where possible to create more harmony. ISIS has given me teachings on how to channel and work with the energy of the Sirinian portal and the keys to ascension, through the Seven Gates of Awareness Teaching (see chapter 18).

The Sirinians are awakened beings with no ego and no personal agenda. Their interest is mainly at a planetary level, even though they may, at times, support individual light workers. They wish the Earth school to prosper so that souls can continue to have this opportunity for education.

Other star beings from different constellations, such as the Pleiades and Orion, also help the Earth. For instance, they mitigate the effects of electromagnetic pollution. They do this not only to aid the planet, but also to temper the harmful energy that our actions and technology discharges into the cosmos.

These star people assist us without being seen and without directly interfering in our lives. However, we can actively seek their help.

Attune: Portals within Ancient Sites and Hidden Relics

The portal of Sirius star emanates high vibrational energy towards the Earth. This is fundamental for the continuation of life on the planet. Other star systems also have portals directed towards the Earth, which work in conjunction with the Sirius portal and further support the experiment. Ancient structures on the planet were designed and built to receive energy from these portals. The energy is then distributed around the Earth through the network of ley lines. People may wander around these ancient sites, not knowing, but perhaps feeling, that they are being bathed in high vibrational light. Apart from the Great Pyramid in Egypt, which is linked to both Sirius and Orion (Bauval & Gibert, 1994), sacred sites, stone circles, and tombs also connect with Sirius, Orion, the Pleiades, the constellation of the Great Bear, and other heavenly bodies. A discipline called "archaeoastronomy" studies these alignments between ancient sites and star constellations (Magli, 2009).

The Egyptian Lineage: The Schoolhouse Door. Egypt is the key to all life on Earth. According to my spirit guide Thoth, Egypt is one of the most important places on the planet, the schoolhouse door. Egypt was specifically built to collect and disperse the energy from the Sirius star and other constellations. A vast etheric star formation surrounds the whole of Egypt, which constantly nourishes the Earth with high vibrational, Sirinian light.

The morphology of the land, the flow of the river Nile, from south to north, and the placement of certain hills are linked to the Sirius star. For example, the hill at the Valley of the Kings ends in a distinct pyramid formation, which collects the light of Sirius and Orion and amplifies its etheric energy.

According to Thoth, ancient pyramids and temples also attune with and aid this flow of light from Sirius. For example, what is now called the Queen's Chamber inside the Great Pyramid, was designed as a healing chamber, and is flooded by the high vibrational energy of Sirius. Other places within some of the ancient Egyptian temples, now mostly closed to the public, have energy fields that feel completely different to the Earth's usual vibration. I have been invited into some of these chambers by native healers, who asked me not to reveal the locations, as these places are sacred to them. Inside the ancient rooms, I could feel the Sirinian vibrations that were present in the golden time of Atlantis. The wise Atlanteans anchored these vibrations in Egypt after the fall of their empire. The local healers knew of ancient symbols that activated the high vibrational energy, but without this activation, the chamber may feel no different from any other room in the temple complex.

The Egyptian Connection across the Globe. The portals within the Great Pyramid and other ancient sites in Egypt are linked to other portals in different parts of the world. According to Hancock and Faiia (1999) connections exist between ancient sacred sites across the globe, from the Great Pyramid to Machu Picchu in Peru, to Easter Island and Cambodia.

In my experience, these connections are mirrored in the etheric realms: high vibrational energy flows between these sites creating a network of light that attunes to the Sirius star and other constellations.

In Machu Picchu, Intihuatana, a monument appearing like a large sundial, connects with Sirius and the Pleiades. Due to its geographical alignment to the Giza plateau, this portal works in conjunction with the Sirinian gate in

Egypt and other gates on the planet. Spiritual practitioners reconnect with such gates, helping us to remember energetically our origin and soul alignment.

As in Egypt and Machu Picchu, other ancient sites across our planet are attuned to Sirius and other constellations. These sites connect to each other through ley lines, straight etheric lines across the Earth's surface. For example, I have experienced a profound energetic connection between the stone circles in Orkney and Stonehenge, and then between Stonehenge and the Great Pyramid. During the autumn equinox 2011, I visited Orkney with other ISIS practitioners. Each morning, we got up early for a sunrise ceremony at the Ring of Brodgar stone circle. Each evening, we finished our spiritual work with a sunset ceremony at the Stenness stones. Following our visit, the spirit guides asked us to visit Stonehenge, revealing to me an energetic line between the two places.

After a few emails, English Heritage granted us private access into Stonehenge in the early morning of 30 October, the Celtic festival of Samhain. When we were amongst the stones, I experienced the incredible energetic connection between all three sites (Orkney, Stonehenge and the Great Pyramid) and the etheric portals of the Sirius Star and the Pleiades.

Hidden Relics of Power. The high energy of the astral portals manifests in objects around the globe, which have been intentionally created and hidden by the Sirinians or by spiritual masters following the Sirinians' guidance. These sacred objects only activate when held by an awakened spiritual practitioner, like the Egyptian healers I mentioned earlier. When held by such a person, the objects create energy fields, which can be used to communicate with the Sirinian beings of light, send healing to the planet, move water and stones, and alter the Earth's surface.

I have not come across any of these objects in everyday life, but I have experienced their etheric power. One day whilst meditating, I became aware of a spirit guide with a large, vibrant aura. He was a master of light. He placed three of these sacred objects on a table in front of me. Even though I saw this psychically, the light from these objects was so powerful that I could feel a force field pushing into my aura and physical body. I could not keep my head straight. The field was so strong that it was pushing my neck backwards. I realised I needed to relax and accept this energy into my body, and integrate it within my own energy field.

I have been told by ISIS that some of these relics are with native tribes, Egyptian healers, African shamans, Mayans, and Tibetan masters. All of these objects will be discovered when sufficient numbers of us have reached a higher level of consciousness that we are able to use their gifts skilfully, for the highest good of all life.

LEARN: THE EARTH SCHOOL CURRICULUM

The Earth school is supported by the high vibrational energies from the Sirius portal and other star alignments. As we walk a spiritual path towards awakening, these portals sustain our efforts. When life is tough, we may think that Earth is a hard place and the school, a harsh way of learning. We do not realise that access to this school is very limited. No matter what our life looks like, incarnating on Earth, and having the opportunity to follow a transformative spiritual path, is like winning the lottery.

One of my friends, Imelda Almqvist, narrates her second son's memories from before he was born, in her book *"Natural Born Shamans: A Spiritual Toolkit for Life"* (2016). He remembers a time in another world, which he calls a "yellow land." Many souls like him lived there hoping to incarnate on Earth, in any life possible, no matter how pleasant or hard.

Incarnation as Soul Lesson. What we sometimes view as terrible suffering, the Sirinians regard as soul lessons in the curriculum of the Earth school; the pitfalls of life are events that our soul has chosen to encounter along its way to rediscovering its own light. The curriculum teaches us through different experiences, both happy and sad. As a result, life on Earth can be bittersweet.

The Sirinian beings have a detached attitude towards life on Earth. In a shamanic journey, I asked to see our world through the eyes of my Sirinian guides. They took me to a woman who had lost her son in a war. The woman was distraught. I asked the Sirinians, "How can this suffering be a good thing?" They showed me how the mother had been full of pride because her son was a soldier in the king's army. She had actively persuaded him to join the armed forces. She had given little thought of the consequences, until war came.

It was only when her son went off to fight that she realised she might lose her child. She started praying—not for her son to be victorious, but for him to be safe. When he died in battle, she understood the futility of her pride. She saw how it may have been better for him to have been a local farmer than a soldier fighting a distant enemy. The Sirinians told me that, as in many cases, the mother and son had a karmic link. Before each incarnated, the son's soul had agreed to help the less aware soul of the mother heal its ego and personality. Prior to this life, the mother's soul had many opportunities to realise the problems that her pride was creating for herself and others. However, it took major suffering—the loss of her son—for her to finally learn the consequences of pride.

The Sirinians showed me that they have compassion for the people on Earth who are going through this difficult schooling of the soul. They respect the choices that each soul makes prior to their incarnation and during their time on Earth.

Entry to the Earth School: The Blueprint for All Life. The beings that inhabit the Sirius star are etheric. They are pure consciousness with no recognisable physical form. However, when they appear psychically to people, they may adopt a relatable form. I used to have a Sirinian guide who appeared as a placid, witty, old man. One day, he showed me that his form was a mask; underneath the mask was pure light.

At some point, some of the Sirinians incarnated to create physical structures on Earth for specific purposes. One of these structures, which is hidden underground, holds the intact blueprint of the Earth. Everything that has been born (including species now extinct) and is capable of being born on Earth is held within this blueprint. Nothing can be created and survive on Earth that is not in the Sirinian blueprint. This is why other alien species cannot settle on our planet. The Earth will not support life forms other than those that have been placed in the blueprint by the Sirinian life engineers.

We all come from one of the star systems that chose to be part of the Earth experiment. Star gates exist in ancient sites, through which we can realign ourselves with our star system of origin, and our purpose of incarnation in this life. This soul memory may be installed as energy codes from the star gate directly into our body. Initially, we may not be aware of what the energy codes do or what they connect us with. However, this awareness may come later as we integrate the vibration within our body. Slowly, we may remember truths that we did not know we understood.

At the same time, many other beings covet the Earth and wish to inhabit and take over our planet. We live in one of the most diverse and beautiful planets in the entire cosmos. The only way to incarnate is to put in a request for an earthly life—to be born as one of the species found in the blueprint. However, this is not always possible. Access is highly restricted, as Imelda's son recalls in the story above. A soul would first need to go through the Council of Nine to apply for the privilege of life on Earth.

Some of the beings who covet the Earth gather etherically around the planet and try to influence people here, negatively. "Since human beings are harming the Earth, and investigating other planets to inhabit, what then?" they ask. Perhaps they think that because we are disrespecting the planet and looking at other planets to move to, such as the moon or Mars, they could force the Council of Nine to consider them as possible inhabitants of Earth.

From Sirius, the beings can observe the light of our collective consciousness and hear the sound of our energy. They have told me that, in the last few years, despite all the negative actions taking place, our collective sound has become much clearer. Our vibration is increasing. We are moving into a new era. Sirius's role is to continue to assist us in the process.

SUMMARY

The Sirinians engineered life on this planet, creating a blueprint of all the potential life forms on Earth. They view Earth as an important school, where souls are able to increase their inner understanding and wisdom and learn to live in harmony with themselves and others. The energy of the Sirius star and other constellations flows through many ancient sites, such as the Great Pyramid of Giza. Star gates exist to constellations that support the Earth experiment and help us increase our inner knowledge and awaken our light.

EXERCISE: ACTIVATION – CONNECTING TO A STAR GATE

The intention of this exercise is to enter the star gate of your soul memory and retrieve self-knowledge from its wisdom codes.

Start by creating sacred space and welcoming your guides and teachers of the light. Ask your guides to take you to an ancient star gate of knowledge where you can retrieve a teaching about yourself and your earthly life. Remain silent to see whether this journey is possible for you now, and only proceed if you receive affirmation.

If you receive a yes, invite the Sirinian beings of light to assist you in your journey. They will help you because when you travel to a star gate and raise your awareness and vibration, more light flows into the planet as well as into yourself. This is helpful to your soul's journey. Wait until you feel the presence of the Sirinians. They are the keepers of all the gates of power on Earth. Feel their strong vibration around your body.

Imagine a beautiful star in front of you. Its light surrounds you. At the same time, another star appears in your third eye. This second star opens your psychic centre, which is permanently aligned with the constellation of your star of origin. The golden starlight of your third eye surrounds you and your aura. Imagine a golden pathway from your third eye to an ancient place on the planet. Follow the pathway in your mind's eye. It may lead you to somewhere in nature or, more probably, to an ancient site. Notice where you are taken.

Once there, you may become aware of guardian spirits who look after the gate. Ask the Sirinians to unlock the gate, so you can receive the energy for the highest good of all. They will mediate between you and the guardians.

When the gate is unlocked, light in the form of high vibrational energy will flow towards you. Feel this light in your physical body. Stay in this space, meditating and receiving. During the activation, you may become aware of symbols, sacred geometry, and colours that further unlock the codes of power within you.

After the activation, you may ask the Sirinians for any further advice. Then thank the guardian spirits, and ask the Sirinians to bring you back.

Find your way back by following the pathway back inside your third eye and into your body. Thank the Sirinian beings of light and your own guides and teachers for the gift of energy you have received. Release them, and ask that before they go, they completely protect and seal the room and yourself.

THE EARTH SCHOOL

The great mystery.
Life on Earth.
Where did I come from?
How did I get here?

Questions without answers.
Only thousands of probabilities.
Was there a big bang in the cosmos,
creating order out of chaos?

Out of the void of nothingness,
was light born through the voice of a conscious thought?
Did God make me in his image?
And if I am God, why am I lost?

I wonder about the swirling colours,
etheric energies and different lights,
seen by my mind's eye,
explaining everything.

How my soul looked for a home,
a place to taste the adventure of life,
to dive into the ocean and crystal lakes,
to climb snow peaked mountains, above the clouds.

To seek the heat of the Earth,
companionship with others.
To find and inspire love,
to taste the fruits of the physical body.

And then what, asked my soul, always seeking;
when you have found the beauty of life,
the clear waters, the depth of the sea?
The light will take me back, where I have always been.

23

The Grace of the Holy Spirit

Spiritual Lesson 23: The Holy Spirit, the essence of God, brings light, truth, and life to the world

The rainbow spirit: On the island of Iona, Scotland, spirit beings of light called the "keepers of the Holy Spirit," speak to me of the time of the Doves.

The Doves were a holy order of monks based on the island, who channelled the Holy Spirit. The monks arrived on Iona at a young age, seeking the experience of the Holy Spirit, to know the essence of God, the holy fire. They never knew when the Holy Spirit would come. Their master, the head of the order, said: "The more impatient you are, the longer you will have to wait." And those who could not abide the wait became angry and left the island. Others spent over twenty years in meditation and isolation in hermitages around the island, waiting to receive the Holy Spirit. While some young, innocent souls were bathed in the grace of the Holy Spirit within months.

When the Holy Spirit came to a monk, the master welcomed him into the holy order of the Doves. The Doves, the channels, shared the blessings of the Holy Spirit with the many pilgrims who came to Iona. The pilgrims sat on wooden benches whilst the Doves sang the chants that invoked the essence of God. The first chant was a blessing about life, "May You Walk in Peace." The second, a blessing to know the grace of God in life, "May You Walk with the

Holy Spirit." The third chant was an invocation for healing, "May the Suffering Be Healed with Peace." Some of the Doves remain around the island etherically. Their chanting continues to support the thousands of pilgrims who still come to Iona.

As I meditate in the ancient chapel, the spirit Doves ask me if I would like to become a Dove and lead others into the order. I accept. Their chanting becomes clearer in a language I now recognise: ancient Greek. I take down the first verse.

THE LIGHT OF THE HOLY SPIRIT

The light of the Holy Spirit permeates both the physical and spiritual realms, creating harmony and liberating from suffering both the dead and the living. Its energy is the light of unconditional love, which helps us awaken from the conditioning of the monkey mind. The Holy Spirit is the helping hand of the Divine Mother that blesses us with understanding. It is the Divine essence that unveils the truth, allowing our blinkers to fall away, so we can experience our authentic, radiant Self.

In the film *Amazing Grace* (2006), there is a beautiful story of the workings of the Holy Spirit. When his ship was caught in a storm, a slave trader had an epiphany. Facing the risk of death in the raging weather, he became aware of the pain of the twenty thousand African people he had traded. He had never before given much thought to the suffering he caused others. The trader changed his life direction, gave all his money to the poor and destitute, to widows and orphans, and became a Christian preacher against slavery. The light of the Holy Spirit lifted the veil of his cruelty, so he could see all people as equal and realise the harm his slave trading had caused.

THE ORIGIN OF THE HOLY SPIRIT

The Holy Spirit has always been on Earth and is not exclusive to any spiritual tradition. It is beyond religion. The Holy Spirit is born from the boundless love of the Divine Mother. ISIS, as a manifestation of the Divine Mother energy, shares her child, the Holy Spirit, with all creation.

When physical life was created on Earth, ISIS guided beings of light, the keepers of the Holy Spirit, to bring the Holy Spirit to the planet and create a link to the essence of God. The keepers anchored the Holy Spirit energy at specific locations on the Earth, identified for their high vibrational energies. These places are portals to higher dimensions of God's consciousness. In doing so, the keepers created places where people can experience their original state of consciousness, the state of unconditional love. One of these locations is the island of Iona.

THE HOLY SPIRIT IN ANCIENT TIMES

Iona did not form part of the Atlantean empire. Instead, it was inhabited by a different race, a spiritually awakened people called the "Lemurians" who ascended into a higher dimension prior to the fall of Atlantis and the great flood.

In the ancient lost continent of Atlantis, the energy of the Holy Spirit was invoked by both men and women with specific chants. The chants were in what is called the "light language," a high vibrational, universal language we do not know in our times. This language is not descriptive, but made of power words that invoke etheric energies of light. Thoth, the ancient Egyptian god of wisdom and learning oversees this language and its teachings.

After the fall of the Atlantean world, the practices that invoke the Holy Spirit were brought to ancient Egypt and safeguarded in the temples by high initiates. At some point, they were given to the Essenes, an esoteric sect of Judaism that flourished for three hundred years, from 200 BC to 100 AD. The Essenes were connected to the ancient Egyptian mystery school. They established a branch of the order of the Doves on the island of Iona, before Christianity, with the support of the druids. The Doves were men and women who, through rigorous spiritual practice, became the channels for the Holy Spirit. The name Iona means "dove" in Hebrew.

In Jesus' time, Joseph of Arimathea became a Dove, a conduit of the Holy Spirit. He travelled to Britain, which was now part of the Roman empire, and re-organised the holy order of the Doves, to include some of the teachings he had received from Jesus. Iona, although not part of the Roman world, was a major holy centre during these times.

After the fall of the Roman Empire the holy order declined in Iona and became exclusively male. It was reinstated by the Irish monk Crimthann, who took the name Columba in Latin (Colm Cille in the Celtic language), meaning "dove." Saint Columba became the head of the order of the Doves and christianised their practices. Columba's version of Christianity was different to that of Rome's. It followed the spiritual traditions of the ancient Egyptian doctrine, which influenced the teachings of the future Egyptian Coptic church. Ancient texts of the time also include prayers that have a distinct druidic character, such as the invocation of the four elements.

In 664, sixty-seven years after Columba's death, in the Synod of Whitby, Oswiu, the King of Northumbria, decreed that the Iona church would no longer follow the teachings laid down by Saint Columba (Adomnan of Iona & Sharpe, 1995). Instead, the church would follow the "superior" doctrine of Saint Peter of Rome. The order of the Doves gradually declined until it was lost in the veils of time.

According to the keepers of the Holy Spirit, many Doves, including some who were students of Joseph of Arimathea, have now reincarnated. These souls may feel a calling to once again become the conduit of the Holy Spirit.

CONNECTING TO THE DOVES AND THE HOLY SPIRIT

Psychically, I have come across the Doves in Iona and Lindisfarne, a place of pilgrimage linked to Iona. (Lindisfarne, also called the "Holy Island," is a tidal island in Northumberland, England). In 2013, Fi Sutherland, a fellow teacher in The ISIS School of Holistic Health, and I were on a retreat in Iona. As we meditated in a sacred place, the Holy Spirit unexpectedly entered our hearts. Psychically, I saw and heard spirit monks, who identified themselves as the "Order of the Doves," the carriers of the Holy Spirit, chanting beautifully in ancient Greek. They explained that as everything is the essence of God, the chants can trigger a remembrance in us of our Divine state and affect a healing. Over the course of several retreats in Iona and Lindisfarne, from 2013 to 2017, the Doves gifted us the three chants they knew in ancient Greek and ISIS gave us the original light language chant.

The Holy Spirit can connect spontaneously with someone anywhere. Some people may not need any intermediary, such as the Doves. However, for others, it may be easier to connect with the Holy Spirit in Iona and other places where the energy is anchored, and the spirit Doves are present. The Doves hold a very high vibration; they invoke the Holy Spirit energy for us to bathe in when we are in these places.

Everything is accessible to us, but we are not always attuned to it. Not everyone has the time or inclination to seek the Holy Spirit, or meditate in seclusion to become a channel. However, some spiritual people may still be touched by it. I have facilitated several retreats in Iona. More than once the Doves have said that some of the people in the group are Doves in training and one time, they invited a participant to become a Dove, a conscious channel for the Holy Spirit.

SEEKING THE HOLY SPIRIT

We are experiencing a duality in our world that has become pronounced. Many people in the West are studying the spiritual arts, seeking an awakening out of the conditioning of the mind and a more harmonious way of living with Mother Earth. Alongside this, many advanced souls have been and are incarnating on the planet. At the same time, the old regimes cling to individualism, division, and ego.

To assist the evolution of our collective consciousness, the keepers have asked me to increase people's awareness of the Holy Spirit. They have said, "There is a need for people who are awakening to rediscover their link with the Holy Spirit."

The Holy Spirit is a force that has the potential to flow through everyone, creating a sense of oneness with all. The chants that invoke the Holy Spirit carry a blessing that can bring everyone light, truth, and life.

The keepers have said that many people unconsciously seek the Holy Spirit, to immerse themselves in the unconditional love and the light of awareness of the Creator. The paradox is that when we consciously seek the Holy Spirit, it cannot be found. The Holy Spirit comes of its own volition, to open the hearts of men and women.

The keepers advise: "If seeking the Holy Spirit, do so with humility and love and without the fire of desire. Desire will abort the experience. So, if you seek the Holy Spirit, surrender to Divine love. Let go of your expectations. Open your heart. Let the Holy Spirit find you." The same is true for becoming a carrier of the Holy Spirit. In order to bring the qualities of the Holy Spirit, Divine love and the light of awareness, to others, we must first develop them within ourselves through spiritual practice.

Since 2013, with the guidance of the keepers, Fi and I have been working in sacred sites and holding ceremonies to raise the vibration of the Earth and awaken the collective consciousness. We sing the chants that invoke the Holy Spirit. When we chant, time stops. The blessing of the Creator flows to the land, touches the participants' hearts, and brings a pillar of light into the Earth. Divine, unconditional love and awareness abounds. The tree of life blossoms. The essence of the Creator, the one being, is reunited with the soul in the body. The eye of the soul opens. The keepers have told us that this is but a fraction of what can happen. All life is blessed during this time.

THE HOLY SPIRIT AS LIBERATOR AND HEALER

The Holy Spirit helps all souls—the dead as well as the living.

One day during a meditation, my spirit guides took me to Egypt. I saw many souls who had been trapped for thousands of years in the astral planes over the country. In ancient times, these souls had misused the high vibrational energies available to them, through black magic. Their actions created much suffering in themselves, the people they hurt, and the land. My guides told me that even though Egypt is the portal of light, there also exists a realm of extreme darkness and evil over the land because of this misuse of power.

My guides asked me to sing the Holy Spirit chants to break the black magic and release the souls. As I chanted, I saw the suffering, caused by the dark rituals, leave the faces of all the trapped souls. They became lighter and eventually, moved to a higher spiritual dimension. At the same time, the land below the astral plane was healed by the divine essence of the Holy Spirit.

Recently, my student Francis asked me if I could send her healing, as she was having a difficult time. At the end of the distant healing, I was guided to sing the Holy Spirit chants. As soon as I had finished, the phone rang. Francis said she had been enveloped in a bubble of bright light and surrounded by love. "I knew I was in the presence of God. It was as if my whole body dissolved into light, and I was one with God's love."

SUMMARY

One of the greatest gifts that ISIS, in her emanation as the Divine Mother, has given to Earth, is the blessing of the Holy Spirit. The Holy Spirit, the essence of the Creator, lifts the veil of the conditioning. Through its blessing of light, truth, and life we become aware of the Divine within.

THE DIVINE WITHIN

From the heart of the Mother
born from love, bringing light
I seek your blessing.

Long ago I walked this Earth in spirit form,
but I have forgotten through the solidity of my mind
how to find my way home.

I searched inside me for the road to the stars,
reaching high for avenues of golden light,
yet on Earth a tiresome life, unpleasant and difficult.

When my heart opened to my inner light,
I wept tears of grace.
Floods of gratitude for the mystery I was born into.

I never knew I could regard life as a journey,
where each day could take me deeper into myself,
away from the drama created by the mind.

Each day, potentially a ray of light,
even though Earth's darkness is heavy,
lifting the veil, I see beauty.

I dream with my feet on the ground;
appreciating the small things, the tiny miracles
that remind me I am not alone.

For many years I too have weathered the storm,
before my heart was touched by the Holy Spirit.
Reborn through the grace of my soul, I seek no more.

24

Our Golden Core:
Awaken, Enlighten, and Ascend

Spiritual Lesson 24: I awake through the heart, and find the path to enlightenment and ascension

The rainbow spirit: I remember a time before life, when I was radiant. I could move through walls, travel immense distances in a split second, and bi-locate. Frustrated, I gaze at this body that keeps me stuck in the physical reality. I feel sad, as if I have lost something so precious: my sense of freedom.

My spirit guides surround me, bathing me in their love. "Do not despair, Fotoula," they say. "What you remember is the state of spirit, the state of pure consciousness. What binds you to the Earth is not your physical body but the conditioning of the mind. Once you overcome the conditioning, your body will transform into clear light, and you will once more become the shining spirit."

BECOMING A CLEAR CHANNEL OF SPIRIT'S VOICE

This book is a collaboration between experience and wisdom. The experience is drawn from decades of personal exploration, spiritual development and clinical practice, and many years of academic study. The wisdom is the channelled voice of enlightened beings. According to ISIS, each human being is an incarnated soul whose eternal spirit never dies. Although the soul incarnates, the spirit, also called the higher self, remains in the ethereal realms. Thus, the human and its soul and spirit work in tandem and are in communication. When we advance spiritually, we become more aware of our link to our higher spiritual self and enlightened beings. ISIS and my other spirit guides said to me: "You do not need to be an enlightened master or guru who knows everything. You need to be a pure channel. Be our voice. Then you will have done your job."

In my work, I often speak words of wisdom and give teachings that I did not know I possessed. The words flow through me, and reach and touch others at a profound level. My guides add,

> The highest teachings and the purest healing come from
> spirit. Your human nature can get in the way, no matter how
> evolved you are. Getting yourself out of the way, so the Divine
> can speak through you, is true wisdom.

> When you read this chapter, a transmission of light can
> take place. The teachings can reignite your cellular memory
> and assist your awakening process by aligning your soul's
> earthly experience to your higher spiritual self.

LIFE: THE LOTUS, THE SWAMP AND THE LIGHT

In ancient Egyptian spirituality, the lotus is a symbol of the soul and a representation of rebirth into the authentic Self. In this next part, the guides have asked me to use the lotus as a metaphor for ourselves, and the swamp it grows in as our life conditions.

Imagine you are a lotus flower growing in a swamp. Around you are mosquitoes and stagnant water. It is pungent and dirty and the mosquitoes annoy you with their buzzing; but this is your food. All this organic matter helps you grow.

As the morning arrives, the sun rises in the sky. The sun inside you responds to the sun in the sky. The light makes the swamp a little more comfortable. Now, you look around and see the beauty of nature. The water in the lake seems to be shimmering in the sunlight. This beauty encourages you to reveal your own goodness; so with the help of the sun, your petals begin to open and reveal your golden centre, the enlightened authentic Self.

Such is our awakening. It is a three-step process: The swamp—life feeds the lotus (us). The light—the Divine opens the petals (our heart). And eventually, the lotus opens fully and reveals its golden centre (our Divine essence).

We are here on Earth to experience both the swamp and the sunlight in order to reveal the authentic Self within. No one likes the swamp. Life can be difficult and uncomfortable; yet, it is the swamp that helps the lotus grow and awaken when the light comes.

AWAKEN THE HEART

The Journey: Practice and Process. Awakening is a process of self-development. It is an inner journey of self-realisation where we grow beyond our conditioned identity and embody the authentic Self. The beginning of the journey of awakening may be the realisation that we are more than our physical body. In the above analogy, this is when the lotus is touched by the sunlight and starts opening its petals.

During the journey, further realisations teach us about our life and primordial nature, and show us the patterns and issues we carry that obscure our authentic Self. The journey requires dedication and commitment to dive deeply into the world within, to discover the love we are, and to live our soul's purpose. A regular spiritual practice, one that creates inner transformation, can help reveal the workings of our conditioned mind and access our Divine Self. Spiritual practice can take many forms. Some people practice yoga, whilst others prefer to chant mantras and meditate. My own practice is based on the teachings of ISIS—the Seven Gates of Awareness, the Rays of Divine Consciousness that transforms my DNA, and shamanic journeying. The exercises and practices at the end of each chapter are designed to support the journey to awakening.

A regular spiritual practice will sustain us on our journey, like food for the traveller. Without it, we may be too weak to continue and give up.

Another important resource in awakening is the purification of karma. Our negative and positive deeds have to be acknowledged, so that we can realise and neutralise the consequences of the seeds we have sown. Karma can be purified through rituals that reveal and transform the lessons our soul needs to learn.

Spiritual practice and karma purification support our journey to awakening. They are resources that help clear the path; they are not the path itself. Awakening is not a mathematical equation: "If you do this, you will awaken." Nor can awakening be reached through desire. Grasping is part of the conditioning. When we covet awakening, we push it further away.

Awakening happens when our soul is ready to consciously embody its Divine nature. A shift takes place, and the programming of the ego mind shuts down. It can happen as a result of a gradual process. It can emerge spontaneously because part of us is ready to hold the whole picture, either permanently or temporarily.

Some of us glimpse this state and then, revert into the conditioning. Some of us awaken suddenly and then find we are unable to function in the world. When we open unexpectedly into the unconditioned state, the structures of the everyday world are gone. This may become too much for our mind to take on and our loved ones, and even ourselves, may think we are insane. Our present world has neither the understanding nor the capacity to support someone who has awakened but is not grounded. The awakened state can be a difficult place to be, if we have not prepared ourselves with inner work. We may not be ready, mentally and emotionally, to experience such a profound shift in awareness.

This is why the conditioning has its place. Restrictive as they may be, the social structures provide a mental safety net until we are ready to let them go. Most of us could not function in our everyday life if we suddenly awoke. Imagine losing all your reference points for how life is and who you are. Imagine having complete awareness of spirit, of what is happening in the future, and of all that took place in the past. How many of us could cope with such an immediate and monumental shift in perspective?

In the awakened state, we exist outside the illusionary planes of the conditioned existence—the collective dream. With adequate preparation and having awakened, we embody pure consciousness. We find ourselves in a space of incredible joy that we know instinctively how to personify. This is a state of being.

The Shadow: Greet and Heal. Paradoxically, the closer we are to awakening, the stronger our conditioned monkey mind can become. The ego-self will make its presence known and any unresolved issues within the ego-shadow will show up at some point to be recognised and healed. The etheric, high vibrational energies that are coming to the Earth at this time support a collective wish of the human heart to awaken, and they encourage this unveiling process.

Sometimes strong feelings, resistance to spiritual practice, and mind chatter arise to help us become aware of and transform the lingering issues. We can feel as if we are backpedalling, falling deeper into the conditioning and the negative emotional states. This is part of the shift. These issues are showing themselves, so that we can heal them and move on.

ISIS gave me the following channelling about the process of awakening, both for individuals and the collective, to help support spiritual practitioners of our times.

> This is a time of transition. Light and dark become more distinct, like two different realities within you and in the world. At times, you may become aware of an expansion taking place, an opening into the stillness, a homecoming into the wise Self and experience moments of clarity and infinite grace touching the Divine within.

> At other times, you see yourself as you have always been, immersed in the same story, filled with doubt, fear, and dissatisfaction. It is as if nothing has changed, and any spiritual opening you experienced never happened.

> It is the same in the world reality. People are waking up to the thirst for the authentic Self, a life in alignment with the soul purpose, a coming together in supportive community. Light is flowing from many hearts, lifting the shadow of injustice, fear, and chaos. Yet, at the same time, the old regimes become even more fragmented, teaching the lesson of scarcity, fear, and separation.

> At this time of transition, the emphasis is on self-healing. Through healing the shadow, both inside and outside, you build a strong foundation for the inner temple of light to rise from your heart centre. Rather than being dismayed by the apparent lack of progress, notice the areas of your life that need more love and healing. Practice spiritual teachings that help you become aware and heal at a deep level. Know that you are healing thousands of years of separation that live within you.

> The path to grace requires focus and determination, surrender and acceptance.

The Breath: In the now. Our breath connects us to the present, this precious, transient, and powerful moment. By focusing on the breath, we focus on the here and now. The present moment is the experience of the silence between breaths. By concentrating on the space between breaths, we connect to our authentic Self. (Both breathing in and out are actions. The silence in between is in-action, a state of being.) Breathing in is an affirmation towards life. As I breathe in, I acknowledge I am alive. I choose life. Breathing out is a release. As I breathe out, I surrender and let go. I surrender to life. The space between breaths is the silence, the nothingness, the space of awareness. (This teaching on breathing was offered by my spirit guide, a Sirinian being of light.)

Conscious breathing also features in many eastern traditions. According to Rosen (2002) in his book *"The Yoga of Breath: A Step-by-step Guide to Pranayama,"* in yoga philosophy, pranayama is the formal practice of breath control, which is seen as the source of life force. In Bön Buddhism, conscious breathing is used to clear the three main meridian channels before engaging in meditation. These channels are the central channel and the left and right channels originating in the base of the spine. The name of this Buddhist breathing practice is Lung-Ro Gu-Trook.

Being Centered. Once, whilst meditating, Thoth asked me to open my eyes and look straight ahead at a middle point. As I did, I realised I was becoming increasingly present and my consciousness was converging, becoming a ball of energy inside my central meridian channel. Each time that my mind became busy, I noticed my consciousness moving away from this central point. Literally, I was losing my centredness.

As I refocused in the present, a shift happened. All thoughts stopped. No thought could enter my mind unless I initiated it. When I felt an energy coming over the right side of my head, I knew it was trying to induce me to create thoughts. And I chose not to engage.

The energy trying to enter my mind was external. In choosing to ignore it and maintain my focus, I became aware of the power of my own spirit. All I could feel was the presence of my being, which was absent of compassion, love, fear, and anger. My being was empty of all emotional and mental states, positive and negative, all of which I understood to be part of the conditioning. There was only a presence, an exceptionally strong, pure, and empty void. This state is also called the "I am presence."

My intense focus of the inner essence remained throughout the evening. A shift in my perception had taken place. I recognised that all I was inside was nothingness, even though my presence was palpable. This is one of the paradoxes of awakening.

We live in a world that identifies with dual states: fear and love, anger and peace, ignorance and wisdom. When we incarnate, we become immersed in the dualities of the swamp. However, none is who we are. Our spirit is beyond life. No matter what happens in the swamp, the golden core of the lotus will never cease to be. Inside, there is always the emptiness of the infinite: the I am presence.

Through the Heart. ISIS has said that the best way to awaken is through the heart. The opening of the heart provides a foundation to support ourselves as we delve into our shadow. In opening the heart and developing compassion and unconditional love for ourselves and others, we remember that we are the love of the Creator.

We may experience glimpses of the awakened mind through intense meditation, ritual fasting, and spiritual practice. However, unless we awaken through the heart, we will not be able to hold onto the immensity and nothingness of the void. Our ego and unresolved issues will pull us back into the conditioning—possibly to a deeper extent. For example, if we assume falsely that we have awakened, we can become prey to our ego mind's delusion that we are special and eventually lose any spiritual progress.

During the awakening of the heart, we can initially become overly sensitive and feel the immense suffering of the world. Then, as our spiritual practice continues, we develop detachment that leads to unconditional compassion. I asked an angel how he could witness all the pain on Earth. The angel showed me that he lives in a permanent state of joy and grace, in which suffering does not affect him. The angels empathise with us, but they do not sympathise. They do not take on our pain.

Eventually, through my spiritual practice, I have come to understand what the angel meant. The more I work with the teachings of ISIS, the more my heart fills with joy. When we become a vessel of Divine love, we grow detached from the dramas and pain we witness as part of everyday life. Rather than bury ourselves in grief, either our own or that of the collective, we grow spiritually to hold a bigger picture. This is unconditional compassion.

Through this awakening process, the heart continues to open to learn the meaning of unconditional love. Counterintuitive as it may seem, I have witnessed people pull away when they feel this love. Many in the western world can feel overwhelmed and unworthy when pure love flows their way. We are conditioned to think that what we receive from partners, parents, and family is the true expression of love. However, the love we receive from spirit and we slowly access within ourselves, is immense, beyond the experience of human, conditional love.

As more of us open our hearts and resonate with the vibration of unconditional compassion and love, our structures and our planet will also begin returning to a state of balance. Unconditional love is a powerful force that can transform the mind from the selfish state of ego to the awakened state of wisdom. At the same time, it can bring our collective consciousness into a state of joy, rather than fear.

ISIS says,

> In order to create a positive shift both globally and in your
> personal life, approach both with a sense of detachment and
> unconditional love and compassion. This is so easy and, at the
> same time, so difficult for you to do. In the earthly reality, you
> are not used to extending unconditional love towards what
> you consider ugly, unskilful, or dark. Yet, transformation can
> only take place through love, despite what the mind thinks,
> that love is weak and ineffective.

The universe was created through an act of love. You are the embodiment of Divine love. Love is the most powerful force available to you now.

Enlighten the Mind

The Conditioned Mind. The conditioned mind is like a computer programme that can manifest thoughts and responses in us according to pre-set parameters. The programme says: "If this happens, you will have this thought, feel that way, and do that." The computer has no interest in us; it is just doing its job.

At some point, I realised that I am stronger than the programme. I can tell the computer what to think. I can interrupt its code, and I can observe what it is trying to do. Each time I take control, I am changing the machine's code, creating a new pathway. At times, I can shut down the machine completely and surrender to the inner I am presence.

After we awaken from the dream of the illusion, we have the potential to grow further into the state of enlightenment. In this state, we bring the light of the world to the illusionary realm of life. We consciously become the Divine will incarnated—able to create miracles, bi-locate, and exist within and outside of the earthly dream. We are the fully opened lotus displaying our inner golden centre.

Guru Rinpoche (also known as "Padmasambhava"), an eighth-century Buddhist master of the Himalayas, was said to have kept the sun shining throughout the night and to have performed miracles that defied normal understanding. Being the Divine will, Guru Rinpoche could affect the conditioned reality.

The Enlightened State. A single awakening experience is only part of the journey. Enlightenment is the full embodiment of our divinity and can only be actualised by someone who has fully grounded the awakened state in her body, and then, moved beyond it into the wholeness of the inner light.

At this time, many of us are experiencing different stages and degrees of awakening, but few are fully enlightened. My guides say that currently, five or six of us on Earth walk in the fully enlightened state. (The number is inexact because one of the beings sometimes leaves the Earth.)

Enlightenment is a state where we are the Divine presence on Earth. Fully awakened into our power, we are aware of who we are at all levels. We know consciously we are a being of light, the pure consciousness of the Creator, the One being.

ASCEND THE SPIRIT

Whilst our current culture may view the body as an obstacle to enlightenment (as something to transcend or overcome or master), ancient spirituality regarded the human body as a temple for the soul. The ancients knew that transformation into what is known as the "shining spirit" or "rainbow body," and ascension, goes through the acceptance, honouring, and metamorphosis of the physical body.

In Bön Buddhism, there is a reference to the ascension process. First, the master realises she is the clear light. In that state, over a period of continuous, prolonged meditation, the body eventually transfigures into the same clear light. All that remains behind are nails and hair. In other schools of Buddhism, this is referred to as the "rainbow body." Ancient Egyptian spirituality uses the term "shining spirit" to describe ascension.

In this state, there is no death process. We exist consciously outside the illusionary world of life and death, in a state of inner peace, nirvana. We no longer experience reincarnation, but can enter into the earthly realm whenever our soul chooses and with whatever form we wish to adopt. For example, the Indian guru Paramahansa Yogananda spoke about an enlightened master called "Babaji," who has been living on Earth for thousands of years, appearing in different forms to his disciples (Yogananda, 2006). Being the intention and the Divine power, we recreate ourselves at will. Being the state of limitless consciousness, we are everywhere and nowhere, knowing that nothing exists.

Even though we ourselves have not yet ascended and are experiencing the wheel of reincarnation, paradoxically, at some level, we have ascended. Life is but a dream, the swamp an illusion, our spirit the only thing that exists. Our consciousness, like the sun, always knows its purity and light, but it is obscured by the clouds of the conditioned mind. Awakening, enlightenment, and ascension are all states of consciousness that are inherent in us.

Summary

The soul's purpose is to awaken from the conditioning, to overcome the social programming and the milliards of thoughts that take us into the past and an unknown future. In the awakened state, the mind is silent and to be engaged only when needed. The best way to full awakening is through the heart; otherwise, unresolved ego issues can pull the seeker back into the shadow and into the conditioning.

In the enlightened state, we become the will of the Creator, the Divine being. Ascension is the state of being fully enlightened when our body transforms into the "shining spirit" or "rainbow body." The body is a mirror to the soul. So, when the inner sun shines freely through the body, through the mirror, the body turns into light. Spiritual practices that create inner transformation sustain us on the road towards awakening, enlightenment, and ascension.

Exercise: Spiritual Practice – Revealing the Divine Light

This practice is an extension of "meditating beyond karma" in chapter six. Here, you aim to centre yourself into your natural state of emptiness.

Start your practice by creating sacred space, welcoming your enlightened guides and teachers. Set your intention to experience yourself in your Divine light.

Bring your awareness to the central channel in the middle of your body. This is called the "pranic tube," "*sushumna*" in Sanskrit. It originates in the base of the spine and travels the full length of the middle of the spinal cord and then up to the third eye, and in a subtler pathway, into and through the crown chakra located at the top of your head. Focussing on this central axis, intend to become perfectly aligned with this channel. If your thoughts take you out of this alignment, gently bring your awareness back.

Then, visualise about thirty centimetres above your head, an intense sphere of light, the eighth chakra. When you are perfectly aligned, the eighth chakra activates and sends rays of light down your central channel. Experience this flow of light into your body.

Now move your awareness from the top of your head to your feet. In this way, you are first grounding yourself. Once grounded, you are now ready to work with your consciousness.

See, feel, or imagine a ball of light inside your central channel. This is your consciousness. Waves of energy radiate out from your consciousness. As these waves continue, the sphere of consciousness expands until it encompasses your whole body.

Stay in this luminous, focused state, surrounded by the sphere of light that you are for a few minutes. (To maintain this state, it may be helpful to chant "Om", the sound of creation, or other sounds that come into your awareness. Let your voice express its own sound and rhythm.) You may also wish to open out your hands and let the light that you are radiate to all beings.

Slowly, bring your hands into prayer position and touch your third eye. In this way, you emphasise the state of centeredness within you, the alignment between body and spirit. You may wish to dedicate your practice to the highest good of all beings.

With your hands still in prayer position touch your throat. In this way, you are emphasising your inner alignment with your speech and communication centre, your throat chakra, also aligned to your spirit.

Bring your hands in prayer position onto your heart, emphasising your alignment to your enlightened mind. Bow to yourself and all life. Give thanks for being the light of the world, walking a human life in a body of light.

Finally close your sacred space by thanking your spirit guides and releasing them, asking that before they go, they seal and protect you and the space.

THE JOURNEY TO ENLIGHTENMENT

I have forgotten who I am,
consciously I chose the veil,
the shadow that masks my light.

I sent my image onto this Earth.
I fashioned it the way I wanted it,
in order to help me remember.

This image, my body, is temporary.
It feels real but is thinner than air
and when it perishes, nothing is left.

Yet this body knows me so well.
Such a pity I choose to ignore it.
Most of the time, I live alone in my mind.

My body tries to speak,
but the voice in my head is louder,
until I scream what I could not silence.

The grief of separation from my light.
I searched to find it but returned empty-handed.
The Divine in me was nowhere to be seen.

Until one day, the mind stopped talking.
It became quiet and still.
No thoughts appeared.

What remained was a presence.
The shining spirit, the pure consciousness.
The body completely aligned, centred on its axis.

The body aligned, reveals the spirit.
The quiet mind, the sense of power.
The open heart, the gift to the Earth.

Afterword:
The Dawn of the Age of Horus

The traveller: In summer 2015, I visit the Joshua Tree National Park in California. The spirits guide me to three portals on the land. They say in order to awake, I need to understand the process of life.

The first portal, the gate of manifestation, was created through the intention for my life, my soul purpose. Walking through the gate, I am told I start life as a column of light. Then, I lose sight of the radiance and identify with the body until, through the process of death, I become the column of light again. The continuous journey of life and death starts and ends at the same point. It is a circle in which I cannot get lost, as I always end up where I started. "What is the point of packing my bags and going on this journey of life if I always return to the same place?" I ask. "This is a journey to gain awareness," the spirits say. "Would you rather not travel, stay at home, and put your feet up?" In my heart, I know I am a traveller, an adventurer, a nomad. That is why I packed my bags and was born into life.

The second portal is the gate of birth, where the rock formations create a vulva. "Nothing in life is guaranteed," the spirits say. "Once you start the journey, with birth, you leap into the unknown. Coming out of the womb is a leap of faith, a surrendering to life."

The third and final portal is the gate of death. This time the rock formations create a sarcophagus. As I lie in the sarcophagus, a raven appears and circles above me, a manifestation of the spirit of death. I am told death is a safety mechanism, the return ticket, the journey back to the purity of my spirit. After life, death frees me from my attachments, taking me back to a space of inner freedom.

These three gates, the spirits say, are the three stages of existence:

a. *Manifestation of my intention creates the journey of life.*

b. *Birth starts the journey into the unknown.*

c.   *Death takes me back to the purity of the spirit I am.*

At the end of the journey, I arrive back at the same point, the point where I began, bringing with me one thing only—the wisdom of inner knowing.

I wrote this book because I believe it to be an important resource in our awakening process, both individually and collectively. I feel that we are at the dawn of the age of Horus, a time of heart opening and spiritual evolution. Many people are realising that the way we live life, does not serve us. There must be more to life than going to work, paying the rent, eating and drinking, and watching television. Those whom I meet through my work understand that as spiritual beings having a human experience, we yearn for the enlightened mind and a peaceful world.

When I was a child, I was filled with light. I had a detached view of the world, as I could see everyone's shining spirit and knew people behaved badly because they were afraid or hurting. As a teen, I became immersed in the conditioning, losing the spiritual connection. The state of inner light was there, but it was veiled. The Divine hand was still guiding me, but from further away. Then in my early thirties, through a series of awakening experiences, the light returned. But the conditioning was there, too. And it is the same out in the world: the light has returned, mirrored in the many spiritual practitioners who seek the inner wisdom and the radiance of their own spirit. But the conditioning lingers. The sectarian, racial, economic, and political divides are evident and if anything, more pronounced.

My book is a path, a guided roadmap on the quest for inner and universal harmony to overcome the conditioning. Not much can change in our lives, and worldwide, unless we effect a transformation from the inside. In order to do this, we need a wider picture. Who am I? Where have I come from? What is life all about? How can I heal and create transformation, both within me and in the world reality?

My answers to these questions are contained in this book. They have come from what I have channelled, practiced, taught, and shared with hundreds of students and clients. I have summarised the wisdom into four parts: To learn who we are, and the lessons we have come here to study, we need to shed the old skin; heal our state of separation, clear our karma, surrender to life (part I). To find out where we have come from, we look to the spirit, our own higher self and the spirit entities of light that support us. We gain a wider, more encompassing view of life from above (part II). When we ground our spiritual experience into our everyday life, we can answer questions on what our existence is about, a continuous journey of learning that has no beginning and no end (part III). And finally, on the road to spiritual awakening, we transform into the spiritual warrior, the radiant being that shines like the sun and the stars, waxes and wanes like the moon, and is in the flow of life with the awareness of spirit. Firmly, we straddle both worlds, the physical and the spiritual, and centred on our axis, we travel the road to wholeness (part IV).

Through the process of writing, I realised the need for a roadmap for the community of spiritual seekers has become more critical, as the divides within and outside are now more evident. This book aims to carry the reader into a realisation of a broader picture and, at the same time, aid individual transformation in the here and now. This in turn, has an effect on how we view the world situation: rather than being angry and dismayed, we detach from the illusionary drama of the collective dream and working with the light within, we create the foundation for a different experience of the world reality. The outside world reflects our inner cosmos. The age of Horus is the evolution into the homo spiritus that we are called to embody.

In a nutshell, I wrote the book to inspire the seeker to remember that, our soul has a Divine origin and that it is the light of one hundred thousand suns. The spiritual practices in this book assist readers in increasing their vibration and connecting with their own Divinity. Healing our conditioning is a journey towards rediscovering our inner light. At the same time, I demonstrate that what we may perceive as the difficulties of earthly life, are in many ways the blessings and gifts that point us towards the truth of who we are. Life is an amazing opportunity to uncover our true nature. Feelings of homecoming are one of the blessings of life's journey. On Earth, we are given this incredible opportunity to know who we are through the process of first losing oneself and then finding oneself.

I have found that people who delve into the teachings contained in the book regularly and practice the exercises in daily life derive a great benefit in their spiritual evolution. Whether your journey with this book continues or has now come to an end, I wish your path to the "top of the mountain" to be filled with light, truth, and life, peace, grace, and incredible joy. May you be the traveller within the worlds, who savours the view and enjoys every part of this special adventure we call Life!

The Journey Back

It ended where it began,
back at the one place;
the same starting and arrival point.

Long ago I packed my bags.
Surrendering to the unknown,
I jumped into the abyss with both feet.

And whilst walking the path of life;
an inner longing for the home I had left,
a deep desire that could not be expressed by words.

So deep it was, searching for meaning.
Why am I here? Why am I travelling this road?
The path is circular bringing me back, always home.

Yet I was excited to be a traveller,
to leave the safety of the port for the expanse of the ocean,
to lose myself in the depth of emotion.

I remember looking forward to the day of departure.
The time of arrival into earthly life.
And the slow realisation of the conditioning.

I forgot who I was; the earthly world consumed me,
losing myself in the process of living,
thinking I was the body I inhabited.

Yet I created this body, to carry me into the experience.
I mourned for its loss
when age slowly took it away, my creation.

Now I rediscovered my path,
the roadmap of the explorer,
where many things are not as they seem.

There were lines on the map that I had to review,
locations that I had to delete, new places that I found.
Never knowing what comes next.

My map is old, the paper scribbled upon many times.
Different hands wrote on it, belonging to the same consciousness.
Slowly I realise the way of understanding.

I am the traveller and the journey.
The map and the hand that wrote it.
The sun and its shadow. I am whole.

References

Adomnan of Iona, & Sharpe, R. (1995). *Life of St Columba*. Middlesex: Penguin Books.

Almond, J., & Seddon, K. (2002). *The book of Egyptian ritual: Simple Rites and Blessings for every day*. London: Thorsons.

Almqvist, I. (2016). *Natural Born Shamans: A Spiritual Toolkit for Life: Using shamanism creatively with young people of all ages*. Winchester: Moon Books.

Auster, P. (2017). *4 3 2 1*. London: Faber & Faber.

Bauval, R., & Gilbert, A. (1994). *The Orion Mystery: Unlocking the Secrets of the Pyramids*. London: Arrow.

Bernhard, T. (2013). *How to Wake Up: A Buddhist-Inspired Guide to Navigating Joy and Sorrow*. Somerville, MA: Wisdom Publications.

Bien, T. (2011). *Buddha's Way of Happiness: Healing Sorrow, Transforming Negative Emotion, and Finding Well-Being in the Present Moment*. Oakland, CA: New Harbinger.

Blavatsky, H. P. (1994). *The voice of silence*. Adyar, India: Theosophical Publishing House.

Botten, M. (2011). *Herakleitos: Logos made manifest*. Peterborough: Fastprint Publishing.

Causton, R. (2011). *The Buddha In Daily Life: An Introduction to the Buddhism of Nichiren Daishonin*. London: Rider.

Chakraborty, U. (2013). Effects of different phases of the lunar month on humans. *Biological rhythmic research, 45*(3), 383-396.

Combs, A., & Krippner, S. (2008). Collective Consciousness and the Social Brain. *Journal of Consciousness Studies, 15* (10-11), 264-276.

Cresswell, J. D., & Lindsay, K. E. (2014). How Does Mindfulness Training Affect Health: A Mindfulness Stress Buffering Account: Current Directions in Psychological Science. *Sage Journals, 23*(6), 401–407.

Cutler, W. B., Schleidt, W. M., Friedmann, E., Preti, G., & Stine. R. (1987). Lunar Influences on the Reproductive Cycle in Women. *Human Biology, 59* (6), 959-972.

Debord, J. M. (2017). *The Dream Interpretation Dictionary: Symbols, Signs, and Meanings*. Detroit: Visible Ink Press.

Easwaran, E. (2007). *The Bhagavad Gita* (2nd ed.). Tomales, CA: Nilgiri Press.

Eliade, M. (2004). *Shamanism: Archaic Techniques of Ecstasy*. Princeton: NJ Princeton University Press.

Emoto, M. (2010). *Messages from water and the universe*. Carlsbad, CA: Hay House.

Faber, A., & Mazlish, E. (2012). *How to talk so kids will listen and listen so kids will talk*. New York: Piccadilly Press.

Foster, R., & Kreitzman, L. (2010). *Seasons of Life: The biological rhythms that enable living things to thrive and survive*. London: Profile Books.

Freud, S. (1994). *The Interpretation of Dreams.* New York: Random House.

Freud, S., Wilson, S., & Griffin, T. (2012). *A general introduction to Psychoanalysis.* Ware, UK: Wordsworth Editions.

Friis-Christensen, E., & Lassen, K. (1991). Length of the solar cycle: An indication of solar activity closely associated with climate. *Science New Series, 254*(5032), 698-700.

Gill, C. (2017). *Plato's Atlantis Story: Text, Translation and Commentary.* Liverpool: Liverpool University Press.

Goleman, D. (1996). *Emotional Intelligence: Why It Can Matter More Than IQ.* London: Bloomsbury.

Hancock, G. (2015). *Magicians of the Gods: The Forgotten Wisdom of Earth's Lost Civilisation.* London: Coronet.

Hancock, G., & Faiia, S. (1999). *Heaven's Mirror: Quest for the Lost Civilization.* London: Penguin Books.

Harner, M. (1990). *The Way of the Shaman.* New York: HarperCollins.

Henning, E. (2007). *Kalacakra and the Tibetan Calendar.* New York: Columbia University Press.

Hobby, K., & Jenkins, E. (2014). Mindfulness in schools. *EarthSong Journal: Perspectives in Ecology, Spirituality and Education, 2*(7), 26.

Holiday, R. (2016). *Ego is the enemy: The fight to master our greatest opponent.* London: Profile Books.

Ingerman, S. (2001). *Medicine for the Earth: How to Transform Personal and Environmental Toxins.* New York: Random House.

Ingerman, S. (2004). *Shamanic Journeying: A beginner's guide.* Boulder: Sounds True.

Ingerman, S. (2015). *Walking in light: The everyday empowerment of a shamanic life.* Boulder: Sounds True.

Jansen, R. E. (2001). *The Book of Hindu Imagery: Gods, Manifestations and Their Meaning.* New Delhi: New Age Books.

Joseph, F. (2009). *Advanced Civilizations of Prehistoric America: The Lost Kingdoms of the Adena, Hopewell, Mississippians, and Anasazi.* Vermont: Bear & Company.

Jung, C. G. (2002). *Dreams.* London: Routledge.

Kalipershad-Jethalal, G. (2015). *Kundalini Yoga Massage: Seven Steps to Activate the Seven Chakras and Power People's Prana.* Bloomington: iUniverse.

King, J. (2012). *Passive aggressive disorder.* Kindle ebook: Alvis.

Kouloukis, J. P. (2013). *The Seasons of Our Lives.* Victoria, Australia: Heart Space Publications.

Liao, W. (2009). *Chi: Discovering Your Life Energy.* Boston, Massachusetts: Shambhala Publications.

Lorenz, K. (1989).*The Waning of Humaneness.* London: Unwin Hyman.

Magli, G. (2009).*Mysteries and Discoveries of Archaeoastronomy: From Pre-history to Easter Island.* New York: Springer.

Marshall, J.M. (2002). *The Lakota Way: Stories and Lessons for Living.* New York: Penguin Books.

Maslow, A. H. (1970). *Motivation and Personality.* New York: Harper & Row.

McMahon, J. (2015). Behavioural economics as neoliberalism: Producing and governing homo economicus. *Contemporary Political Theory, 14*(2), 137-158.

Meyer, J. (2008). *The power of forgiveness: keep your heart free.* New York: Hachette.

Miller, M. (2015, October, 1). Bronze Age steam room may have been used by select Orkney settlers for rites. *Ancient Origins,* (14): 37 Retrieved from http://www.ancient-origins. net/news-history-archaeology/bronze-age-steam-room-may-have-been-used-select-orkney-settlers-rites-020550

Murray, A. (2000). *Suicide in the Middle Ages: The curse on self murder.* Oxford: Oxford University Press.

Neumann, E. (2015). *The Great Mother: An Analysis of the Archetype.* Princeton: Princeton University Press.

Paine, N. (2012). *This Force of Memory: A Surgeon's Story of Addiction and PTSD.* Ebook.

Pert, C.B. (1999). *Molecules of Emotion: The science behind mind-body medicine.* New York: Touchstone.

Phillips, M., & Frederick, C. (1995). *Healing the Divided Self: clinical and Ericksonian hypnotherapy for post-traumatic and dissociative conditions.* New York: WW Norton.

Radin, D. (2010). *The Conscious Universe: The Scientific Truth of Psychic Phenomena.* New York: HarperCollins.

Rajkotwala, S. (2017). *The Year Of Talking To Plants: The plants and fairies talk in their own words.* CreateSpace.

Ramachandran, V. S. (2012*). The Tell-Tale Brain: Unlocking the Mystery of Human Nature.* London: Windmill books.

Ralls, K. (2013). *Medieval Mysteries: A guide to history, lore, places and symbolism.* York Beach, Maine: Ibis Press.

Reichard, J. (2011). *Grandmother Spider: The Creatrix: Celebrate the Divine Feminine.* San Francisco, CA: Bush Street Press.

Reis, S., Morris, G., Fleming, L. E., Beck, S., Taylor, T., White, M., ... Austen, M. (2015). Integrating Health and environmental impact analysis. *Public Health, 129*(10), 1383-1389.

Roof, W. C. (2003). Religion and Spirituality: towards an integrated analysis in M. Dillon (Ed), *Handbook of the Sociology of Religion.* Cambridge: Cambridge University Press.

Rosen, R. (2002). *The Yoga of Breath: A Step-by-step Guide to Pranayama.* Boston: Shambhala Publications.

Salzberg, S. (2003). *Faith: Trusting Your Own Deepest Experience.* London: Element.

Saraswati Satyananda, Swami (2008). *Surya Namaskara: A Technique of Solar Vitalization.* Bihar, India: Yoga Pubns Trust.

Scharmer, O., & Kaufer, K. (2013). *Leading from the emerging future: from ego system to eco system economies.* San Francisco: Berrett-Koehler Publishers.

Scogna, J. R., & Scogna, K. M. (2014). *Junk DNA: Unlocking the Hidden Secrets of Your DNA.* CreateSpace.

Shapiro, D. (1996). *Your body speaks your mind: understanding how your emotions and thoughts affect you physically.* London: Piatkus.

Shine, B. (1991). *Mind Magic: The Key to the universe.* London: Cox and Wyman.

Sjoo, M., & Mor, B. (2013). *The Great Cosmic Mother: Rediscovering the Religion of the Earth.* San Francisco: HarperOne.

Smith, C. G. (2017). *Ho'oponopono book: healing your life with the ancient Hawaiian secret power-prayer: practice of love and forgiveness.* Ebook.

Smith, R. T. (2009). *Cosmos, Earth and Nutrition: The Biodynamic Approach to Agriculture.* Forest Row, UK: Sophia Books.

Stephenson, B. (2006). *From Boys to Men: Spiritual Rites of Passage in an Indulgent Age.* Rochester: Park Street Press.

Stuart, D. E. (2014). *Anasazi America: Seventeen Centuries on the Road from Center Place.* Albuquerque, New Mexico: University of New Mexico Press.

Taylor, J. E., Deane, F. P., & Podd, J. V. (2007). Driving fear and driving skills: Comparison between fearful and control samples using standardized on-road assessment. *Behaviour Research and Therapy, 45*(4): 805–818.

Tasso, J., & Miller, E. (2010). The Effects of the Full Moon on Human Behavior. *The Journal of Psychology, 93,* 81-83.

Temple, R. (1998). *The Sirius Mystery: New Scientific Evidence for Alien Contact 5, 000 Years Ago.* London: Century.

Tick, E. (2014). *Warrior's Return: Restoring the Soul After War.* Boulder: Sounds True.

Tindle, H. A., Chang, Y. F., Kuller, L. H., Manson, J. E., Robinson, J. G., Rosal, M. C., ... Matthews, K. A. (2009). Optimism, Cynical Hostility, and Incident Coronary Heart Disease and Mortality in the Women's Health. *Initiative Circulation, 120*(8) 656-662.

Tournier, P. (2012). *The Seasons of Life.* Eugene: Wipf and Stock.

Tucker, J. (2009). *Life Before Life: A scientific investigation of children's memories of previous lives.* London: Piatkus.

Wasserman, J. (2015). *The Egyptian Book of the Dead: 20th Anniversary Edition.* San Francisco, CA: Chronicle Books.

Wangyal, G. (2002). *The Door of Liberation: Essential Teachings of the Tibetan Buddhist Tradition.* New York: Wisdom publications.

Wei-an, C. (2000). *Taming the Monkey Mind - A Guide to Pure Land Practice.* New York: *Sutra* Translation Committee of the U.S. and Canada.

Weinhold, B. K., & Weinhold, J. B. (2008). *Breaking free of the co-dependency trap.* Novato, CA: New World Library.

Williams, F. (2017). *The nature fix: why nature makes us happier, healthier and more creative.* New York: Norton.

Xygalatas, D. (2014). *The Burning Saints: Cognition and Culture in the Fire-walking: Rituals of the Anastenaria.* New York: Routledge.

Yogananda, P. (2006). *Autobiography of a Yogi.* Los Angeles, CA: Self-Realization Fellowship.

Zweig, C., & Abrams, J. (1990). *Meeting the shadow: Hidden Power of the dark side of human nature.* New York: Penguin/Putnam.

Acknowledgements

Writing this book has been quite an undertaking; 100,000 words, 24 spiritual lessons, stories, exercises and poetry. I could not have accomplished this incredible task without the loving support of my friends, family, teachers, clients and students.

My dedication would have waned numerous times without my dearest friend and co-teacher in The ISIS School, Fi Sutherland. Fi was in touch with my spirit guides who encouraged her to encourage me. Thank you Fi for your enthusiasm, motivation, correction of the Greek-English, care and love.

My editor, Lisa Thaler did an amazing job. Thank you Lisa for your professionalism, dedication and support. Thank you Eryn Strachan of Moonwood Arts, designer of the book cover, for your inspiration, talent and creativity.

I wish to thank my friend Laura, for her encouragement and for believing in me. I thank my friend and colleague Claudia Wolff who brought my work to Germany and shared her knowledge of sacred sites, some of which I reference in this book. My friend Ian Shanes supported me with his affectionate humour and channellings from my grandmother, who always asked, "What is happening with your book?"

I would like to take this opportunity to thank one of my teachers, who wrote the foreword for the book, Sandra Ingerman. I have met many spiritual teachers and shamanic practitioners in my work but very few have Sandra's integrity, love and care, and the professionalism to never take power from their students. Being part of shamanicteachers.com and her teacher training gave me a firm foundation and understanding of the responsibility of being a teacher.

I would like to thank my parents, siblings Stella and Mika, wee nephew Akis and my ancestors. My parents offered their continuous love, support and encouragement, and contributed to the editor's fees. On a spiritual level, I feel this publication ends a karmic theme: my grandfather was a scholar of ancient Greek who wrote several books on the Platonic dialogues that have not seen the light of day. My mother tried to publish her children's stories when I was young, but surrendered her dreams due to the abortive cost. Publishing this work releases the old karmic pattern for them and me.

My clients have been some of my biggest teachers. Every session offers incredible opportunities for learning for them and for me. Their experiences, listed in the book, will teach others who are travelling the same healing journey.

I would like to acknowledge all the help I received from the spirits of the land, the local and universal deities, the Crone-Cailliach-Hecate, Maiden-Brigit-Persephone, Mother-Danu-Demeter and all the other deities, discarnate shamans and wise ancestors, fairies, power animals, magic beings, standing stones, oak trees and ancient drums.

Finally, I would like to thank my spirit guides, teachers of the Light, in this life and other incarnations, who instructed me in meditations, dreams, channellings and through life experiences. With their contribution, this book has been created. My eternal gratitude goes to the Creator for this amazing life, ISIS, THOTH-DJEHUTI, HTHOTH, ANUBIS and the saint Dionysius Areopagitis.

Further Information

Fotoula, through The ISIS School of Holistic Health, offers a rich programme of spiritual teachings in retreats, workshops and practice groups in Glasgow, Scotland, rural Germany and online, and at times in other parts of the world. The School currently offers six main teachings, aiming to help people in their spiritual journey of awakening through the practice of chanting, meditation, shamanic journeying, ceremony, group work, nature work and pilgrimages to sacred sites. We also offer training in meditation and spiritual practice. Programmes include:

The Path of ISIS: The Seven Gates of Awareness
The OSIRIS Ascension Teachings
The Rays of Divine Consciousness
The ISIS School Shamanic Practitioner's Course and workshops
The Priestess/Priest of the Moon
Meditation

For further information on the courses offered and programme, please visit:
www.theisisschoolofholistichealth.com
or www.facebook.com/theisisschoolofholistichealth